P9-BII-772

developing
sustainable
planned
communities

EDITOR
Jo Allen Gause

PRIMARY AUTHORS
Richard Franko
Jo Allen Gause
Jim Heid, Jr.
Steven Kellenberg
Jeff Kingsbury
Edward T. McMahon
Judi G. Schweitzer
Daniel K. Slone

Urban Land Institute

Copyright © 2007 by ULI–the Urban Land Institute

All rights reserved. No part of this book may be reproduced in any form or by any means, electronic or mechanical, including photocopying and recording, or by any information storage and retrieval system, without written permission of the publisher.

ULI–the Urban Land Institute
1025 Thomas Jefferson Street, N.W.
Washington, D.C. 20007-5201

Library of Congress Cataloging-in-Publication Data

Developing sustainable planned communities.

    p. cm.

1. Planned communities—Environmental aspects.
2. Real estate development—Environmental aspects.
3. Sustainable development. I. Urban Land Institute.

  HT169.55.D48 2007

  307.76′8–dc22

                         2007020428

ISBN: 978-0-87420-991-4

10 9 8 7 6 5 4 3 2 1

Printed in the United States of America.

BOOK AND COVER DESIGN

John Hall Design Group
Beverly, Massachusetts
www.johnhalldesign.com

Jennifer Mineo
Design Assistant

JACKET PHOTOGRAPHS

Front cover, clockwise from top: Peter Bastianelli Kerse; Countryside Properties; © Ryan Hawk; © Barbara Karant/Karant + Associates, Inc. Back cover, clockwise from top: Uwe Schneider; © 2007 EDAW/ Photography by Dixi Carrillo; Ed Rosenberger.

ULI–THE URBAN LAND INSTITUTE

The mission of the Urban Land Institute is to provide leadership in the responsible use of land and in creating and sustaining thriving communities worldwide. ULI is committed to:

- Bringing together leaders from across the fields of real estate and land use policy to exchange best practices and serve community needs;

- Fostering collaboration within and beyond ULI's membership through mentoring, dialogue, and problem solving;

- Exploring issues of urbanization, conservation, regeneration, land use, capital formation, and sustainable development;

- Advancing land use policies and design practices that respect the uniqueness of both built and natural environments;

- Sharing knowledge through education, applied research, publishing, and electronic media; and

- Sustaining a diverse global network of local practice and advisory efforts that address current and future challenges.

The Institute has long been recognized as one of the world's most respected and widely quoted sources of objective information on urban planning, growth, and development. Established in 1936, the Institute today has more than 35,000 members in over 90 countries, representing the entire spectrum of the land use and development disciplines.

PROJECT STAFF

Rachelle L. Levitt
Executive Vice President, Information Group
Publisher

Dean Schwanke
Senior Vice President, Publications and Awards

Jo Allen Gause
Senior Director, Residential Development
Project Director

Nancy H. Stewart
Director, Book Program
Managing Editor

Lori Hatcher
Managing Director, Publications Marketing

Abby Bussel/Engine Books
Manuscript Editor

Betsy VanBuskirk
Art Director

Craig Chapman
Director, Publishing Operations

Karrie Underwood
Administrative Manager/Digital Images Assistant

Authors and Reviewers

PRIMARY AUTHORS

Richard Franko is an architect and a principal with Mithun, an integrated design firm in Seattle that works internationally on sustainable environments.

Jo Allen Gause is the senior director of residential development at the Urban Land Institute. She has managed a variety of books and conferences on topics related to real estate development practice.

Jim Heid, Jr., is the founder of UrbanGreen, a real estate development and advisory firm focusing on strategies for successfully incorporating sustainability, place making, traditional neighborhood design, and conservation into community developments.

Steven Kellenberg is a principal and vice president in the Irvine, California, office of EDAW/AECOM. He specializes in large-scale new-community and mixed-use development, and in sustainability-based planning and design.

Jeff Kingsbury is the managing principal and cofounder of Greenstreet Ltd., a real estate development, brokerage, and consulting firm. His practice focuses on leveraging sustainable strategies in the planning, development, marketing, and sale of new communities.

Edward T. McMahon, the ULI/Charles Fraser Senior Resident Fellow for Sustainable Development, is a nationally recognized authority on sustainable development, land conservation, and urban design.

Judi G. Schweitzer, president of Schweitzer + Associates, is a consultant to banks, pension funds, developers, and landowners whose goal is to create community developments that are beautiful, livable, and valuable.

Daniel K. Slone, a partner in the law firm McGuireWoods LLP, is national counsel for the U.S. Green Building Council and for the Congress for the New Urbanism. He advises developers and municipalities on codes, development and utility agreements, conservation easements, and governance documents for developments using sustainable principles.

OTHER CONTRIBUTORS

Alexa Bach
Sustainability Consultant
UrbanGreen
San Francisco, California

Rebecca Bryant
Writer
Fayetteville, Arkansas

Clair Enlow
Writer
Seattle, Washington

Anne B. Frej
Director, Office/
    Industrial Development
Urban Land Institute
Washington, D.C.

Gregory H. Kats
Principal
Capital E
Washington, D.C.

Terry Lassar
Lassar Communications
St. Louis, Missouri

Milt Rhodes
Principal
New Urban Water Works
Raleigh, North Carolina

Julie D. Stern
JDS Communications
Falls Church, Virginia

Stella Tarnay
Tarnay & Associates
Washington, D.C.

REVIEWERS

Richard F. Galehouse
Principal
Sasaki Associates, Inc.
Watertown, Massachusetts

Franklin A. Martin
President
Martin Community
    Development, LLC
Boise, Idaho

Jonathan Ratner
Director of Sustainability Initiatives
Forest City Stapleton
Denver, Colorado

Acknowledgments

MANY INDIVIDUALS CONTRIBUTED THEIR TIME AND TALENTS to this book, and to each one I would like to extend my sincere appreciation. First, special gratitude goes to the primary authors whose passion for sustainable development motivated them to take time from their busy professional schedules to write chapters. I am also grateful to those who wrote case studies and feature boxes, shared information through interviews, and provided photographs. Many thanks to the developers, architects, planners, and designers of the projects featured in this book, who worked to accurately describe their efforts and supplied the attractive visuals that bring this publication to life. Much appreciation goes to those who reviewed manuscript chapters and provided comments and clarifications that helped make the book more concise and more practical.

Several others brought their research and writing skills to this effort and improved the quality and content of the text. Thanks go to Jennifer LeFurgy and Alice Early, both freelance writers; Cheryl McClune of Roni Hicks & Associates; Christine Rombouts of Carlsson PR; and Jenny Paek and Lauren Good of ULI.

Very special thanks go to Abby Bussel of Engine Books for editing the text and ensuring that the information was clearly written and presented to make it most useful to our audience. And a big thank you to John Hall of John Hall Design Group, who created the book design and united all the parts under a rigorous deadline.

I would like to thank the ULI staff members who worked on this publication: Rachelle Levitt and Dean Schwanke provided direction and insight; Nancy Stewart managed the complex production process; Betsy Van Buskirk managed the design and layout; Craig Chapman coordinated the publication process; Lori Hatcher worked to ensure that the book reaches a wide audience; and Karrie Underwood provided technical and organizational assistance with the hundreds of photographs submitted for consideration.

And to everyone else who had a hand in this work and could not be mentioned in this limited space, I am sincerely grateful.

Jo Allen Gause
Project Director

Foreword

HUMAN ACTIVITY IS RAPIDLY ALTERING THE EARTH'S FRAGILE ECOSYSTEMS. Despite growing evidence of our destructive behavior, we continue to emit excessive amounts of greenhouse gas, from our daily commutes to the energy consumed by our buildings, exacerbating climate change and global warming. We continue to clear-cut our forests, pave our fertile farmlands, and pollute our water resources. These actions seriously threaten the earth's carrying capacity. We are taxing these ecosystems at an ever-increasing rate. The world's population is growing and people are living longer and consuming more. Many scientists believe that humans are causing the next great wave of extinctions and a massive reduction in our ecosystem's biodiversity.

In light of this grim picture, what is a real estate developer to do? In the next 30 years, the U.S. population is projected to grow by 94 million. These new residents will need places to live, work, shop, and learn. The answer is neither slow growth nor no growth. The answer must be sustainable, providing for the health and prosperity of many future generations. And these communities will be planned under local government guidelines and developed by the real estate industry. The challenges before us are complex, but not insurmountable. Our industry faces many questions and we need to respond with creative solutions. How can we most responsibly accommodate growth? Is there a way to reduce human impact on the environment? Can we do this profitably and equitably? Can we create a more environmentally responsible future?

The answer to the latter question is a resounding yes! For example, using currently available technologies for energy-efficient buildings, water conservation, and transit, New York City has just released a plan to accommodate one million additional residents while reducing overall energy consumption by 30 percent and increasing parklands. Chicago, San Francisco, Boston, Washington, D.C., and many other cities are generating similar plans. The message is clear: The move toward greener communities presents enormous opportunities for planners, architects, investors, and developers who understand the ways in which environmentally responsible development can be achieved.

A growing library of green design and planning reference materials is at our disposal. A key addition to this body of resources is the book you hold in your hands, *Developing Sustainable Planned Communities*. This practical guide to environmentally responsible development provides reality-based, economically viable insights into how to shape design and development processes that reduce environmental degradation, increase market satisfaction, and build healthy communities.

There is a reason that this book is about developing green communities, not green buildings. We are faced with systemic issues. We need to find systems-level solutions. This book provides thoughtful approaches to integrated planning, design, and development that we will need to create a more sustainable world.

Environmentally responsible development will succeed only if it also is economically viable. The first step is to select the best places to accommodate the country's projected growth. We must be very judicious in our use of land, water, and other limited resources. As a society, we reap the greatest return on public investment when we maximize the use of our existing infrastructure. And so, as outlined in this book, our greener future begins by selecting development sites that are transit-oriented, walkable, and suitable for higher densities.

It is estimated that there are 1 million acres of brownfields in America. If we redevelop them at an average density of 20 units to the acre (49 units to the hectare), we could produce 20 million new homes on despoiled lands. Many brownfields lie underutilized on our cities' waterfronts. Others are next to rail line rights-of-way, which are also the easiest places to build new light-rail systems. The redevelopment of these areas would have enormous market appeal. In Great Britain, 78 percent of all new houses are being built on brownfield sites. Surely, we can take advantage of the brownfield inventory in our country, too.

To support the preservation of our watersheds, forests, and natural and agricultural lands, greenfield development should—must—be guided by environmental principles. Communities need to support greater density and a mix of uses on these sites so that they consume fewer acres. Adjacency to existing and planned mass-transit infrastructure is a top priority. Without access to car-free travel and walkable communities, we are simply building more sprawl and putting more vehicles onto our roads. Small building

footprints and efficient energy and water-management strategies are key components, too. This book provides examples of green practices in all settings—urban, suburban, and rural.

Biophilia is the innate human desire to be connected to nature. And so, as human settlements become denser, they must also become greener, filled with trees, parks, gardens, bike paths, and walkways. Every child should grow up within a ten-minute walk of a park or a safe play area.

The demand for green buildings is rapidly growing. Fortune 500 companies are increasingly seeking green office spaces. Private citizens want to reduce energy costs and live in healthy indoor environments. Green buildings not only make economic and market sense, but, in the near future, consumers and regulators will demand them.

Taken together, these trends provide us with an enormous opportunity. The ideas and methodologies documented in *Developing Sustainable Planned Communities* can help us to imagine a more sustainable future.

Jonathan F. P. Rose
President
Jonathan Rose Companies LLC
New York, New York

Contents

Developing Sustainable Planned Communities

EDWARD T. McMAHON

1 Introduction

Based on the three pillars of sustainability—environment, society, and economy—the Loreto Bay community on Mexico's Baja Peninsula has made sustainable development its primary goal.

IMAGINE ENTIRE COMMUNITIES conceived and constructed in harmony with nature. No degraded resources. No wasted energy. No toxic materials. Lots of green space. Such places would be beautiful, walkable, healthy, and designed to last.

And they are being built now. The past two decades have seen the emergence and increasing marketability of a new kind of development. Whether referred to as "green" or "environmentally sensitive," a sustainable community can produce a triple bottom line for residents, developers, and the planet: environmentally friendly, economically profitable, and socially sustainable developments.

Few would argue with such benefits. The challenge is in realizing them. It is easy to label a community sustainable; making it so requires a commitment to thinking differently about what development means. A sustainable community is a holistic entity. Like an ecosystem, sustainable development is about interrelationships. From conception through development and maintenance, a sustainable community balances environmental, social, and economic imperatives. It is about more than energy-efficient buildings. It is about reducing the impact of development on the natural environment and creating a mix of uses and housing types. It is about regionally interconnected public transportation, green spaces and stormwater management systems that reduce runoff. A community that fosters a healthy relationship between people and nature is sustainable.

A Greener Future

An early response to the 20th-century's spread of soulless subdivisions and their commercial-strip counterparts was the rise of large master-

LEFT: DARREN DEWARDS PHOTOGRAPHICS; OPPOSITE: ED ROSENBERGER

Daybreak, South Jordan, Utah. Sustainable communities foster an intimate relationship between people and nature.

Top: United Kingdom developer BioRegional Quintain Ltd. is planning to build a carbon-neutral community in Middlesbrough, where residents will live in individually designed "sugar cube" apartment blocks. Below: Issaquah Highlands in Washington has banned culs-de-sac and front-loaded garages in favor of shared front yards.

planned communities such as The Woodlands near Houston, Texas, and Irvine Ranch in Orange County, California. Realized in the 1970s, these projects and others like them have stood the test of time because of their focus on the physical elements of community design that enhance livability, facilitate social engagement, emphasize open space, and incorporate a mix of uses and housing types.

Sustainable communities share many of these same characteristics, but they place greater weight on environmental sensitivity. Such communities sit lightly on the land and incorporate many environmentally friendly products and strategies. Green building practices stress energy efficiency, water conservation, and native landscaping, and improve indoor air quality with nontoxic paints, carpets, and other materials.

However, sustainable communities do more than incorporate ecologically sensitive building technologies and materials. They integrate green principles into every aspect of a community's planning, design, construction, and maintenance. Choosing a sustainable site is also important. It is difficult to be truly green if a project is constructed on prime farmland, a historic site, or endangered-species habitat. Ideal locations for sustainable communities include brownfields, decommissioned military bases, vacant parcels, and infill sites. If a greenfield site is unavoidable, sustainable communities must minimize site infrastructure and grading, maximize sediment control, limit landscaping to new or

restored native vegetation, and provide easy access to public transportation.

And the development community is taking these challenges seriously. Based on data collected in a joint 2003 survey, *Residential Green Building SmartMarket Report*, the National Association of Home Builders (NAHB) and McGraw-Hill Construction have forecasted a surge in environmentally responsible efforts: "By 2010, the value of the residential green building marketplace is expected to boost its market share from $7.4 billion and 2 percent of housing starts last year to $19 billion to $38 billion and 5 to 10 percent of residential construction activity."

And with good reason. Buildings consume 37 percent of the nation's energy and 68 percent of electricity, according to the U.S. Department of Energy. Buildings also produce about 30 percent of the country's greenhouse gas emissions. With global warming and other damaging effects on

TOP: ZEDFACTORY.COM; BELOW: FUSIONPARTNERS, LLC

the environment on the rise and an increasingly savvy home-buying public demanding healthy, energy-efficient houses, the development community's future can only be one color: green.

Shades of Green

There are many "shades of green," ranging from full-spectrum green to one-dimensional strategies with few ecological or social benefits. "Greenwashing," which occurs when a conventional project is dressed up with slick, nature-oriented marketing, is among the worst offenses. These developers and builders recognize that "green" has become fashionable, so they use their marketing budgets to try to reposition their projects.

A more genuine shade of green is the "conservation development," or what some people call a "low-impact development." These communities conserve a substantial amount of open land by clustering houses in walkable neighborhoods. They reduce the surface area paved with impervious materials and use a variety of techniques to reduce stormwater runoff and protect wildlife and natural settings.

In his 1969 book *Design with Nature*, landscape architect Ian McHarg advocated a careful analysis of the site to foster a greater sense of harmony between natural systems and the built environment. His ideas, along with those of Randall Arendt, a well-known land use planner, have influenced a generation of planned communities, ranging from Prairie Crossing, a conservation community outside Chicago, to The Woodlands, one of the largest and most successful master-planned communities in the country.

The developers of these communities recognized that neighborhoods that engage the natural world were good for both people and wildlife. In fact, many conservation-minded developers take pride in helping to restore the land, removing invasive species, improving water quality, and building trails.

Unlike conventional developments, where natural features are often replaced with automobile-oriented environments, turf grass, and undifferentiated housing stock, conservation developments have grown in popularity because homebuyers value natural open spaces, native plants, wildlife, and beautiful surroundings.

Arcosanti, located in the high desert of central Arizona, was conceived in 1970 as an antidote to wasteful land use practices. The experimental town is designed according to the concept of "arcology" (architecture + ecology), developed by Italian architect Paolo Soleri.

ARCOSANTI FOUNDATION

5

Right: At the Island-
Wood Wetland Lab
on Bainbridge Island,
Washington, many build-
ing materials were locally
sourced, recycled, and
reused to help connect
the project to its site and
surrounding ecosys-
tem. Below: All native
plantings were removed
during construction of
the Four Seasons Resort
Scottsdale at Troon
North in Arizona and
then transplanted back
into the natural plant
groupings found and
documented on
the site.

TOP: ©MITHUN; BOTTOM: © 2007 EDAW/PHOTOGRAPHY BY DIXI CARRILLO

While they demonstrate outstanding site planning and careful approaches to natural systems, some of the early manifestations of conservation development could be labeled "grass green," because they mainly addressed horizontal land development issues, albeit in a thoughtful way. A more comprehensive approach addresses not just land development but also a wide array of issues involving the design, materials, and building methods for new homes, offices, and businesses. The home-building and real estate industries have established standards for houses and other structures based on sound environmental principles.

The nonprofit U.S. Green Building Council, founded in 1993, for example, has created the Leadership in Energy and Environmental Design (LEED) Green Building Rating System, a nationally recognized benchmark for high-performance sustainable building practices. These standards ad-

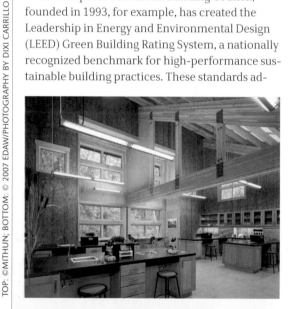

dress everything from indoor air quality to energy efficiency and construction-waste management.

The NAHB has also developed green building guidelines for residential construction, and the U.S. Environmental Protection Agency (EPA) has created the Energy Star program to help businesses and individuals protect the environment through superior energy efficiency. The EPA has certified some 300,000 homes that are at least 15 percent more energy efficient than the standards set by the 2006 International Energy Conservation Code.

Sustainability, however, is more than effective insulation, high-performance windows, or efficient heating and cooling systems. In the *Ecology of Place*, Timothy Beatley, one of the world's leading experts on the subject, notes that creating sustainable communities is not simply a matter of preserving a few wetlands, saving a few acres of open space, or establishing a few best management practices. It is a matter of considering ecological limits and environmental impacts throughout the entire development process, from the energy efficiency of buildings to the proximity of a regional transportation system. It is also about people. Truly sustainable communities take a holistic approach that benefits the residents, the natural environment, and the developer. It is full-spectrum green.

Sustainable communities are not just greener. They can be healthier and safer than conventional developments. Winston Churchill once said, "We shape our buildings, and afterwards our buildings shape us." His point, of course, was that the physical character of our communities affects who we are and how we relate to one another and to our surroundings.

Sometimes the consequences of development patterns and resource usage are obvious. When neighborhood green space is lost to development, children lose a place to play and their parents lose a place to socialize. Long commutes, one result of sprawl, contribute to air pollution but also to the loss of free time. The more electricity we use, the higher our utility bills will be and the more greenhouse gases we will emit into the atmosphere.

However, many consequences of development choices are less obvious, particularly in the areas of physical and mental health. A growing body

Located on the banks of Virginia's Rappahannock River, the neotraditional town of Haymount will be a showcase for sustainable planning strategies.

of research shows that how we design our communities and buildings has a profound effect on human health. One example is the relationship between walkable communities and childhood well-being. According to federal transportation studies, approximately half of all school children walked or rode a bicycle to or from school in 1969. Today, fewer than 15 percent walk to or from school, a statistic that speaks to the health care crisis facing our youngest citizens.

Another effect of sprawling development patterns is what author Richard Louv calls "nature-deficient disorder." In his book *Last Child in the Woods*, Louv argues that children need to have a stronger connection to the natural world, if they are to truly flourish as healthy citizens of the planet. He points out that our schools may teach students about threats to the Amazon rain forest, but conventional development patterns do little to encourage children's personal rela-

tionship with the natural terrain outside their own doors.

Sustainable communities link citizens to nature and to one another to create more healthy and vital neighborhoods. And they involve residents in community governance and environmental stewardship. Several of the projects profiled in this book, for example, have community stewardship organizations—nonprofit organizations dedicated to long-term conservation and education efforts.

Converging Ideologies

The last several decades have seen the emergence of planning ideologies and strategies that emphasize somewhat different approaches to land use and community development. Traditional neighborhood development, transit-oriented development, conservation subdivisions, smart growth initiatives, and green development all have similar goals, but their approaches vary.

JOHN A. CLARK CO./HAYMOUNT LIMITED PARTNERSHIP

Dongtan Eco-City

IN 2005, the Shanghai Industrial Investment Corporation (SIIC) partnered with the global design firm Arup to create a plan for China's first large-scale sustainable city. Located in the Yangtze River delta on the island of Chongming, Dongtan will be developed as an ecologically sensitive city containing more than 500,000 people by the year 2050. The 21,250-acre (8,600-hectare) site is a former agricultural area adjacent to one of Asia's most important wetlands, where migratory birds stop during their cross-continental flight. In order to both accommodate China's rapid growth and sustain the wetlands, the mayor of Shanghai and the Chinese premier set a requirement that the land be developed as a model city with a minimal ecological footprint. Dongtan will also help China learn how to reduce its industrial pollution and serve as a case study for the hundreds of master-planned cities China intends to build over the next 20 years.

Dongtan Eco-City will contain a mix of uses connected by pedestrian pathways, rail, and canals. Most of the buildings will have green roofs and none will be over eight stories tall.

The first phase of Dongtan is planned as a town with three compact, pedestrian-oriented villages containing about 3,000 dwellings in total. The development will continue to grow as a series of towns connected by bicycle routes and public transportation corridors. Ideally, people will not have to walk more than seven minutes from any part of the city to reach a bus or train station and residents will have easy access to social infrastructure, such as hospitals, schools, and work. In keeping with the aim of limiting carbon monoxide emissions, vehicles will be required to run on either hydrogen or battery power; owners of fuel-burning cars will have to park outside of the city and use public transport within the city. The first phase of Dongtan Eco-City, which will accommodate a population of 10,000, is scheduled for completion in 2010, coinciding with the opening of the World Expo in Shanghai.

Because of the existence of large wetlands on the southern part of the island, planners are converting adjacent agricultural land to a wetland state to create a buffer zone between the city and the wetlands' mudflats. This buffer zone, at its narrowest point, will be 2.2 miles (3.5 kilometers) wide. Only 40 percent of the land area of the Dongtan site will be dedicated to urban areas. The design team aims to prevent pollutants (light, noise, emissions, and water discharges) from reaching the wetlands area.

Wastewater will be captured, purified, and reintroduced to the city, while organic waste will be used as biomass for energy production. There will be no landfill in Dongtan. Human sewage will be processed and used for energy recovery, irrigation, and composting. On-site farmers will use organic agricultural methods to grow food for the city's inhabitants.

The city will be largely powered by renewable energy—wind, sun, and biomass.

Electricity and heat will be supplied from several sources: a combined heat-and-power (CHP) plant that runs on biomass in the form of rice husks, which are the waste product of local rice mills; a wind farm; biogas extracted from the treatment of sewage and from food waste; and the gasification of municipal solid waste. Any fossil fuel used will be offset to ensure zero-net annual carbon dioxide emissions.

Dongtan incorporates many traditional Chinese design features and combines them with a sustainable approach to modern living.

Dongtan's buildings will be required to have high thermal performance and use energy-efficient equipment and mechanisms. In some cases, the buildings will generate their own energy using photovoltaic cells and micro-wind turbines. Green roofs will improve building insulation and water filtration and provide potential storage for irrigation or waste disposal.

ARUP

When available, labor and material will be sourced locally.

The city's planners are not only concerned with the city's long-term environmental health, but also its social and economic sustainability. Although some residents may commute to Shanghai for work, Dongtan will provide employment opportunities for the majority of people who live in the city. Chongming's existing local farming and fishing communities will have new marketing opportunities with the development of Dongtan, enhancing the island's environmental and social sustainability at the same time.

The developers, planners, and designers of Dongtan hope to create a high-quality, commercially viable environment that will set a new paradigm for city building.

9

The Gerding Theater at the Armory in Portland, Oregon, was the first building on the National Register of Historic Places to achieve LEED Platinum status.

UWE SCHNEIDER

Traditional neighborhood development combines the character of old neighborhoods with new technologies and an emphasis on walkability. It restores the street to its proper role as an integral part of the public realm: a place shared by pedestrians and vehicles. It also emphasizes the value of regionally appropriate architecture and craftsmanship with modern floor plans that support contemporary lifestyles.

Conservation developments, which are typically found in rural and exurban settings, focus on cultural and natural resource protection and restoration. These master plans cluster houses to protect large blocks of green space and foster a more harmonious relationship between people and nature.

Transit-oriented development is designed to combat traffic congestion and protect the en-

vironment by placing high-density, mixed-use communities near regional subway stations, trolley lines, and light-rail systems.

Smart growth embraces many of the ideas promoted by the other types of development, but also identifies appropriate areas for new construction and renovation, typically within or near existing communities.

Green building design stresses resource efficiency in building design, materials, and construction. Its best practitioners emphasize a holistic approach rather than a checklist of technologies or features. It is also characterized by a heightened awareness of the relationship between building materials and human health.

Sustainable development is a convergence of all these ideologies. Regardless of the planning strategy, successful projects take a comprehensive approach, which means integrating green principles and practices into every aspect of a community's planning, design, construction, marketing, and maintenance.

Barriers to Sustainable Development

Sustainable communities reduce energy consumption. They make more efficient use of land, provide more transportation choices, reduce infrastructure costs, and respect a community's natural beauty, history, and ecosystems. However, despite these benefits, sustainable communities represent only a fraction of recent development in the United States. This is because applying sustainable principles is often more difficult than implementing conventional development practices.

The major impediments to sustainable communities include inflexible local regulations, outdated market perceptions, high development and entitlement costs, financing by formula, and high-density development without amenities.

Most local zoning, subdivision, and land use regulations make it easier and faster to build single-use developments. For example, local regulations frequently mandate a separation of housing, shopping, and offices, and provide little flexibility in lot size or street width. Public officials should make zoning and subdivision regulations more flexible to encourage conservation development, green building practices, mixed uses, pedestrian-friendly streets, and other sustainable concepts.

Yet such reforms would only be part of the solution. Because sustainable development is unfamiliar territory to some developers and builders, it is perceived as risky. Outdated assumptions often inform current market and demographic analyses, which prevent developers from building projects for significant groups of consumers with specific needs, tastes, and preferences. A 2003 article in *Professional Builder* magazine reported that more than 90 percent of homebuyers said they were willing to pay more for green building features, with 20 percent willing to pay an extra $10,000. Yet when asked the same question, builders believed that less than half of homebuyers would pay more for green features. This disconnection between consumer attitudes and builder perceptions causes some developer to shy away from sustainable development.

High development impact fees and land assembly costs, which can often increase lot and

The Water and Power Department in Loveland, Colorado, created this xeriscape garden to demonstrate and promote landscape-related water conservation among city residents.

© 2007 EDAW/PHOTOGRAPHY BY DIXI CARRILLO

Right: A sustainable
approach to stormwater
management is to divert
rainwater to an on-site
wetland for filtering
before discharging it off
site. Below: Density can
be made more appealing
through creative design
and the landscaping of
adjacent open space.

ABOVE: © 2007 EDAW/PHOTOGRAPHY BY DIXI CARRILLO
BELOW: JOHN STAMETS

building expenditures, can also be a deterrent. A shortage of infill sites, for example, can make smart growth more expensive and complicated. To make infill projects financially viable, local and state governments should provide more incentives for the reuse of historic structures, brownfield redevelopment, downtown revitalization, and transit-oriented development.

A lack of comparables, the secondary financing market, and bank procedures can make it difficult to secure funds for sustainable development projects. In general, banks finance projects in a formulaic manner, so that only standard types of developments with predictable outcomes receive financing. In addition, excessive parking requirements that are often imposed by lenders add to the cost of a development and may conflict with the goals of both the developer and the community.

Many worthy projects, including infill and greenfield developments, can meet with community opposition. The public may perceive compact development as an undesirable neighborhood addition, but that may be because many high-density projects come without compensating features. Well-designed, higher-density projects with green space and community gathering

places will sell better. For many people, the character of the neighborhood is far more important than the size of the lot.

The Benefits of Sustainable Development

The concepts of green building and sustainable development have been around for many years, but they have only recently gained traction in the marketplace. Guidelines from the Environmental Protection Agency, the Department of Energy, the U.S. Green Building Council, and the NAHB are making it easier to understand basic principles and standards of sustainability. What's more, federal, state, and local governments are offering incentives and tax credits to encourage sustainable practices and are passing legislation requiring energy-efficient and green building techniques. And, the mainstream media—*Vanity Fair*, *Newsweek*, and *USA Today*, among others—has jumped on the bandwagon with cover stories and articles about green building practices and sustainable lifestyles.

But why should a developer or builder want to build a sustainable community? One reason, according to Peter McMahon, president of the Kennecott Land Company in Murray, Utah, is reputation. He argues that sustainability is good business because a company's reputation can be enhanced by building green, which, in turn, can create new development opportunities. McMahon believes that Kennecott's reputation as a sustainable-community developer has given it access to land, capital, and talent that is unsurpassed in its market. He notes, for example, that the best young talent is attracted to cutting-edge

Dockside Green

SITUATED ON A FORMER INDUSTRIAL site on the inner harbor of Victoria, Canada, Dockside Green is planned as a socially diverse, ecologically restorative, and economically sound community. The codevelopers of Dockside Green—Vancity Enterprises and Windmill Development—envision a community for 2,500 people that meets the highest standards of sustainability. The developer's goal is to achieve LEED Platinum certification for all 26 buildings in the community—an

Situated in the heart of Victoria, British Columbia, Dockside Green is being developed on 15 acres (6 hectares) of former industrial land adjacent to the Upper Harbour and downtown.

ambitious target, considering there are only a handful of Platinum buildings in the world. The developers have backed up their commitment by agreeing to pay a penalty of up to C$1 million to the city if the stringent green building standards are not met.

Dockside Green, which will be developed in phases over the next decade, is striving to be greenhouse gas–neutral, meaning there will be no net emissions of greenhouse gases from the development. This will be achieved through use of an on-site biomass energy cogeneration plant, which will produce heat and power from wood waste obtained from local industry, a geothermal heating system, solar water heaters, and photovoltaic power.

The project's sustainable features do not stop there. Sewage will be treated on site and reused for toilets and irrigation. Potable water use in commercial buildings will be approximately 65 percent lower than in traditional development, achieved largely through the use of reclaimed water for toilets and low-flow fixtures. Reclaimed water collected from rain cisterns located throughout the development will irrigate green roofs, water features, and landscaping.

To further promote sustainability, the transportation plan includes car sharing, a mini-transit system using biodiesel fuel produced on site, and the integration of bicycle paths and pedestrian walkways.

CHRIS FOYD/ COURTESY OF BUSBY PERKINS+WILL

companies with solid reputations. Likewise, the entitlement process is made easier by a commitment to sustainability. As proof, McMahon points to the "Clean Utah Certificate" that was awarded to Kennecott by the state of Utah. This certificate simplifies regulatory approvals and gives the company greater access to capital and, as a result, a better return on investment.

A Marketable Advantage

Sustainable development has changed dramatically in recent years. What started out as a charismatic environmental movement has evolved into a rapidly growing sector of the U.S. real estate industry. Developers and builders have proven that they can construct high-quality, high-performance structures and communities in a profitable and professional fashion. A growing body of evidence suggests that green buildings command premium prices and lease up faster than conventional buildings. In fact, they are becoming more marketable than other real estate endeavors. And the market for green buildings and sustainable communities is certain to grow due to concerns about global warming, energy dependence, and the rising cost of gasoline and home heating and cooling fuel.

In addition to a developer's reputation, there are many good reasons to build green: improved indoor-air quality; reduced dependence on foreign oil; decreased construction waste; increased energy efficiency and lowered operating costs; fewer materials used in construction; decreased development costs due to tax credits and incentives; lowered infrastructure costs; streamlined approval processes; and increased market advantage.

Building sustainable communities is gaining credibility around the country. Today, public officials and building agencies are often willing to work cooperatively with developers who are able to implement green building practices in ways that benefit society at large.

JIM HEID, Jr. • JEFF KINGSBURY

2 Sustainable from the Start

MUCH LIKE A ROBUST ECOSYSTEM, a sustainable community is more than the sum of its green parts. Today's most ambitious green projects are distinguished by their ability to evolve, foster strong and healthy human interaction, and mitigate the negative effects of development. The most successful projects create a living system that makes a site more vital than it was before development took place.

Sustainability should not be treated as an afterthought or a checklist. Realizing the potential of a green project requires a holistic, inquisitive view of sustainability that aligns with some of today's best practices in design and planning, place making, programming, construction, marketing, implementation, and governance. A sustainable community is an evolving organism that needs an appropriate framework of tenets and techniques to facilitate its evolution in an environmentally and financially responsible manner. Beyond reducing impacts, the development team should create a successful partnership with the land, instituting an ethos that will allow builders, tenants, and residents to play active roles in their community's evolution.

Defining Sustainability

Sustainable design is not easily defined. In fact, it is a development approach complicated by an increasingly confusing universe of government and industry rating systems, manufacturer protocols, market preferences, and regulatory codes. As a result, anyone who embarks on the creation of a sustainable community can become quickly overwhelmed, if not weary, in an attempt to prioritize the issues, hire the consultants, and select the certifying agency that will offer the greatest market traction.

There is no perfect sustainable strategy or "silver bullet." Instead, there is an emerging set of practices (both proven and exploratory) that affords a solid baseline from which to start. As the definitions and options surrounding sustainability increase, it is essential for developers and landowners headed down the green community path to take three small, but significant, steps:

- Define sustainability within the context of the industry and as it applies to the project at hand;

- Define ways to measure sustainability and institute those metrics early on; and

- Define the achievable big benefits early on and focus resources to ensure their success, upping the green ante in each successive stage of development.

© JAY GRAHAM

14

The vision for Dunes
Country at Furnessville,
Indiana, focuses on
diversity, ecology, re-
gionalism, and longevity.
The project integrates
neo-traditional planning
with the latest in green
building technology.

One of the challenges of sustainability is that it means many things to many people. The most universally accepted definition comes from the Brundtland Commission, convened by the United Nations in 1987. At this landmark meeting, the participating organizations and individuals defined sustainable development as "development that meets the needs of the present without compromising the ability of future generations to meet their own needs." Today, the words "sustainability" and "green" are used interchangeably, but they can mean very different things. Throughout the design and planning process and into the entitlement and implementation phases, it is very important to define sustainability objectives so that a project can be evaluated based on its intended goals in comparison to accepted standards.

The most common mistake developers make is to tout a development as one that will be totally sustainable, without knowing what this means or how it will be achieved. Savvy members of the public may greet the announcement with skepticism and raise questions that will test the integrity of the proclamation: Will the developer ensure that jobs created by the project go to the local community? Will the community provide a range of housing options, including permanently protected affordable units? Will the community produce more energy than it consumes in every aspect, including its transportation regimen? Will fresh food be available from sources within a reasonable distance of the site, and without the negative attributes of industrial agriculture? For every commitment the developer makes toward a more sustainable approach, opponents and concerned citizens may find an aspect of the project

that is not sustainable. As a result, the negatives, perceived or real, will obscure the positives. In the end, the project and its proponents will face what Ed McMahon, ULI's Senior Resident Fellow for Sustainability, refers to as "the perfect becoming the enemy of the good."

Therefore, developers should determine the aspects of sustainability to commit to publicly, while privately exploring technologies and strategies that may enhance the project. Nowhere in the field of real estate development is the adage '"under promise and over deliver" more relevant.

Once the initial deliverables have been established, the question of how to measure fulfillment of those goals needs to be determined. This is where many of the existing and emerging certification programs and standards can be helpful. By reviewing criteria for green developments and construction, smart growth, and healthy communities, the development team should create its own yardstick of sustainability.

It is important to emphasize that sustainability cannot be achieved á la carte—take one of these and one of those. Interrelationships must be respected and a framework of resource efficiency, community connections, social equity, economic success, and environmental stewardship must be addressed. The emphasis and techniques each development team chooses in programming and planning its project is what creates unique solutions. Developers must be realistic about balancing their capacity for research and innovation with the challenges of implementing unproven techniques and processes. Staff, consultants, investors, and lenders must be committed to a cohesive strategy and set of goals. One of the best tools for creating this alignment is through the development of a compelling and clearly articulated vision.

LESLIE WASSEN-FRONTIS GROUP/DUNES COUNTRY PARTNERS, LLC

The Visioning Process for Sustainable Development

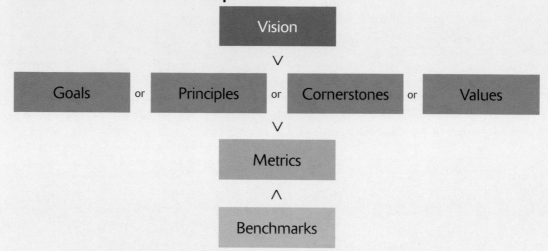

Planning for a sustainable community begins with the creation of a vision statement that will guide the development process. Goals, principles, cornerstones, and values all provide direction for achieving the vision. Metrics are the yardsticks that measure performance and benchmarks define project success.

Creating a Vision

Visions and vision statements should motivate a project team to work together toward fulfillment of an ambitious mission. Even recognizing that the stated goals may never be fully achieved, a well-written and powerfully communicated vision can influence and guide all decisions during the course of a project's evolution. The vision needs to be embraced and repeated across design, physical construction, and operations to unify every action that leads up to the completion, in the built sense, of a new community. And it should endure long after construction is complete and the developer has left the site, inspiring residents and visitors to advance—rather than simply maintain—the purpose for which the community was built.

When creating a vision statement, it is important to remember that, "There is a fine line between vision and hallucination." While vision statements need to motivate their audience to reach for "stretch goals," they should not be so unrealistic as to lack any practicality. The vision statement for a sustainable community should reflect the holistic nature of integrated planning and design, but be based on real-world conditions. Rules of thumb for a vision statement include:

1. Keep it short. A full-page statement is not a vision—it is a manifesto.

2. Use precise and meaningful language. Avoid jargon and obscure language. A vision statement is most effective when the people on the front lines of implementation can use it as their compass in guiding daily activities.

3. Make it actionable. Give the statement a sense of urgency and purpose.

4. Avoid marketing lingo. While a vision statement will guide the marketing message and strategy, it should not read as a sales pitch.

5. Vet it. Solicit comments from admired colleagues and peers to test its viability and appeal.

Finally, one of the key pitfalls of creating a vision statement is underestimating the time and level of dialogue required to create an enduring message. Too often, the envisioning process is relegated to a one-day exercise that is tightly programmed and involves only the design team and senior project management. In envisioning, the process is as important as the product. Attendance and participation by a cross-section of the project team (if not the full team) is critical, if the statement is to have broad acceptance and understanding. Set aside plenty of time to discuss, explore, and debate various options. Envisioning is an inherently iterative, sometimes messy, process that defies tight schedules and linear thinking. Set aside several half-day sessions to create a vision statement. The ability to sleep on discussion points and test-drive ideas with a broad range of people (staff, consultants, marketers, buyers) allows the statement to evolve until it has a laserlike precision unique to the project at hand.

Tools for Achieving the Vision

In development circles today, there are several camps exploring a range of options to help implement the vision, including tools—goals, values, principles, and cornerstones—that the entire development team can use to advance a project's design and execution:

Goals. Goals are a tried-and-true tool for providing detailed guidance in a vision statement. They are used to define a development team's basic agenda in specific terms. For example, a goal may be "to create a diversity of housing options for a wide range of buyers." A correlating objective may be "to achieve price points that can be purchased by x percentage of buyers from the designated market."

Principles. Principles appeared on the scene about 20 years ago, as an alternative to goals and objectives. Providing a less quantitative directive to describing the roadmap to the vision, they are often an important part of the marketing message for a community. Using the housing diversity example again, a principle might be "to ensure that a diversity of residents from different socioeconomic backgrounds can live in the community."

Cornerstones. In recent years, cornerstones have become a popular tool for defining core characteristics of a development. They tend to be very succinct, powerful words or phrases that provide a clear sense of purpose and direction. They are memorable and easily communicated. Continuing the housing product example, a cornerstone would be stated simply as "diversity." Brevity, however, is both an asset and a liability for cornerstones. The simplicity of language can obscure the subtext that should support the overall cornerstone concept it is meant to capture.

Values. Designed to express a unique "voice," values should articulate the developer's beliefs.

A garden community three miles (4.8 kilometers) northwest of downtown Denver, Highlands' Garden Village is located on a 27-acre (11-hectare) infill site. Effective recycling and reuse programs have made the community a model for environmentally conscious development.

JONATHAN ROSE COMPANIES, LLC

I'On, a community
in Charleston, South
Carolina, uses vernacular
architecture to appeal to
its market.

While goals may be achieved and principles may
evolve as conditions change, values should endure. By overtly stating values in planning and
marketing literature, a development often attracts buyers and users in whom its values resonate. In the housing diversity example, a value
statement might be, "We believe that people
from all walks of life should be able to live in our
community, regardless of economic means."

Whichever technique a developer chooses
to employ, the same advice for crafting a vision
statement applies: Avoid jargon, be precise and
succinct, and solicit input from others. For both
inspiration and comparison, read competitors'
statements. Because many of the current ideas
for sustainable community development are
coalescing into a common set of trends and language, research into leading-edge projects may
reveal that a developer's uniquely crafted idea is
already in use elsewhere.

Measuring Success

Metrics and benchmarks have long been used in
real estate development to assess the financial
performance of projects. Metrics are specific
measurements of performance such as internal
rate of return (IRR) or return on investment.
Benchmarks are standards by which performance can be measured. For example, an IRR
of greater than 20 percent is a development
industry benchmark for good performance.
Nonfinancial benchmarks are new to the development process, but are an effective way to
evaluate an evolving or completed community's
adherence to its stated vision. Achieving a sustainable community requires fostering a project
culture where the scorecard of success is much
broader than an IRR or absorption schedule.
Benchmarks and metrics for sustainability
provide a more balanced measurement of a
community's success.

Examples of metrics that speak to the sustainability agenda (but not an exhaustive list) include
vehicle miles traveled, annual energy consumption, tons of waste diverted, and potable water
consumed. These are standard fare metrics that
reflect the notion that sustainability is about
reducing consumption. More progressive approaches use metrics that assimilate a number
of connected ideas—carbon footprint as a way

I'ON COMPANY

21

Noisette:
Measuring Success
With Cornerstones

NOISETTE IS A 3,000-ACRE (1,214-hectare) restoration project encompassing the downtown core of North Charleston, South Carolina. One of the largest sustainable urban redevelopment projects underway in the United States (completion is targeted for 2018), the project will redevelop a former U.S. naval base, breathe life into existing historic downtown neighborhoods, and establish an urban core complex called the River Center.

The project was conceived through a public/private partnership between the Noisette Company and the city of North Charleston. The Noisette Company, which led the development process, spent significant time working with community groups, city representatives, and architecture and planning firms to create a master plan that would realize the partnership's vision: to "create the good life in ways that don't compromise the ability of future generations to do the same."

The Noisette Company decided that truly sustainable communities are founded on three core values: social justice, environmental responsibility, and economic viability. They turned these values into three cornerstones—people, planet, and prosperity—that will guide the project team throughout the development process. Realization of the cornerstones can already be seen in elements of the master plan such as environmental restoration, infrastructure improvements, expansion of parks and recreational areas, enhanced retail and mixed-use areas, and the integration of arts and culture. Noisette will be home to South Carolina's first LEED-certified elementary school and has encouraged the creation of a special tax district to benefit green school development in North Charleston.

Noisette's vision and cornerstones embody the "Sanborn Principles," established

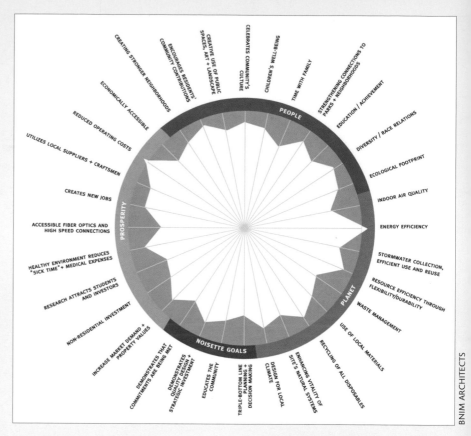

BNIM ARCHITECTS

by a group of urban design visionaries in the 1990s as a foundation for sustainable communities. The principles include:

- healthy indoor environments;
- ecological health;
- social justice;
- cultural creativity;
- beauty; and
- physical and economic accessibility.

To ensure that Noisette realizes its vision, embraces its cornerstones, and implements its principles, the project team is using several tools to measure success. To assess the quality of the built realm, the team partnered with the U.S. Green Building Council to develop the Noisette Quality Home Performance Standards, which are special green building criteria for all residential development on the site, and to establish

green building standards for redevelopment of buildings on the 380-acre (154-hectare) former naval base. Recognizing that integrative design is essential to create a livable, sustainable community, the team developed the Noisette Rose, a flexible tool created to establish and measure specific sustainable goals for the individual building projects within the community. Each radial line in the rose diagram demonstrates the level of achievement within a particular goal. The larger the white rose at the center of the diagram, the closer the development team is to realizing its goals for sustainability.

The Noisette Rose was created to provide a flexible tool to facilitate goal setting and measurement to chart the success of the community's development.

to measure energy reduction, types of energy used, transportation modes, and contribution to greenhouse gases. Resident health indicators are even more complex, but they evaluate important issues, including physical fitness, air and water quality, and social and mental wellness.

Selecting and Managing the Project Team

More than any other type of real estate development, sustainable communities require a cohesive project team that is aligned in its values, working style, and ability to collaborate. This is easier said than done.

A project team for creating sustainable communities includes a broad range of dedicated specialists, each bringing a detailed knowledge to a multitude of interrelated and sometimes competing issues. Identifying the necessary skills and finding the right consultants to provide those skills are critical to a developer's ability to innovate and succeed. Too often a developer will read an article on the latest sustainable luminary, bring that person on board, and end up with a revolving door of consultants and approaches. At the end of several years' work and the expenditure of a few million dollars,

a master plan may emerge looking more like a documentary on sustainable design rather than a financially feasible, executable plan built upon a clear and compelling idea. This is not to say that leading-edge thinkers shouldn't have a seat at the table. They play an important and valuable role, but their input should be balanced against the perspectives of implementation-focused, market-savvy specialists.

Of equal importance to knowledge of sustainable systems is the ability of consultants to work in a collaborative manner. Sustainable design is, at its core, a whole-systems approach to thinking about design, development, construction, and operations. It cannot be accomplished in isolation or in a series of "discipline silos." It requires that the consultant team regularly meet to discuss and evaluate ideas, test those ideas for alignment with the vision statement and business strategy, and refine the plan accordingly. For example, while an initial master-planning workshop may not appear to benefit from the marketing team's presence, the ability to absorb critical decisions in the master plan will allow the marketers to be better messengers of how the project's vision and values are manifested in the physical plan when they interact with buyers.

The mixed-use community of Baldwin Park in Orlando Florida, was designed to enhance the natural environment and attract wildlife through the use of native and wetland aquatic plants. The Audubon Society helped guide the community's environmental conservation and wetlands restoration efforts.

GLATTING JACKSON KERCHER ANGLIN

23

Helpful Hints for Selecting the Right Consultant

THE SELECTION OF CONSULTANTS should be a thoughtful, organized, and equitable process. Ask questions that will result in a clear understanding of how a consultant thinks and works. Here are some tips for achieving better consultant selection:

■ **Prepare a Request for Qualifications (RFQ).** Keep it brief and to the point. Ask the consultant to do the same. Don't be swayed by quantity over quality. Ask the team to clearly describe its approach and methodology before asking about deliverables and fees. Think of specific questions that will help to determine who is best equipped to work with the development team.

■ **Solicit a list of candidates.** Ask colleagues in the industry to recommend professionals who are doing the best work today. Talk to peers and colleagues. Call project staff at other well-respected communities you admire. Compile the names of firms whose working style is similar to that of the development team. Research Web sites and industry publications. Call consultants to inquire if they would be interested in responding to your RFQ.

■ **Based on RFQ responses, shortlist a few firms.** Carefully select two or three firms. If possible, interview those shortlisted in their offices. This will provide a sense of the company's culture and values. The subtle messages an office environment communicates will be a powerful indicator of the firm's operating style.

■ **Interview the people (and the firm).** Focus on the staff members who will be doing the work and how they interact with the development team. Ask them to illustrate the relevance of their experience to the project. This is a great way to understand how they think and if they truly appreciate the development team's values and work ethic. Don't be dazzled by quantity of work—look for quality of thought and experience. Ask for references and follow up.

■ **Use the interview process to assess capabilities and skill sets, including communication.** Can the consultants clearly convey an idea? The iterative process of testing and refining community concepts requires clear thinking and the ability to articulate ideas to a broad range of stakeholders.

■ **Consider team chemistry.** Will the consultants be intellectually committed to ensuring project success? Will they work well with other development team members?

Selecting a consultant team requires both finding talented professionals and ensuring chemistry among them. A developer who simply assembles high-profile experts may be creating a recipe for disaster. Every firm brings a strong individual agenda and set of values to the table. Matching individual personalities to project needs and the developer's own culture is an effective approach to team selection. The chemistry of the consultant team is an intangible quality that should not be overlooked.

One of the paradoxes of the developer-consultant relationship is the lens through which each sees their roles. The developer, who faces a constant flow of financial demands, looks for forward movement. Consultants are always in pursuit of the perfect, elegant solution. Given the opportunity, the search could go on forever. Consequently, enlightened developers know how to set clear parameters for what is important to continue to test, explore, and evaluate, and for what needs to be brought to conclusion quickly. Setting a realistic time frame is an invaluable asset to consultants. A developer should draw on its team's experience to determine research and decision-making schedules.

Too often, consultant fees are spent prematurely, or unnecessarily in the crafting of renderings, detailed drawings, or extensive computer studies. Keep in mind, however, that the Achilles heel of many projects is the lack of high-quality base-mapping, which identifies cultural and natural characteristics of the property. To make the best use of the team's talent and capabilities, and set a strong foundation for project planning and financial modeling, do not skimp on getting base-mapping done early and correctly. It will save money many times over in reduced design time, more accurate drawings, and yield analysis.

Multiple Players, Multiple Challenges

Ten years from now, it may be a reality that every land development has a sustainable component. This means changing the way developers think about the buildings they construct, the infrastructure they install, and the community associations they create and fund. In 2007, however, sustainable land development is an emerging art being practiced by a passionate, intellectually curious few. The increasingly visible discussion about sprawl, the loss of community, traditional neighborhood design, and focus on environmentally responsible development has attracted a whole new range of people to the community development arena. While the community devel-

24

Jackson Meadow's developers emphasized community and interpersonal relationships. Their primary goal was to create a place where "people care for each other and the land." Located outside Minneapolis, the development is surrounded by 250 acres (101 hectares) of open space.

opment business was once largely the purview of entrepreneurial land developers who did not build homes and were driven by a zeal for creating enduring communities (e.g., James Rouse with Columbia, Robert Simon with Reston), today the business is split somewhat unevenly into three general areas: homebuilders, land and community developers, and legacy landowners.

Each of these initiators of community development has different motivations and interests in the development process. And each has a different set of threshold issues that could prevent them from successfully developing in a sustainable manner. Conversely, each proponent also brings a unique skill set that, if properly focused

and directed, can play an important role in advancing the concept of sustainable development.

Homebuilders. Historically, homebuilders often bought lots from land developers, leaving the entitlement, planning, and design process of new communities to others, but they have emerged as a major development force over the past decade. With the increasing focus on revenue growth and unit production by publicly owned homebuilders, there is significant motivation to capture the increased profit perceived to accompany land development, while also gaining tighter control over lot inventory.

Because builders are intimately involved in the construction of homes, they have the ability to

PETER BASTIANELLI KERSE : KATHLEEN DAY-COEN

research, manage, and execute high-performance structures that are an important part of the resource efficiency discussion. The downside is that homebuilders are driven by speed and the bottom line. The need for an iterative, exploratory design process that accompanies sustainable communities is not often a practice embraced by homebuilders. This needs to change, if they are to become effective players in the sustainable community business.

Land and community developers. These developers have migrated to larger and more complex deals, focusing on community-building rather than simply looking to generate lots. They have pioneered a range of techniques to resolve the challenges of both the capital markets and the builders with whom they must work. They also tend to embrace vision-driven projects.

Land developers understand the long-term nature of community development, and the resulting value created over time. As such, they have the ability to produce a capital structure that allows for more deliberate front end costs that support a sustainability agenda—innovative infrastructure, enduring conservation stewardship entities, communal open spaces, and main street amenities. The challenge for land developers lies in their relationship with third-party builders, with whom they must negotiate to ensure that desirable architectural and high-performance construction features are included in the purchase price. Depending on the market's level of interest in their developed land, this can be a tough negotiation that often results in compromises on the most visible and resource-consumptive part of the community—the buildings.

Legacy landowners. Individuals who control unique land assets due to inheritance or change in land-use priorities are known as legacy landowners. This group is changing the character of community development. Not satisfied to sell their property to the highest bidder, they often have an emotional attachment to the land and a personal desire to change the way it is developed. Their common motivation is to ensure that when the property is developed, they feel a sense of pride for having demonstrated constructive social change. This group is inexperienced in the community development process, yet it also holds great potential to transform the face of sustainable development.

CITY OF SAN FRANCISCO

Measuring Sustainability on Treasure Island

THE REDEVELOPMENT of Treasure Island, a former U.S. Navy base in the center of the San Francisco Bay, is on track to become a self-sustaining community. At buildout in 2018, the 450-acre (182-hectare) development will include 6,000

Aerial view of Treasure Island

residential units (30 percent affordable to low- and very low-income residents), shops, hotels, entertainment facilities, and a 300-acre (121-hectare) park and organic demonstration farm. Every home on the island will be within a 15-minute walk of a transit hub and the residential solar power system will be designed so that excess electricity generated by photovoltaics on Treasure Island's buildings will be redirected to the city's power grid.

The environmental underpinnings of the redevelopment are detailed in a 150-page Sustainability Plan, including a list of performance criteria. The plan establishes specific metrics for measuring progress in terms of various sustainability goals. Current performance is continually assessed and compared to the sustainability goals at buildout. The table at right provides a comparison of Treasure Island's sustainability performance in 2006 and its projected performance at project completion. The metrics identified reflect the sustainability goals that have been established for development.

Treasure Island Sustainability Metrics

Category	Metric	Current Performance	By 2018
Population			
Number of People	Population estimate	2,700	13,500
Site Design and Land Use			
Density	Dwelling units per acre/hectare	8.23/3.33	75.6/30.59
Access to retail services	Miles/kilometers to retail for majority of residents	4/6.44 (off-island)	0.5/0.80 (on-island)
Landscape and Biodiversity			
Open space	Percentage of land allocated as open space	23	56
Tree preservation	Number of mature trees	not known	Preserve mature trees where feasible
Xeriscaping	Percentage of xeriscaped landscaping	<5 (estimate)	100 (% of new landscaping)
Transportation			
Walkability	Block length in feet/meters	1,000 to 2,000/305 to 610	300 to 400/91 to 122
Transit connectivity	Miles/kilometers to transit	<1/4/0.40 bus; no ferry	<1/4/0.40 shuttle; <1/2/0.08 ferry/bus
Transit frequency	Number of transit rides per weekday[1]	65	600
Parking	Cars per dwelling unit	1.66	1
Mode share	Weekday peak hour, non-auto mode share	26	55
Energy			
Energy use	Electric use per sq f/sq m	N/A	12.7kWh/1.18
Energy use	Peak electric power demand	10MW	17.4MW
Renewable energy	Percentage of energy from on-site renewable sources	0	5
Carbon emissions	CO_2 emissions (pounds/kilograms) per capita[2]	7,740/3,510	3,030/1,374
Water			
Water use	Per capita potable water use (gallons/liters per day/capita)	193/730	70/264
Wastewater reuse	Percentage of wastewater recycled	0	25 (average wastewater flow)
Stormwater	Percentage of impervious surfaces	64	39
Solid Waste			
Diversion rate	Percentage of waste diverted from landfill	67[3]	95
Health, Safety, and Security			
Exposure to physical risks	Earthquake, climate change, flooding vulnerability	High	Low
Community and Economic Indicators			
Community facilities	Community facilities (sq f/sq m)	N/A	25,000/2,322
Community diversity (families)	Percentage of households with children	17[3]	35
Community diversity (age)	Percentage of residents <18 and >64 years of age	30[3]	31
Affordability	Percentage of affordable housing	23	30

Note: Data apply to Treasure Island only.
1. Calculated based on LEED ND methodology: number of buses stopping within 0.25 mile (0.40 kilometer) of a majority of dwelling units, and number of ferries (times 3) stopping within 0.5 mile/0.08 kilometer.
2. Applies to energy and transportation carbon sources, and includes offsets and sequestration; calculated using Greenhouse Gas Protocol.
3. San Francisco citywide data.

Source: Exhibit K, Treasure Island Sustainability Plan, October 2006;
http://www.sfenvironment.com/articles_pr/2006/article/120606.htm.

SERENBE

Serenbe: A Landowner's Passion to Protect the Land

SERENBE IS A 900-ACRE (364-hectare) community being developed in the heart of rural Chattahoochee Hill Country in Fulton County, Georgia, about 45 minutes southwest of Atlanta. Every facet of Serenbe is being designed with environmental sustainability in mind and the notion that a community is a living part of its natural surroundings, not something to be built at nature's expense.

Serenbe came about when, one day, Steve Nygren (the developer) went out for his jog and spotted a bulldozer in his neighborhood. Afraid that developers were clearing out all of the woodland, he decided to take action to preserve the natural landscape. Although there was no development

SERENBE

taking place—the bulldozing was only for a landing strip for his neighbor's personal plane—Nygren bought as much land as he could afford in addition to the 60 acres he had owned since 1991. He and his wife Marie then gathered a group of the largest property owners in the area with the idea of convincing them to share his passion to protect the land from the typical growth patterns of suburban development. Many discussions later, and after forming the Chattahoochee Hill Country Alliance in 2001, this group established a land use plan promoting sustainable development coupled with environmental preservation. The plan, which was adopted in 2002, represents the first

plan in the region that was developed by a community through a grassroots initiative.

Serenbe is being developed in the heart of 40,000 acres (16,187 hectares) protected by the Chattahoochee Hill Country land use plan. Developer Serenbe Properties outlined a set of defining principles to ensure the protection and enhancement of quality of life for Serenbe's future residents:

■ a healthy lifestyle
■ expression of regional character
■ diversity of age and economics
■ environmental conservation
■ environmentally responsible development
■ community design integrated with natural setting
■ education and self-development
■ interaction with educational and arts organizations
■ high-technology connectivity

Serenbe is designed to flow with the topography to disturb the natural landscape as little as possible. The community is laid out with continuous pathways to encourage walking. Native plants and organic landscaping techniques are used to eliminate the need for chemicals and lawn maintenance. Tree clearing is limited to only trees absolutely necessary for building, and many of the trees and native plants that must be moved are placed elsewhere at Serenbe.

Serenbe's plan calls for 80 percent green space. At buildout in 2008, there will be 220 homes, including single-family, multifamily, and live/work units, and 95,000 square feet (8,826 square meters) of commercial buildings. All homes are built to the

standards of the EarthCraft House Program, a local green building program. These standards include energy efficiency, low maintenance, air quality, water conservation, and resource-efficient building materials and systems. The residents are able to reduce utility bills and protect the environment.

A biological wastewater treatment system was installed rather than a traditional sewer system. Using inexpensive recycled water techniques, treated effluent water is reused for irrigation and future water supply for toilets. Other wastewater is treated in a two-stage chemical-free passive system that incorporates non-disruptive filtration and dispersion. The result is cleaner water, reclaimed through means that require less energy and less supervision by the operator, and amount to savings on water bills.

Above: The Blue Eyed Daisy Bakeshop at Serenbe recently achieved Silver LEED status, making it the smallest building in the nation with this designation. Left: Serenbe is designed to flow with the topography to disturb the natural landscape as little as possible.

Moreover, instead of using concrete spillways that concentrate storm runoff, Serenbe stormwater runoff is directed into natural systems of vegetated filter strips and shallow channels of dense vegetation. These natural filters remove pollutants while dispersing water flow.

Serenbe, born out of the vision of one man, suggests that it is possible to build a community that brings compact residential and commercial development to a pristine rural setting while still preserving the natural landscape. But, first and foremost, there has to be a commitment to build in a new and better way.

Because they are often more patient in their view of how quickly land needs to be developed, they have the significant benefit of time to explore, test, and create studies, a master plan, and an execution strategy that can incorporate the best current and forward-thinking practices and technologies. While this group holds a significant potential to advance national models of sustainability, its lack of working capital, inexperience, and discomfort with the inherent risks that go with land development are not insignificant hurdles. Both an asset and a liability, the inexperience of many legacy landowners means they may lack discipline in following a rigorous process for development. Failure under the weight of naivete or under-capitalization will reinforce the notion of some pundits that sustainable community development is a fantasy. Partnering with an experienced community developer is a good alternative.

Having an Exit Strategy

Determining an exit strategy at the onset of a project increases a development team's ability to focus and control the vision associated with each step of the sustainable community process. For example, if the goal is to sell the land soon after crafting a vision, energy should be spent carefully detailing a set of covenants and restrictions that will codify the developer's vision and ensure its implementation by the buyer. If the goal is to take the community through to a detailed level of implementation, energy and dollars should be spent researching and resolving tough design and construction issues as well as on developing design standards and restrictions.

In order to effectively change the way a finished community looks—and lives—developers must understand the practical process by which a community gets built. The homebuilder, land developer, and legacy landowner have different options for converting their vision into reality. A vision is only as good the development team's ability to implement it, and if it spends all of its time and energy on crafting a superior vision without understanding what will sell, to whom, and when, the vision may only become a paper exercise. The feature box on the next page ("Pad, Paper, or Finished Lot") explains the three most common ways developers exit a project.

Miller Showers Park in Bloomington, Indiana, addresses a number of quality-of-life issues, including the ecological health of an important stream, alternative transportation, public recreation, and community connectivity.

RATIO ARCHITECTS, INC.

29

Pad, Paper, or Finished Lot?

THE PROCESS OF COMMUNITY development is as much about envisioning, planning, and design as it is about execution and exit strategy—how to effectively get paid for the value created by a development and eventually end developer involvement. Many legacy landowners and novice developers are long on vision and short on exit strategy. Defining an exit strategy requires a comprehensive assessment of the development process and a determination of the point at which departure is desirable. Costs are measured not only in dollars but also in terms of control and risk to the vision.

The development generally has three options to monetize the value it has created:

■ **Pad Sale.** The developer may choose to create large tracts of land that show a generalized road system, utility concept, and product types and then sell these parcels or pads—5 to 50 acres (2 to 20 hectares)—to a homebuilder or another land developer. The goal is to exit the project as quickly as possible. If the developer has limited capital or the market is hot, a few pad sales can facilitate investment in other parts of the project. In this type of exit, the developer gives up significant control of the finished product. While restrictive conditions can be attached to the purchase agreement, the developer must monitor the completion of the work to ensure its compliance with the initial intent or commitments made during the entitlement process.

■ **Paper Lot Sale.** With zoning entitlement in hand, the developer may choose to begin detailed design and engineering of the project's initial phase, including roads, parks, open space, and organization of lots, and product type. The subdivision process, known as platting or mapping, can take anywhere from 90 days to two years, depending on the jurisdiction. Upon approval of a preliminary plat, the developer has increased the land's collateral and can often secure more favorable financing. The final plat creates even more value. However, because of its specificity, the final plat may be less appealing to large builders who may prefer greater freedom in developing the land they purchase. With plat in place there is a more defined plan that affixes community concepts more definitively than in a pad sale that may only be accompanied by a nonbinding concept plan.

■ **Finished Lots.** The sale of finished lots creates value and maintains greater developer control over the community vision. However, it introduces risks in terms of both construction cost escalation and unknown conditions (e.g., bedrock, underground water flow, hazardous materials) that can add to the project's cost and extend its timeframe. Typically, developers delivering finished lots also take on responsibility for the design and construction of the public realm, including parks, streetscapes, open space trails, and main street cores and plazas. By building the public realm, the developer can test ideas and concepts, refine designs in the field, and perfect the character of the community. The ability for homebuyers to experience a neighborhood is critical to sales success in communities that are seeking to resonate with buyers who value green development.

Aligning the Product with the Market

The community development landscape is littered with projects that began with a great vision but, for a variety of reasons, failed to be realized. A cursory glance by observers often reduces the cause and effect to the belief that the project vision was not aligned with the marketplace. In some cases, overly optimistic developers have brought a concept to market before its time. Yet in other cases, failures in execution due to inadequate due diligence are at the heart of the problem. One of the most crucial due diligence steps for real estate development projects in general—and for sustainable development projects in particular—is to conduct a market study. Developers should be as thorough as possible in trying to understand how deep the local market need is for non-traditional development and what this market values.

Green development is receiving increased media attention and becoming more widely desired by consumers. However, there are "shades of green" and sustainability is not an all or nothing proposition. Depending on the market, a sustainable development can and should incorporate different solutions. A concise market study will determine how receptive consumers are to sustainable principles and, in turn, will help the development team prioritize project components.

A market study should test consumer preferences; however, it may be difficult to determine how much of a premium the local market will pay for sustainable features. While it is not really possible to determine the costs and profit margins associated with features such as LEED certification, walking trails, and open space, it is more important to determine how the differentiated product will fit within the marketplace and make for a sound business strategy. Surveys will test for the depth of market potential, while focus groups will help refine particular concepts and ideas.

Traditional market study tools may be used, but because there are relatively few sustainable communities up and running and consumer knowledge may be low, the tools must be used in a creative manner. Management consultant Tom Peters points out that "customers are your rear-view mirror"—they respond to what is already in the marketplace. This "rearview mirror" approach does not address what could sell, given the right product targeted to the right market. When a development is based on what has succeeded in the past, it becomes more susceptible to market shifts.

Developers of sustainable communities confront special challenges in assessing the market: consumer misconceptions of sustainable development; lack of data on comparable projects; and appraisers and lenders wary of non-traditional products. That is why a thorough market study that uses information in new ways can help offset some of these challenges and help ensure appropriate design and marketing.

The first VCR, fax machine, and minivan all famously received negative ratings when initially tested through market research. Some potential pitfalls can be avoided with due diligence and confidence in a strong product. A close second to "location, location, location" in successful real estate development is "research, research, research."

MARKET RESEARCH TOOLS AND STRATEGIES

Sustainable development has gained market traction in the last decade and there is a growing body of knowledge available on the economic and environmental performance of such early communities. It must be remembered, however, that certain sustainable practices and features may work in some parts of the country but not in others due to different climatic conditions, regulatory constraints, and consumer preferences. A useful market study will be a sophisticated mix of standard research methodology and creative detective work. The resources discussed below are some, but not all, of the tools appropriate for market research on sustainable communities.

Home sales data. Of course, a thorough understanding of the housing market is a necessary part of any market research effort. In addition to the multiple listing service (MLS), the local homebuilders' association, banks, appraisers, title companies, and local government and economic development resources, major markets have local or national companies that track the new-home market in depth. Some track

sales, starts, closings, completions, permits and/or lot supply. Each of these statistics can illuminate a piece of the housing market puzzle. Understanding the current supply—what's selling, what's not selling, and why—is important to help set a baseline for the market.

However, these sources give a limited picture of the sustainable features that are included in new homes or communities. MLS data in particular can be misleading, because they may not include custom homes sales, which are often principal-to-principal transactions. Since custom homes are in the higher price bands of a given market, the exclusion of these transactions from the MLS can distort the perception of the prices a market can and will support. A good place to find out about existing green developments is at the local planning department. Whether or not there are any comparable sustainable communities in an area, the main

Community developers are recognizing that green buildings, such as 717 Texas in Houston, are good for the bottom line—as well as the environment.

JOE AKER

DEVELOPING SUSTAINABLE PLANNED COMMUNITIES

objective is to determine if a market will support and pay for product differentiation. If so, sustainable development can be a way to achieve that differentiation.

When comparing specific developments or products, which may be akin to comparing "apples and oranges," an adjusted pricing analysis can help two projects be compared where features of a given project are adjusted up or down relative to a subject site. This is a specific feature-to-feature comparison of the primary competitors to a new development. The study should not only assign values to conventional home and community attributes such as lot size, interior finishes, and shared amenities such as a pool, but also to sustainable features such as low-VOC (volatile organic compounds) products, energy-efficient appliances, and community assets (bike trails and access to open space).

The market study should also include an analysis of the density of newer development projects. Some insight can be gleaned on how sensitive a market may be to greater density, often a characteristic of sustainable development. Some local governments and markets embrace density, especially around transit stations, while others avoid it.

Homebuilders and developers should not focus only on the competition from other new homes and ignore the resale market. The fact is resale neighborhoods can be more direct competitors to new home developments than other new homes, particularly when a new home community is differentiated from the majority of the new home market. For example, most communities have an established older neighborhood with mature trees and charming architecture. Such neighborhoods are often close to downtown, in a historic district with pre–World War II homes, and within walking distance of parks and services. Houses in these high-demand areas usually command premium prices and sell quickly. Analyzing the days on market and price differential between these homes in comparison to homes of similar age and size in conventional neighborhoods can provide some perspective on the relative price elasticity of the market and what it may be willing to pay for new homes that are differentiated from conventional new properties.

Mashpee Commons, in Mashpee, Massachusetts, conforms to traditional Cape Cod design principles and includes scattered affordable units.

CORNISH ASSOCIATES

33

The U.S. Department of Housing and Urban Development's HOPE VI program has facilitated the transformation of thousands of former public housing projects into mixed-income neighborhoods. In order to increase appeal of the Holly Park neighborhood in Seattle, the project's developers integrated the affordable and market-rate units.

Demographics. Demographics are socioeconomic groups that compose a market niche. Information on age, income, occupation, household composition, familial status, commuting times and patterns, and number of vehicles provides insight into the characteristics of a given population and, to some extent, their housing needs. The market study should also include examination of mobility rates and migration trends, the primary drivers of household formation and housing demand.

Some market research firms have aligned demographic data with spatial analysis to form geodemographic neighborhood classification systems, with the basic tenet being people with similar cultural backgrounds, means, and perspectives naturally gravitate toward one another. They emulate their neighbors, adopt similar

TIM GRIFFITH

34

social values, tastes, and expectations, and share similar patterns of consumer behavior toward products, services, media, and promotions. Such programs can help to target certain demographic profiles based on consumer behavior and identify the groups that may value sustainable communities and green products.

In an attempt to seek even further refinement of demographics, psychographics are being used to measure attitudes, interests, opinions, beliefs, and lifestyles. In the 2000 book *The Cultural Creatives: How 50 Million People Are Changing the World*, Paul H. Ray and Sherry Ruth Anderson identify three major psychographic subcultures in the adult population of the United States: Traditionals (24 percent); Moderns (50 percent); and Cultural Creatives (26 percent). Cultural Creatives value many of the guiding principles behind sustainable development, such as the sanctity of nature, altruism, ecology, and social justice. Because of its values, this subculture may likely shun newly built conventional subdivisions. Instead, its members may be drawn to resale neighborhoods or new communities that embody the values that are important to them. Effective market studies will seek out and examine these segments and determine how they apply to sustainable communities.

Surveys and focus groups. Surveys are not an effective method to determine the depth of market potential, but they can provide a helpful research tool to test sustainable community concepts, features, and amenities. The trick is to ask the right questions in the right way. Consumers cannot always articulate preferences for a product for which they may have no knowledge or experience. The various definitions of sustainability and associated terms (environmentally sensitive development, green development, smart growth, responsible development) add to the confusion. Consumers may not have the vocabulary to describe what they want, but instead rely on familiar images, which may only be conventional development patterns. People may also have disparate perspectives on the same concept. For example, "urban density" can mean different things to different people. While often used during the planning and entitlement phase, Visual Preference Surveys (VPS) are a tool to help bridge the communication gap by allowing a survey group or community to express its preferences without having to come up with the vocabulary to describe it. VPS utilizes images, photographs, and renderings of design elements, buildings, and communities accompanied by questionnaires to determine preferences.

A focus group is a good way to gather information on a market regarding a specific issue or product. Prairie Holdings Corporation, for example, conducted focus groups while planning Prairie Crossing, a pioneering conservation development in Grayslake, Illinois. The project centered on a farm and focus group participants were, at first, surprisingly negative to the concept. The concern was not the noise, odor, or pests associated with a farm, but rather suspicion that the adjacent agricultural lands would be developed as conventional suburban sprawl in the future. Upon learning that the adjacent farmlands would be protected through a conservation easement, participants were not only enthusiastic about the concept, but also believed the home sites to be worth a premium.

USING MARKET RESEARCH TO SHAPE THE PLAN

Once the market study is completed, the next step is to use the findings to inform how the community is financed, positioned in the market, designed, and sold. Sustainable communities are unique to many markets and uncharted territory to some lenders, so it is essential to make the most of the market research to explain why sustainable projects are financially viable, environmentally responsible, and attractive.

Due to the conservative nature of the capital markets, one of the challenges in advancing sustainable developments is access to funding. Lenders and appraisers have been trained to think of standardization as a means to minimize risk. Therefore, when making the case for funding, the developer of a sustainable community may need to present the project in a more conventional way, by emphasizing the proven attributes of the development and minimizing the innovative qualities, while still honoring the overall vision. For example, while sustainable developments have often exceeded the market in terms of absorption and price premium, these factors cannot be relied on in the *proforma* assumptions. Instead, when

35

Located in the Baoshan district of Shanghai and built as a model of ecologically sensitive urban development, the new town of Luodian has a Swedish architectural theme and offers a mix of housing choices.

seeking capital, developers should emphasize the fundamental merits of the project such as a good location, a product mix that is aligned with the target market, and a competitive pricing strategy.

Results of surveys and focus groups will help prioritize a community's sustainable features. Often potential homebuyers' top concerns are affordability, privacy, little or no traffic congestion near homes, and convenient access to shops and schools. Depending on the results of the market survey, the marketing plan should include how certain sustainable elements such as energy savings, natural amenities, and walkability offset these concerns.

Sustainable development necessitates collaborative effort on the part of the development team throughout the project's critical path. The right information at the right time can have benefits to both the front end and the back end of the development process. An iterative approach, rather than a linear approach, requires that the marketing, sales, and leasing disciplines define the market strategy and inform the planning and design teams at the earliest stage of a project's inception. Such a process, though perhaps more time intensive upfront, can be cost-effective in

the long run if challenges are identified early on and consensus among the entire development team can be attained. Many experienced developers contend that the single largest cost savings can be the timing of implementing sustainable goals and design practices. The earlier in the planning process such practices are considered and evaluated, the higher the return on both soft- and hard-cost investments.

A thorough market study for a sustainable community will arm the development team with the proper tools to ensure a successful project. Research must include a creative and in-depth analysis of existing conditions in combination with what the target market values.

Leaving a Legacy

The processes for creating sustainable communities are as unique as the sites they will occupy. Each one must be customized to meet the personality of the sponsor, the uniqueness of the site and its context, and the financial structure of the project. Starting with a clear vision and developing the tools to implement that vision is essential. Selection of a talented team of people with good chemistry and a commitment

SWECO FFNS ARCHITECTS

Understanding the Market Potential for Sustainable Development

	Why	What	How
New Home Sales	To understand the current environment of new home products and projects on the market, as well as the pipeline of pending projects from municipal records to provide an assessment of future competition.	What does the current supply "look like" in terms of product, place, price, and promotion? Is there variation in the pricing of new home communities, indicating a demand in the market to pay for differentiated products like sustainable developments?	■ Metrostudy, a leading provider of housing market information tracks. www.metrostudy.com ■ Hanley Wood Market Intelligence tracks 75 of the top U.S. housing markets. www.hanleywood.com/hwmi ■ Local government agencies track local housing market data.
Resale Home Sales	To understand how trends in the resale market, which usually make up the majority of home transactions, can affect new home sales.	Is there variation in sales, market times, and pricing among resale neighborhoods, indicating a demand in the market to pay for differentiated products like sustainable development?	■ Multiple Listing Service www.mls.com
Demographics	To understand the key variables affecting demand for real estate: population; employment; age; income; household composition; migration; mobility, etc.	Which market segments are projected to increase or decrease? How does the current supply fulfill those various market segments? Are there opportunities to gain market share? Are there opportunities to fulfill an underserved segment?	■ www.census.gov ■ www.claritas.com ■ Local economic development agencies
Psychographics	To understand the key variables affecting lifestyles, beliefs, opinions, interests, and values, which are better predictors of consumer behavior than demographics alone.	Known as PSYTE, clusters, PRIZM, Personicx, or MindBase, these segmentation products group consumers by values (psychographics) and where they live (geodemographics).	■ www.americanlives.com ■ www.esri.com ■ www.claritas.com ■ www.mapinfo.com ■ www.acxiom.com ■ www.yankelovich.com
Consumer Trends	To understand broader consumer and societal trends and how other industries are responding to meet those needs, wants, and desires.	What sort of consumer trends are surfacing and how can they affect new communities?	■ www.yankelovich.com ■ www.faithpopcorn.com ■ www.trendwatching.com
Analogs	To understand the lessons learned from other projects in other markets.	What did the developer do to create a sustainable community versus a conventional community? What was the incremental cost? Did the market pay for it?	■ www.casestudies.uli.org

Source: Greenstreet Ltd.

to the developer's vision is critical to a successful process. Developers should avoid the common pitfalls that come from not spending appropriate time and dollars on initial market research and determining an exit strategy in the early stages of the project.

Finally, one of the primary differences between a sustainable development and a good planned community is the conscious effort to create a legacy, a healthy community that continues to evolve after the developer has left the scene. A strong original vision, thoughtfully and comprehensively executed, will instill an ethos of sustainability and establish frameworks for evolution.

3 Integrated Planning and Design

More than half of the new coastal community of WindMark Beach, Florida, is dedicated to open space, parks, and native preserves.

A MIXED-USE PROJECT IN CINCINNATI earns LEED Silver; the project cost 10 percent more to build than conventional construction. Across the street, a mixed-use project of the same size earns LEED Gold and only incurred an additional cost of 2 percent. What made the difference in this hypothetical example? Integrated planning and design looks beyond the traditional linear design process; it incorporates sustainability upfront and uses a holistic approach to the development process.

Integrated planning and design has two dimensions. The first involves the design process itself, which requires collaboration between multiple disciplines and stakeholders, especially during the initial stages of planning. In an integrated process the design team does not work in isolation. The developer, architects, planners, engineers, major contractors, and other key team members become involved at the start of a project. This early collaboration lays the foundation for developing a sustainable community. Guided by a clearly articulated vision statement and set of principles, the integrated team works together throughout the life of the project and seeks strategies, systems, and products that best support a sustainable outcome.

The second dimension of integrated design is a shift toward whole-systems thinking—an approach that considers the linkages and interactions between project elements and seeks solutions that address multiple problems at the same time. For a community-scale development, it is critical to understand the interconnections between natural systems, infrastructure, and building design, and leveraging what are known as "solution multipliers." For instance, drainage swales that improve stormwater quality will not be optimized unless the size of underground storm drains is reduced. A local shuttle/transit system concurrently requires a reduction in travel lanes in order to provide more green space, improve stormwater quality, or reduce heat gain.

Thinking in a more holistic manner about a site's natural systems, infrastructure, community context, and urban form can result in achieving a higher level of performance at a lower cost. This chapter examines the integrated planning process and key design considerations for a sustainable community.

The Integrated Process

Historically, planning for community-scale development projects has been linear, starting with land acquisition, market analysis, and engineering studies and followed by conceptual planning,

COOPER, ROBERTSON & PARTNERS

Above: The Sanctuary's infiltration swales allow runoff from a parking lot to be absorbed into the ground instead of collected and discharged off site. Right: Employees who work at Intech Park, located near Indianapolis, Indiana, benefit from the office park's natural setting. Wetlands serve as the primary method of stormwater management, and existing natural features were preserved and enhanced.

ABOVE: LANDDESIGN;
RIGHT: RATIO ARCHITECTS, INC.

design, and construction. At each step of this process, plans are compared to both market and financial parameters and appropriate adjustments are made.

The problem with this approach is that it does not consider the interrelationships between systems, either constructed or natural. Nature does not operate in a linear fashion. It is cyclical and interconnected. Impacts on landform, soils, sunlight, hydrology, flora, or fauna ripple through each other, often with unforeseen consequences.

Cutting-edge projects today are incorporating high-performance development practices, such as low-impact stormwater design, reduced-water landscape systems, and energy conservation features. Each of these features can generate financial savings and environmental benefits. But if not linked together and understood as an interconnected network, certain synergies and gains may be lost.

Integrated planning starts with a fundamental shift in the project team's mindset. The team must think about its goals in a different way, in which interconnectedness and cause-and-effect are part of every decision. If this adjustment does not occur, the team may abandon high-performance

practices in the face of a tight schedule, budgetary constraints, or skepticism from many fronts. The mindset shift must occur at the highest management levels; otherwise the team will not be empowered to make tough decisions.

Another early requirement is to bring the right design team members in at the right time. For example, ecologists are typically hired only to secure the wetland permit, the landscape architect comes on at the end to "shrub things up," and the traffic engineer negotiates the roadway plan approval process. As Sandra Mendler points out in *The HOK Guidebook to Sustainable Design*,

"The project delivery process itself must change from a serial collection of discrete tasks performed with little interaction between players to a collaborative and self-conscious effort to integrate design strategies between all disciplines and all players in the project delivery process . . . integrated design demands a more inclusive team working much more closely together than is traditionally the case."

Integrated planning also means connecting with the larger community context in order to achieve the so-called "triple bottom line" of social, economic, and environmental sustainability. The word "sustainability" suggests long-term viability. If the surrounding community is not prepared to nurture and sustain a new addition, a project's innovations and low-impact practices may deteriorate.

Successful sustainable projects must respond to real-time market dynamics and opportunities. An integrated process acknowledges the importance of the marketplace, and is realistic about the extent to which increased costs can be absorbed by higher pricing. The building program should include the green features that buyers and tenants want, not solely what the development team thinks they should have.

A key ingredient in the integrated planning process is a comprehensive understanding of the site's environmental context. Opportunities to link into or preserve regional green infrastructure networks, natural lands, wildlife corridors, drainage systems, and subsurface water networks should be identified and leveraged. Regional transportation plans and water quality requirements must be researched.

The planning process should begin with clearly articulated and measurable goals and objectives for sustainability. Whether it is a 50 percent reduction in potable water, a 30 percent reduction in off-site vehicle trips, a post-development wildlife corridor system superior to predevelopment conditions, or a net-zero energy community, goals energize the process and provide tangible targets. The sustainability program should address every aspect of community development, from energy, water, and indoor environmental quality to natural habitat, green infrastructure, urban form, mobility, education, and social equity.

Whole-systems thinking is the crux of an integrated planning and design process. Specific cause-and-effect interconnections between natural and built systems can be leveraged to increase benefit and reduce costs. Tough decisions must be made about which sustainable practices and green features to include and which are not merited. In the final analysis, an integrated

planning approach is the surest way to go green without breaking the bank. A developer who utilizes an integrated process is in a better position to achieve a higher standard of sustainable design, save money, and enjoy a high return on investment.

Site Selection

Site selection must be made with both the regional and the local context in mind. A site next to a transit corridor will reduce fossil-fuel emissions; a project adjacent to a wildlife corridor may provide the means to preserve it in perpetuity; locating housing close to jobs will reduce vehicle miles traveled. An integrated design process optimizes a development's relationship to its surroundings.

Historically, site selection for community-scale projects has tended to be "opportunistic." Developers seek out parcels when they become available for purchase at a reasonable price with acceptable risks. Often the land is identified, evaluated through due diligence, and a vision,

The ability to link into an existing or proposed transit system adds to a project's ability to reduce automobile emissions. The Sacramento Regional Transit District's stations offer amenities such as parking and bicycle storage areas.

© 2006 DIXI CARILLO

41

The drainage system at High Point, a mixed-income community in West Seattle, protects the nearby Longfellow Creek from stormwater runoff.

SVR

program, and design are developed to fit the site's context, unique characteristics, and market setting. Although this traditional approach does not prevent the use of green development concepts, it may limit the depth and degree of environmental benefits offered by a sustainable approach.

To achieve a truly sustainable development, a change in thinking about site location is required. Rather than looking for a good piece of land to build a sustainable project, developers should search for a sustainable piece of land. Some parcels provide a greater opportunity to maximize sustainable attributes and minimize ecological impacts. The obvious examples are the redevelopment of brownfields and regeneration of declining urban areas. It is also true that many greenfield sites can be developed with minimal negative impact and provide manifest social, economic, and ecological benefits.

When pursuing a sustainable outcome as part of a business plan or vision statement there are certain site conditions that lend themselves to this goal at the lowest cost and greatest positive effect. The following list of attributes expresses characteristics for brownfield, infill, and greenfield locations:

Previously developed or impacted lands. Although often more expensive in the short term, infill and regeneration can save money and natural resources in the long term by using or expanding existing infrastructure, minimizing energy costs, improving indoor air quality, and decreasing commuting time for residents and employees.

Lands contiguous to existing regional infrastructure. Avoiding leapfrog development is key to attaining regional sustainability. To the extent a site can bolt onto existing systems, especially transportation infrastructure, substantial costs, both economic and environmental, can be avoided. So-called "corridor development" creates patterns that more readily support multimodal transportation and provides jobs, housing diversity, and parallel regional drainage and open space networks.

Internal natural lands of high ecological value. Traditionally, such lands have been avoided like

High Point Drainage System

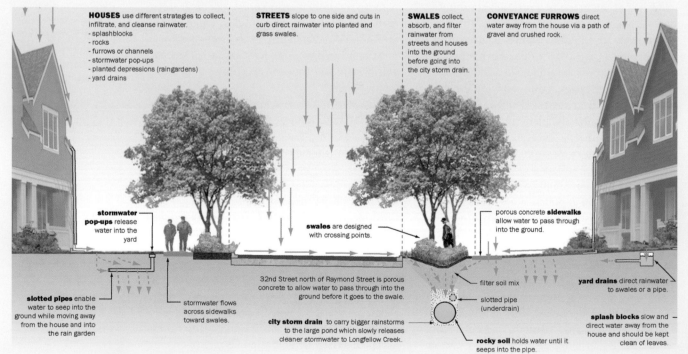

HOUSES use different strategies to collect, infiltrate, and cleanse rainwater.
- splashblocks
- rocks
- furrows or channels
- stormwater pop-ups
- planted depressions (raingardens)
- yard drains

STREETS slope to one side and cuts in curb direct rainwater into planted and grass swales.

SWALES collect, absorb, and filter rainwater from streets and houses into the ground before going into the city storm drain.

CONVEYANCE FURROWS direct water away from the house via a path of gravel and crushed rock.

stormwater pop-ups release water into the yard

swales are designed with crossing points.

porous concrete **sidewalks** allow water to pass through into the ground.

slotted pipes enable water to seep into the ground while moving away from the house and into the rain garden

stormwater flows across sidewalks toward swales.

32nd Street north of Raymond Street is porous concrete to allow water to pass through into the ground before it goes to the swale.

city storm drain to carry bigger rainstorms to the large pond which slowly releases cleaner stormwater to Longfellow Creek.

filter soil mix

slotted pipe (underdrain)

rocky soil holds water until it seeps into the pipe.

yard drains direct rainwater to swales or a pipe.

splash blocks slow and direct water away from the house and should be kept clean of leaves.

The Alcyone apartments in Seattle contain live/work units that help reduce commuter traffic.

the plague due to concerns about the difficulty of permitting and entitlement procedures. Conversely, leveraging development to conserve large portions of undeveloped land can provide immense ecological and social value. Known as conservation development, this strategy is one of the most effective means of preserving on-site and off-site natural resources.

Adjacent natural lands of high ecological or connective value. Identifying and conserving the "missing links" within major drainage corridors, ridgelines, or wildlife movement corridors to create a more comprehensive regional system is one of the most significant contributions a sustainable greenfield development can make.

Existing county or city conservation initiatives, incentives, and programs. Counties and cities that encourage a joint public/private process in regional resource preservation can be effective partners in the development process.

Local government-promoted healthy city concepts. Reflecting a growing concern for resource conservation, more and more cities and counties are adopting green building ordinances. Green development projects in these jurisdictions can often move through the entitlement process quickly, resulting in cost savings for the developer.

Market demand and demographics favorable to green building. Some regions and markets

exhibit a higher interest in (and willingness to pay for) sustainable practices. They have more disposable income or have embraced the more holistic aspects of community.

Existing or planned transit networks. Factors affecting transportation are often first-tier determinants of sustainability. The ability to link into an existing or proposed bus or light-rail system adds to a project's ability to reduce vehicle miles traveled. Vehicles miles traveled are a key indicator in the generation of greenhouse gases.

Opportunity to provide on-site or adjacent jobs/housing balance. The closer jobs are to housing, the smaller a new development's impact will be on the environment. Finding a site close to a major employment center, creating one next to housing, and providing jobs and housing on-site are all ways to reduce average commuter times.

Local utility companies that support alternative power generation. Alternative power generation is slowly entering the world of realistic considerations. Finding a site serviced by a utility company that has a flexible, progressive attitude can make a difference in reducing energy costs or pioneering a new technology.

In summary, thoughtful site selection can increase the positive influences of sustainable

JOHN STAMETS

43

44

development. The value of green building and land development practices can be multiplied when integrated into a larger framework of community or subregional land conservation, transportation infrastructure, or public policy.

Green Infrastructure

A primary attribute of a sustainable community is a rational and robust green infrastructure, a network of open spaces consisting of both natural lands and the constructed public realm. The network can encompass natural features at every scale, from a major river corridor to a minor wash in a residential backyard, from a city sports park to a downtown vacant lot. It constitutes the lungs of a community, forming its outdoor living room, hallway, and backyard. Rather than a hodgepodge of leftover land, green infrastructure's hierarchy of connected open spaces provides a wide range of ecological and human benefits.

A healthy green infrastructure consists of both "hubs" and "links." Hubs anchor green infrastructure networks, providing origins and destinations for wildlife and ecological processes. Links are the connections tying the system together. A new or regenerated community should include both components, depending on the character of a site, its natural systems, and the surrounding open-space elements to which it could be linked. The green infrastructure concept differs from a traditional city park and recreation system in three ways: it emphasizes ecology not just recreation; it becomes part of a larger regional system; and it provides a framework to guide growth and urban form at the community and neighborhood levels.

CONNECTING THE (GREEN) DOTS

Without connectivity, green infrastructure is not infrastructure at all—it is disconnected and limited in ecological value. Connectivity allows the whole to be more than the sum of its parts. It provides organization and structure for the public realm and supports biodiversity in the natural world. And many of the parts are preexisting— they just need to be perceived and defined as a coherent network.

Most communities contain extensive areas of natural land—ridgelines, reservoirs, floodplains,

Birkdale Village, in Huntersville, North Carolina, is a 52-acre (21-hectare), pedestrian-oriented, mixed-used community. The developers and designers worked to evoke appealing design elements of the past within a format that would be successful for today's retailers, residents, and office workers.

LANDDESIGN

45

INTEGRATED PLANNING AND DESIGN

Belmar: Retrofitting Suburbia With Compact Development

BELMAR, LOCATED IN THE DENVER suburb of Lakewood, is an example of how to retrofit an established low-density community with compact, sustainable development. Belmar's developers, Continuum Partners, LLC, envisioned the project as a model antidote to sprawl in aging suburban communities. Before Belmar, Lakewood did not have a downtown, only a mall that was nearing obsolescence. Belmar's development team aimed to reduce auto dependency by creating a place where residents' daily needs could be met within walking distance of home.

Located ten minutes west of Denver, Lakewood is Colorado's fourth largest city. Like many American suburbs, Lakewood's growth was fueled by the proliferation of World War II–era military bases and associated factories. Lakewood is home to the Denver Federal Center, which with 10,000 employees in 20 agencies is the largest federal compound outside of metropolitan Washington, D.C.

In 1966, the 1.4 million-square-foot (130,000-square-meter) Villa Italia—the largest shopping mall in the mountain/plains region—opened to great fanfare and was, until its closure in 2001, Lakewood's de facto commercial and civic center. Lakewood officials knew they wanted to redevelop Villa Italia, but it proved difficult as the mall had a complicated ownership structure involving separate landowners, ground leases, and

CONTINUUM PARTNERS LLC

Above: The city of Lakewood was built as a low-density community of single-use subdivisions. Belmar's traditional street grid incorporates mixed uses and encourages pedestrian activities. Below: Before Belmar was constructed, the Denver suburb of Lakewood did not have a downtown and residents had to depend on an aging mall for their shopping needs. Now residents come to Belmar to meet, shop, and attend public festivals.

140 lease subinterests. In order to untangle and streamline the redevelopment process, the city formed a 30-member Mayor's Villa Advisory Committee and established the Lakewood Reinvestment Authority, which would provide public financing and other urban renewal resources. The city then selected Denver-based Continuum Partners as its development partner.

The city and Continuum agreed that the former mall site should contain a mixed-use, pedestrian-friendly community that would serve as Lakewood's downtown. At Belmar's buildout, which is projected for 2010 to 2012, the 104-acre (42-hectare) site will have 1.1 million square feet (102,193 square meters) of retail, restaurant, and entertainment space; 800,000 square feet (74,322 square meters) of office and hotel space; and 1,300 residential units in an urban mix of townhouses, lofts, live/work units, and condominium and rental apartments. Belmar also contains 6,500 acres (2,630 hectares) of parkland.

A radical departure from the low-density, automobile-oriented development of Lakewood's past, Belmar has a tightly knit street grid with a range of housing and retail options. All buildings in Belmar feature ground-level windows and doors on all sides to enhance the streetscape and pedestrian experience. A multitenant speculative office building has earned LEED Silver. The most

visible expression of Belmar's sustainable agenda is a wind farm built on a parking lot, an idea that began as an art project. Belmar's reuse of a grayfield site allowed the developer to take advantage of existing infrastructure and services, including bus lines.

At first, some Lakewood citizens objected to the mall's closing, as they did not want an empty lot or a boarded-up building. However, the first phases of Belmar have been a success and residents appreciate their new urban conveniences. Initially, Belmar

contrasted sharply with the area's low-slung mini-malls and big-box stores, but gradually these places have remodeled and attracted new tenants, resulting in a ripple effect in the surrounding neighborhoods.

poor geologic or soil areas, or dense wood-lands—that have been officially preserved or are not attractive for development due to topography, cost, or permitting reasons. These repositories of existing ecological systems should be seen as the primary anchors of green infrastructure. They provide the basic armature for connectivity: Municipalities often use such lands to build large regional and community parks, where human activity and ecological systems can coexist harmoniously. The park system at Stapleton, a new community developed on former airport property in Denver, is a good example of a series of new open spaces that take advantage of existing adjacencies. The parks helped to regenerate degraded drainage ways—in this case, creek corridors—through native vegetation, wetland reclamation, and storm-water retention and cleansing components.

In turn, drainage and riparian systems—rivers, streams, valleys, washes, and creeks—and patches of residual open spaces in developed areas can provide continuity for wildlife and human movement. Abandoned rail corridors and utility easements can serve a similar purpose: With the existing right-of-way intact, they are valuable linear pathways that provide continuous access across areas that lack other types of linkages. All of these systems can be linked to residential streets and other populated areas, providing environmentally beneficial connectivity on a microscale: habitat

for bird species and reduced ambient heat and glare for pedestrians, homes, and businesses.

Carefully integrated and preserved open space can add significant economic value to a development project, offsetting the reduced saleable acreage. Buyer surveys consistently indicate that the top two most valued amenities in new communities are access to natural lands and walking trails. In fact, conservation developments that preserve substantial amounts of natural land often enjoy sales premiums of 15 to 35 percent.

In summary, green infrastructure places natural systems on equal footing with constructed systems. It provides a framework for development by identifying the land areas that are appropriate for preservation, recreation, and circulation. By providing interconnectedness, a whole-systems approach that leverages maximum ecological and real estate value is achieved.

Sustainable Community Form

Many experts believe that, after location, the primary determinant of how a community-changes the environment is its fundamental physical form and the interaction between its internal components. The size of the development footprint, mix of land uses, density, and internal patterns of connectivity have a profound influence on energy use, vehicle trip miles, water

Mountain House, located in California's San Joaquin Valley, is designed to provide an internal balance of jobs and housing to mitigate traffic impacts. It is also located near existing transportation facilities.

TOM FOX/SWA GROUP

INTEGRATED PLANNING AND DESIGN

Sereno Village Apartments is an affordable community built near a major bus transit hub in Vallejo, California.

Sereno Village Apartments is an affordable community built near a major bus transit hub in Vallejo, California.

© 2005 DIXI CARILLO

consumption, and development impacts on local and regional ecosystems.

It is at the regional level that the shaping of sustainable community form must begin. Communities are not sustainable entities when conceived as independent islands of development. To be socially, economically, and environmentally sustainable, they must be integral components of larger systems, both natural and constructed. There are four key factors that can determine how effectively new development will interact with regional systems: green infrastructure, transportation corridors, jobs/housing proximity, and the creation of urban cores.

As noted earlier in this chapter, linking or contributing to local or regional green infrastructure networks can increase a community's health by giving it "lungs" to breathe, increasing its biological diversity, and defining the geography and edges of its form. The built-environment counterpart to green infrastructure is transportation infrastructure. Approvals for high-density devel-

opment along transit routes are easier to secure; traffic mitigation requirements are reduced and potential population growth increases the impetus for municipalities to take advantage of multimodal technologies, such as rapid-transit bus and light-rail systems. When major employment centers are either physically or economically disconnected from housing, dramatic impacts on the environment result due to long commutes, energy use, and pollution. Sustainable developments can avoid these impacts by incorporating well-balanced employment districts within the community or selecting sites that are accessible to major employment centers via public transportation.

Convenient transportation options should be a seamless part of everyday life in a sustainable community. And the community should offer conveniences, too. Urban cores should provide access to all aspects of daily living, shops, and services. Mixed-use programming allows multiple needs to be met during a single transit ride

48

Seven Principles for Building Green Infrastructure

1. Green infrastructure functions as a framework for both conservation and development. By making green infrastructure the framework for conservation, communities can plan for interconnected, green, open-space systems. Where isolated islands of nature exist, green infrastructure planning can help identify opportunities to restore the vital ecological connections that will maintain and protect those areas.

2. Design and plan green infrastructure before development begins. Restoring natural systems is far more expensive than protecting undeveloped land. Constructed wetlands and other restoration projects often fail to function as well as their natural counterparts over the long term, so it is essential to identify and protect critical ecological hubs and linkages in the early stages of planning.

3. Linkage is key. A strategic connection of system components—parks, preserves, riparian areas, wetlands, and other green spaces—is critical to maintaining vital ecological processes and the health of wildlife populations.

4. Green infrastructure functions across community boundaries and at different scales. Green infrastructure systems should connect urban, suburban, rural, and wilderness landscapes and incorporate green space elements at state, regional, community, and parcel scales.

5. Green infrastructure is grounded in sound science and land-use planning theories and practices. Experts in conservation biology, landscape ecology, urban and regional planning, landscape architecture, geography, and civil engineering are critical to the successful planning and design of green infrastructure systems.

6. Green infrastructure is a critical investment. Strategic placement of green infrastructure can reduce the need for gray infrastructure, freeing funds for other community investments. Green infrastructure also reduces a community's susceptibility to floods, fires, and other natural disasters.

7. Green infrastructure engages key partners and can involve diverse stakeholders. Successful master plans forge alliances and relationships between public and private organizations. Such plans can potentially assuage opposition to new development by ensuring stakeholders that growth will occur only within a framework of conservation and open-space lands.

---

or automobile trip, increasing both the duration of stay in a single district and the opportunity for shared parking lots. Land, water, air, and energy impacts are reduced at significant levels.

Cores can be developed at various scales and levels of complexity, including neighborhood, district, village, city, and metropolitan. They can have a dramatic impact on energy and resource conservation by supporting the basic needs of a neighborhood or community; facilitating social, political, and spiritual interaction; and, through the concentration of population, triggering the construction of regional transit, commercial, and cultural projects.

COMPACT DEVELOPMENT

Much is being made of higher-density or compact development, and for good reason. Although the "D" word is anathema to most established residential communities, it nonetheless holds a key to sustainable development. Higher density reduces trip lengths, promotes walking, supports regional mass transit, and reduces development footprints. It also provides more tangible social and cultural benefits by encouraging more connected support systems and a stronger sense of community.

Densities are, of course, relative. What would be considered high density on a greenfield site would be a waste of land in a metropolitan downtown. But relatively higher density makes a community more sustainable. The benefits are abundant: shorter vehicle trip lengths; increased feasibility for mass transit building programs; energy savings; reduced infrastructure materials and costs; more affordable housing; and land conservation.

ACCOMMODATING DIVERSITY

As is so clearly evident in the natural world, there is a strong correlation between sustainability and diversity. Communities that reflect the diversity of a region's population will likely be more adaptable to economic and cultural shifts over the long term. Incorporating a range of housing types and price levels will result in healthy communities that express the inherent diversity and richness of our society. This range allows people to evolve through the natural progression of life without being forced to leave the community where they have developed roots, friendships, and meaningful support systems. Cities, towns, and villages around the world have proven that a mixture of demographic segments, building types, and

High Point: A Green Mixed-Income Community

HIGH POINT IS A MIXED-INCOME redevelopment project of 1,600 homes in West Seattle, Washington. The project replaces 716 run-down housing units that were built in the 1940s to provide housing after World War II. Beyond housing, the project provides ample community amenities, including a neighborhood commercial center, health and dental clinics, a new library, an expanded community center, a neighborhood athletic field, and many small parks.

High Point is a 120-acre (49-hectare) development in West Seattle that was formerly public housing but has been transformed into a sustainable community under the U.S. Department of Housing and Urban Development's HOPE VI program. Mithun, in conjunction with the Seattle Housing Authority, created a new mixed-income

neighborhood that offers close proximity to jobs, cultural amenities, and public transportation. High Point's planners sought to integrate the project's streets and housing into the surrounding community; create diverse housing types; provide open space; and use resources efficiently. Planners also devised an innovative stormwater manage-

ment system that was the first of its kind in Washington.

High Point features homes with a number of sustainable amenities, including gas-fired, high-efficiency, closed-loop boilers for both on-demand domestic hot water and radiant baseboard heaters; a quiet whole-house fan with a two-speed timing switch to remove moisture; airtight drywall installation meant to reduce moisture penetration and inhibit mold growth; low-e–coated and argon-filled Energy Star windows; low off-gas vinyl flooring with recycled content; and low-VOC paint and sealed cabinet construction to reduce emissions.

Thirty-five High Point units are designated as "Breathe Easy Homes" and are intended for families at risk for asthma. They feature positive-pressure house ventilation systems with air filtering, tempered fresh air supplies, and heat recoveries to improve indoor air quality; linoleum flooring in living areas and bedrooms, recycled-content vinyl flooring in bathrooms and kitchens, and low-pile carpeting to reduce allergens; HEPA-filter vacuums to remove allergens; and walk-off doormats to lessen the amount of dirt entering the home.

The High Point neighborhood makes up 10 percent of the Longfellow Creek watershed, which had the greatest Coho salmon return counts for Seattle-area creeks. When High

Point was a public housing project, stormwater carried spilled oil and other pollutants into a series of underground pipes that emptied directly into the creek. The new plan calls for narrow streets, which reduce runoff. Runoff flows into planted areas and slowly filters into the groundwater. When there is too much rain for the soil to absorb, the excess flows into a pond at the northern end of the neighborhood. The pond's overflow runs into the creek, but now it is far cleaner. Porous pavement sidewalks and streets reduce impervious surfaces, while compost-amended soils increase soil storage and infiltration (see illustration on page 42). However, High Point's innovative stormwater management ideas were not included under Seattle's stormwater management codes. Landscape architect SvR worked closely with the city to ensure that its proposed system could manage the site's stormwater.

(see illustration on page 42).

Above: High Point, a HOPE VI development, contains market-rate and subsidized housing. Left: High Point includes open spaces and public parks. Its Viewpoint Park overlooks Elliott Bay and downtown Seattle.

High Point is expected to reach completion in 2009. It will contain market-rate units and housing for seniors and those earning up to 60 percent of the Seattle-Bellevue area's average median income.

ABOVE: © MITHUN; TOP RIGHT: DOUG J. SCOTT

densities leads to more interesting and economically sustainable neighborhoods.

Diversity of housing types is good for the bottom line, too, because it broadens a project's reach in the marketplace, which results in higher absorption rates. A well-designed sustainable community should support a wide range of family types, income levels, individual values, and lifestyle changes and choices.

Thoughtful neighborhood design can increase physical, social, and economic sustainability. Besides reducing auto trips, good neighborhood design can increase economic value, longevity, social interaction, and neighborhood support networks. Sustainable neighborhoods should offer a diversity of housing types; internal public gathering and open spaces; tree-lined streets and sidewalks; integrated natural and cultural elements; interconnectivity with other neighborhoods; and reasonable access to services, recreation, and shopping.

Sustainable Mobility

What is sustainable transportation? The University of Winnipeg's Center for Sustainable Transportation, defines it as a system that "allows the basic access needs of individuals and societies to be met safely and in a manner consistent with human and ecosystem health, and with equity within and between generations; is affordable, operates efficiently, offers choice of transport mode, and supports a vibrant economy; and limits emissions and waste within the planet's ability to absorb them, minimizes consumption of nonrenewable resources, limits consumption of renewable resources to the sustainable-yield level, reuses and recycles its components, and minimizes the use of land and the production of noise."

The goal is to provide access to work, goods, and services with the least expenditure of energy, time, and emissions. The success rate of such an approach is measured by "trip capture" within the bounds of the community. The idea is to have as many jobs as possible within the community, so that the trips to jobs outside the community are minimized.

Another effective technique is to allow as many trips as possible to use efficient, nonpolluting, and low-energy means of mobility. Rail transit is an obvious mode of choice, but as

much or more of a reduction in vehicle trip miles can be accomplished with walking, cycling, and emerging technologies related to bus rapid transit. Low-speed vehicles (LSV), such as neighborhood electric vehicles (NEVs), and car-share programs are being explored in a number of communities as alternative means of movement.

THE D-FACTORS

How should concepts of sustainable mobility be incorporated into the planning process? Fehr & Peers, a California-based transportation consultant, has identified five factors that lead to a higher level of sustainability in community design. Dubbed the "D-factors," they are measurable within a traffic model and can be used as a tool to refine plans that maximize trip capture.

Density of dwelling units and jobs per acre. Increasing density around hubs or cores raises the probability of synergies and shared trips to meet needs and services, and allows other modes of movement to become viable sooner. In greenfield environments, pushing average densities above 7 to 15 dwellings per acre and jobs above 0.5 to 0.7 FAR, although still modest by urban standards, starts to make buses, NEVs, and shuttle systems worthy of consideration. In infill projects, densities from 15 to 65 units per acre can create walkable, transit-ready neighborhoods without the cost or environmental impact of high-rise development.

Trees planted along streets can reduce the effects of the sun's heat.

© 1998 DIXI CARILLO

51

Diversity of land uses and jobs/housing balance. By placing shopping, entertainment, medical, educational, daycare and other services close together, fewer and shorter trips are required to meet daily needs. And a balance

WWW.MIKETORREY.COM

Recycling of construction waste is mandatory at Terramor, a new community in southern Califormia, and the use of recycled building materials was encouraged throughout the community. Construction waste was incorporated into common area hardscaping.

between employment and housing opportunities within a community gives residents the choice to live and work without long commutes.

Design of the pedestrian/cycling environment. Creating meaningful pedestrian linkages and designing them in a manner that meets safety and aesthetic preferences encourages people to walk and bike to local destinations.

Destination accessibility. Redevelopment around existing cores and the construction of multi-use cores for new communities reduces environmental impacts, saves significant infrastructure investment, and provides unique market and lifestyle choices.

Distance from premium transit. Studies show that an estimated 20 to 30 percent of the population in the United States would prefer alternative forms of mobility. The key is to locate housing and jobs within walking distance of a clean, well-designed transit stop.

It should be noted that only one of the D-factors involves mass transit. Much can be achieved by reducing trips, saving energy, and moderating congestion without mass transit.

THE MULTIMODAL COMMUNITY

When developing a comprehensive transportation plan for a sustainable community, there are initial and long-term strategies for the efficient and economical movement of people and goods. The first, a multimodal master plan (MMMP), is a critical tool for developers of both greenfield and infill communities to implement connectivity options and alternative means of transport. Plan components include a hierarchy of standard surface streets with various combinations of dedicated on- and off-street lanes for different types of vehicles; a walkway and trail network connected to key service nodes; transit centers (near concentrations of residences and jobs); local and regional transit routes (bus or shuttle systems connecting neighborhoods to district and community cores); multimodal corridor reservations (short-term use as bikeways/trails, long-term use for transit); and new technology programs (NEVs and car-share programs).

While multimodal transit offers a far more energy-efficient alternative to sprawling, disconnected community design, its critics argue such a system is not feasible in the suburbs due to low densities and decentralized activities. The concept of "transit-ready design" offers a compromise between multimodal skeptics and those who believe that, eventually, most suburban locations will implement transit out of either foresight or desperation. Initially, most greenfield developments do not meet the density or compaction thresholds needed for economical mass transit. However, as areas start to grow over time, a preexisting planning framework, based on the D-factors, will allow these thresholds to be met faster and more effectively. The key to transit-ready design is to identify spatial requirements for future facilities and set those areas aside or find temporary uses for them. A transportation corridor, for example, can be designed and engineered with an eye toward its future development, while serving as a bike and NEV path in the short term.

Landscape Design

Landscaping can be a haphazard patchwork of decorative settings or it can be used as a tool to make communities more sustainable, contributing to a balanced, multispecies living environment. Landscapes, both natural and constructed, can modify microclimates, reduce water usage, and treat groundwater. Developers who tap into

new technologies and understand the basic traits of natural systems can build more sustainable communities from the ground up.

LEVERAGING CLIMATIC CONDITIONS

Microclimates—localized areas or specific sites with unique, sometimes problematic, climatic conditions—can be modified by a multitude of planning and design decisions. Landscaping, for example, can be used to produce or reduce negative climatic impacts on communities, neighborhoods, and homes. By paving and building without regard to natural systems, developers lose the protection offered by shade trees, alter wind patterns, and pave surfaces that absorb, rather than deflect, the sun's heat. The result may be a cold, windy, inhospitable environment, with buildings that lose heat unnecessarily, or a hot roof that increases the temperature indoors.

"Urban heat islands," areas in cities that are hotter than their surroundings, are a common problem. They occur on hot summer days when dark-colored surfaces like roofs and asphalt paving collect and store the sun's heat. Heat islands contribute to poor air quality and increase the amount of energy needed to cool interiors. One way to combat this problem is to install lighter-colored surfaces. Green roofs, covered with grasses or plant material, are an increasingly popular alternative. Another way to reduce the effects of the sun, especially in suburban areas, is to plant shade trees in strategic locations around buildings, in parking lots, and along streets. Shading of southern and western exposures with deciduous material substantially decreases solar penetration during the summer months and allows for interior solar heat gain in the winter. The energy savings of well-placed trees can be 10 to 50 percent.

REDUCED-WATER LANDSCAPES

As the U.S. population continues to grow, water resources are becoming increasingly precious. Native, naturalized, and introduced domestic plant species, when used with high performance irrigation technology, can help to reduce landscape water consumption as much as 50 percent.

Landscape design in a sustainable community typically has several zones organized roughly as concentric circles. The core zone, the most urban, is dominated by high-traffic areas that are typically finished with hardscape and planted

Community gardens can be integrated into new and rehabilitated communities, such as this victory garden in Miami Beach.

© 2006 EDAW/PHOTOGRAPHY BY DIXI CARILLO

Water moves through three ponds at Kunming Eco-Community in China. The water is aerated as it changes elevations from one pond to the next and cleansed as it moves through planted terraces.

with species that can survive high levels of pedestrian activity, and limited planting space and sunlight. The next outer zone encompasses the majority of residential neighborhoods and suburban business districts. Plant materials here would be a mix of domestic and naturalized species. Naturalized species are those that originated elsewhere, but don't require much water. The most outlying zone is the transition area from urban to rural. Here a mix of naturalized and species native to the local environment would dominate. Native species require the least water and are most appropriate to transition to outlying natural lands. Of course, in reality, pieces of natural open space penetrate into the interior rings and urban environments can be found closer to the periphery in some communities. Selecting plant species that are appropriate for each zone can result in a better environmental fit, leading to an overall reduction in water consumption, better plant health, and improved wildlife habitat.

Where human activity meets wilderness, special care must be taken to protect the integrity of sensitive and threatened plant and wildlife systems. One potential threat is the disruption of ecological processes through the introduction of species that are not indigenous to a region. When non-natives are used along open-space edges, they can become an invasive force, choking out naturally occurring species.

For the community development team, the greatest opportunity for water conservation—and costs savings—is in the landscape and irrigation design of public spaces, including arterial and collector streetscapes, parkways, parks, and residual open spaces. And there are a variety of practices that can be put into place, including low-water or xeriscape planting techniques; on-site weather stations; centralized irrigation control; soil moisture sensors; drip irrigation; and low-water maintenance procedures. All require a commitment to ongoing monitoring and maintenance.

HARDSCAPE MATERIALS

A sustainable landscape comprises both living plants and hard materials, the latter used to construct pavements, steps, walls, ramps, fencing, and other structures. In general, durable, locally produced materials are a better choice than those that are disposable and imported.

Products such as recycled plastics are now available for decks, walkways, and marinas. Recycled rubber tires can be used to create soft paving surfaces for playgrounds and athletic fields. Recycled glass may find its way into aggregate mixes in both Portland cement and bituminous concrete. Crushed concrete can be useful

JESSICA LEETE

as an aggregate in the construction of roads and sidewalks, resulting in a reduction of embedded energy—that is, the total energy (and greenhouse gases) required to dig, crush, and transport the material. Sidewalks broken into pieces can be used to build low retaining walls and larger pieces of concrete from demolition sites can form erosion-control systems on stream banks and waterfronts. And crushed stone, gravel, and stone dust are increasingly being used for walkways, driveways, and light-duty roads. These materials allow for a good deal of water infiltration, but they also erode easily; care must be taken in the application of such materials on sloping surfaces.

WORKING LANDSCAPE

Home gardens and small-scale agricultural practices are making a comeback. They can occur on many scales and provide numerous environmental, social, and economic benefits (eliminates transportation impacts, increases social interaction, provides opportunity for exercise, and feeds the local economy.) Vegetables, herbs, and fruit trees are becoming a common part of the landscape palette at a variety of scales. When space

allows, avocado groves or vineyards can be established. When space is limited, homeowners can use pots to grow herbs and dwarf variety citrus.

Community gardens, which provide plots for people to grow their own crops, are easily integrated into new and rehabilitated developments; they are an important element of a total recreational amenity package. Additionally, plants that produce fruits or have edible features (fruit trees, sunflowers, leafy vegetables, herbs, root vegetables) can easily be incorporated into private or public landscapes.

The landscape we introduce into a community is our most obvious and tangible bridge to the natural world. By utilizing new technologies and rediscovering the basic behavior of natural systems, we can reduce energy and water consumption while creating more habitable environments for daily living. In the wide array of sustainable practices, landscape can provide measurable environmental benefits at relatively low costs.

Reducing Energy Consumption

Energy-saving strategies, both high- and low-tech, can be implemented across all aspects of community design. They are not just good for the environment, but can benefit the bottom line for both the developer and end user. Passive solar techniques, which reduce heat gain in the summer and capture heat in the winter, can reduce energy costs with little investment. Such efforts reduce the country's reliance on non-renewable resources, net energy demand, and greenhouse gas emissions.

The development team can create a master plan in which it is easier to design buildings that optimize sustainable performance features. Likewise, a building that optimizes green performance features can have a favorable effect on a community's infrastructure, from size and cost

Above: Heron Bay, in San Leandro, California, is committed to the preservation and enhancement of nearby wetlands and habitat for endangered species. While controlling access to the habitat areas and wetlands, edge conditions of the development allow for a shoreline trail and wildlife viewing areas. Left: A cooling fountain in North Carolina's Birkdale Village creates a comfortable microclimate during the warm-weather months.

TOP: TOM FOX/SWA GROUP; LEFT: LANDDESIGN

Mayfield, in Fremont, California, has been the catalyst for accelerating redevelopment of the surrounding low-density warehouse and office-park area.

to spatial need and required loads. As a sort of chicken and egg challenge, the linkage between building and context must be continuously guided and evaluated, if maximum performance is to be achieved at minimum cost.

Building orientation is critical to the successful integration of passive solar energy strategies into new construction. The master plan establishes street alignments that affect building orientation throughout the community. The specific sun angles necessary to achieve the energy- and money-saving advantages of passive solar design vary widely from location to location. In Minnesota, it is all about capturing the winter light. In Phoenix, it is about cooling the afternoon air in the summer. Near Melbourne, Australia, a new neighborhood development calls for housing product variances based on solar exposure. Each builder is asked to design plan forms that optimize solar orientation in the winter for both indoor and outdoor space, since Melbourne has cold and damp winters.

The use of plantings to modify solar gain is another age-old strategy. Early consideration of tree planting may modify lot widths in certain locations, street right-of-ways, building setbacks, and landscape budgets. In fact, solar-oriented landscape design offers one of the most favorable cost/benefit ratios in sustainable development.

Often master developers feel they are limited in how much they can control the construction practices of builders and land buyers. The areas developers do control, however, are the public open space and parks systems—the green infrastructure discussed earlier in this chapter. There are a number of technologies that can be employed in this realm, including energy-efficient lighting, LED street lights, fluorescent trail fixtures, and energy-generating photovoltaics (PVs). Other savings can come from the required use of NEVs for maintenance crews and community-service employees. These approaches reduce costs and air-quality impacts and inspire residents to do their part for the environment.

ALTERNATIVE POWER SOURCES

Much has been reported in the press about alternative power sources such as wind farms, PVs, geothermal systems, and hydrogen cells. But are any of these within the economic grasp of

TOM FOX/SWA GROUP

57

The master plan and landscaping for Seminole Community College integrates the natural and built environments. The campus is organized around two herbaceous wetlands in the middle of the property.

developers? The answer is yes, with the caveat that regional disparities in energy cost, green power programs, tax credits, and other variables are so wide-ranging that each project team must identify for itself the opportunity for financially viable alternative energy technologies. The possibilities include the following techniques.

Photovoltaic cells. PVs—which convert solar light into electricity—are an easily installed alternative energy source. PV technology is well established and there are multiple purveyors in most regions. Many new communities are

GLATTING JACKSON KERCHER ANGLIN

implementing solar energy programs on either a mandatory or an optional basis for homebuyers. More progressive applications are using microgrid concepts that generate power on nonresidential buildings (for example, a large food market) and subsidize local neighborhood electrical consumption. The economic attractiveness of PVs varies from region to region, depending on power rates, climate, local utility programs, and state-level renewable portfolio standards (RPS). The most practical application is integrating a modest amount of solar cells into the roof construction and selling power back into the grid to reduce overall energy use and cost.

Community microgrids. Microgrids are an emerging type of energy (and water) infrastructure of a scale that lies comfortably between individual building systems and regional public-utility systems. Traditional examples are the central heating and cooling plants for a college campus or a multibuilding corporate headquarters complex. The basic idea is that power, water, heating, and cooling systems designed at the neighborhood, block, or district scale are fundamentally more efficient than those designed separately for individual buildings. It is often difficult to make graywater or power generation work within a single building because the capacity swings are too big between what is needed at peak requirement times and what is produced on average. But if the system spans several buildings that have different schedules and cycles of occupancy, the various peaks can offset each other if on-site storage is supplied.

Hydrogen cells. An emerging technology is the hydrogen fuel cell, which typically extracts hydrogen from natural gas and leaves only water as a byproduct. It then uses the hydrogen in a fuel-cell process to create electricity. Although currently expensive, fuel cells offer clean energy with no measurable impact on air quality or greenhouse gases. The need for cell replenishment every five years or so adds to the cost, but, as with most emerging technologies, prices are likely to come down significantly over the next three to five years.

Microturbines and cogeneration. Microturbines are basically compact gas turbine generators. Although not as clean as fuel cells, microturbines are less expensive and the power they produce is either grid-connected or stand-alone. Microturbines have the unique ability to produce electricity and heat simultaneously. When both of these products are used, it is called cogeneration. Cogeneration, now being used in apartment complexes, condominiums, supermarkets, pools, and green campus development, captures heat thrown off of mechanical systems in large buildings that can be applied to other uses.

Wind. Wind is an easily convertible and renewable resource, although it is not in reliable supply everywhere. New product development is currently underway to better integrate vertical-axis wind turbines into building architecture with reduced footprints and noise generation. On large greenfield sites, turbine fields can be isolated from residential areas.

Geothermal. Geothermal technology takes advantage of the earth's mass to offset dynamic temperature fluctuations above ground. This is done by installing a grid or series of vertical tubes into the earth to a depth greater than five feet and pumping a highly stable fluid such as water underground, where it is maintained at about 55 degrees Fahrenheit. The fluid is then pumped back up and used to either heat or cool rooms.

Organic waste. At the community scale, much research is underway on how to convert the biomass of various types of naturally occurring waste materials, such as from plants and livestock, into a solid or liquid fuel that can be used to produce electric power, heat, chemicals, or biofuels. The opportunity for new community development to tap into this type of energy production lies in identifying agricultural operations, landfills, and other local sources.

How real are these technologies? The answer lies in the rate of increase in the cost of energy, which, of course, has a direct relationship to the payback period for higher-cost technologies. It also depends on the regions of the country, which have different energy costs, utility programs, government incentives, and, of course, climates. But don't rely on preconceptions. A little bit of research into alternative energy sources can result in big savings.

NEXT GENERATION ENERGY STANDARDS

Two new standards for community energy set a higher bar for reduced environmental impact. An aggressive goal for a number of new communities around the country is zero-net resource use, meaning that a development has to work within the site's natural solar and water budget.

Santaluz, in San Diego County, uses drought-tolerant, water-conserving landscaping, including native and naturalized plant species.

DENISE RETALLACK

Shady Canyon, in Orange County, California, contains a golf course that earned Audubon Society certification.

TOM FOX/SWA GROUP

It cannot use one kilowatt-hour of electricity beyond what is generated from the sun or the wind and it cannot use one ounce of water beyond the amount that naturally hits the ground. Since this is a difficult feat, the energy or water used over the natural budget can be offset by credits purchased through carbon transfer programs emerging around the country.

Although zero-net energy sounds highly improbable, it is technically feasible at the new-community scale. Lennar's Treasure Island, south of San Francisco, is planning to use PV panels and strict conservation measures to generate sufficient power during the day (contributing to the grid) to offset peak utilization periods at night (drawing from the grid), resulting in a zero-net off-site consumption on an annualized basis.

The greenhouse gas–neutral standard requires that a development produce no net greenhouse gas emissions. The goal is for sufficient renewable energy to be produced on site from a variety of sources (biomass cogeneration, PVs, electric vehicles, and geothermal systems), so that the remainder of energy production that creates greenhouse gases is offset by other green power techniques such as the use of biodiesel fuels, power from Green Power–certified sources, and the purchasing of Green Power certificates.

By understanding the two fundamental approaches to making energy more sustainable— reducing the need for energy and supplementing existing sources with cleaner, low-impact energy—the community developer can reduce a project's carbon footprint cost effectively. Energy is the number one interest of the end user because it cleans the environment and saves money at the same time.

Water Usage Strategies

Like other components of a sustainable community, water is best dealt with in an integrated, holistic manner that involves both reducing the use of potable water and lessening the impact of stormwater on natural systems. The truly sustainable water program starts with "total water balance planning." That is, understanding how to best replicate a site's natural water system—how much water is introduced by rainfall, how much is absorbed into groundwater and aquifers, and how much leaves the site through natural drainage systems in both quantity and quality. Developing a comprehensive strategy that mimics these characteristics as much as possible will lead to the least impact on natural systems and maintain ecological sustainability over the long term. Such a strategy encompasses potable water, recycled water, and stormwater.

Because only about 1 percent of the earth's water is potable, first-tier technologies for

Stormwater Management as Civic Art

THE AQUEDUCTS OF ROME, the Step-wells of India, and the lavoirs of France were designed to establish a public presence for water within an urban landscape. Today, the stormwater master plan can be used as an opportunity to develop functional, civic-minded infrastructure.

Water is fundamental to the existence of life, but rain can be both a blessing and a curse—problems can arise from too much or not enough of it. Consequently, management of rain and surface water must be an integral part of the built environment.

It is incumbent upon those who design and maintain the landscape to use water management infrastructure in a way that reduces physical impacts. Stormwater facilities that store, treat, infiltrate, and distribute can become valuable elements in the urban landscape. Like the early fountains of Rome, water infrastructure elements can also serve as "place makers."

Conventional stormwater engineering focuses on controlling large rain events and typically relegates stormwater management facilities to underground pipes or places them behind chain link fencing. Today, however, conventional

practices are being challenged by management efforts that are part of broader hydrological reforms. These efforts maximize value by integrating infrastructure, natural, and community resources into multipurpose facilities.

The following principles offer a framework for integrating rainwater management into community development plans:

- Rainwater is a valuable resource.
- Water management infrastructure is an integral element of neighborhood design.
- The foundation of a stormwater master plan starts with the lot.
- Engineering elements must not detract from character- or location-defining elements of the neighborhood.
- Streets play a significant role in generating runoff and can help filter it into the ground.
- End-of-pipe elements should be designed as carefully as the architecture or urban design.
- Vegetation and managed terrain must be supported by permanent management measures that provide long-term support for ecosystems.

The tools of modern stormwater management—ponds, canals, cisterns, dry detention depressions, conveyance swales, and flow dissipaters—can be designed so that they do not confuse or detract from their surroundings; they can be defining elements of a community. Architecture, landscape, and other design elements arising from the study of the local and regional context enhance the built environment and strengthen the public realm.

Features such as the shallow depressions or recessed areas within neighborhood parks, squares, or greens can hold rainwater during more small rain events, reducing the need

to construct long runs of extensive drainage networks and other costly infrastructure. Retention and detention ponds can satisfy "wet weather" regulatory requirements.

Introducing a "hard" edge in prominent locations presents an opportunity for public promontories for walkers or other pedestrians. Instead of shallow slopes around a pond, portions can have a vertical edge that allows people to be closer to the water. Where water-table elevations permit, canals, channels, or other water networks can be plugged into developed sites to provide water access and views for neighborhood residents.

Above: A canal in I'On, Mount Pleasant, South Carolina, serves a dual purpose: stormwater management and civic art. Left: The stormwater management system adds character to New Town at St. Charles, in St. Charles, Missouri.

Considering the intrinsic benefits of rainwater—both as a natural resource and as a visual element—should lead to using water as more than just a decorative element in neighborhood development. Proper management of water serves multiple purposes; it is best not left solely to engineers or to the public works department. Stormwater management can be part of the civic art that enlivens our communities.

—*Milt Rhodes*

Milt Rhodes is a planner and urban designer based in Raleigh, North Carolina.

TOP: MILT RHODES; LEFT: TONY SEASE

The Jeffrey Open Space Trail, in Irvine, California, is a three-mile (4.8-kilometer) spine that connects to residential neighborhoods. Established through a series of community workshops, the primary design concept was inspired by the works of Frederick Law Olmsted and uses simple grading and plant massing.

DENISE RETALLACK

reducing indoor potable water use are well established and generally understood by the public, especially in the arid western states. Low-flow faucets, toilets, washers, showerheads, and dishwashers have become commonplace. More innovative technologies such as waterless urinals and tankless water heaters are readily used in Australia and Europe, but are just now making inroads in the United States.

In a typical small-storm event, water evaporates from the soil surface (a form of consumptive use); in the case of larger events, stormwater quickly runs off. If this rapid runoff is harnessed on site a portion of the water could be used for human consumption or landscape irrigation. In addition, water can also be kept on site by lessening outflow through detention devices, reusing wastewater effluent, recharging into under-

ground aquifers, and reducing landscape water requirements.

RECYCLING TECHNIQUES
Recycling graywater, such as the outflow from showers and washing machines, which has a low organic content, is an increasingly popular alternative. With minor treatment, graywater can be adapted for use in landscape irrigation or toilets. Typically, such techniques work best when implemented on a medium to large scale.

But for a sustainable community development team, the greatest opportunity for water conservation is in the landscaping and irrigation design of arterial and collector streetscapes and parkways, parks, and other open spaces. On-site rainwater, for example, is a drastically underappreciated resource for water conservation.

62

Rainwater can be used for landscape irrigation, water features, cooling tower make-up water, and toilets. It provides a relatively clean source of water, and can be collected and reused with relatively little treatment or filtration. Rainfall harvesting can involve simple or complex technologies and can serve parks, schools, apartment complexes, and individual residences. Large-scale projects may incorporate harvesting basins to collect water for landscape irrigation. And small-scale projects may include individual rain collection devices—fitted with hoses to facilitate irrigation functions—that are positioned at the end of downspouts to collect roof runoff.

STORMWATER MANAGEMENT

Maintaining healthy water quality in our streams, rivers, and oceans has been one of the earliest and highest priorities in sustainable community design. Government agencies at every level have intervened in development practices to ensure storm runoff is controlled in both peak quantity and urban pollutants. The sustainable community incorporates innovative techniques to reduce and cleanse project outflows and does so in a manner that is carefully integrated into the fabric of the community. Such techniques can often reduce infrastructure costs and create open-space amenities that lift development values.

The detention (capture and slow release) and retention (total capture without release) of stormwater runoff are standard practices that reduce peak project outflows while providing percolation into the underlying groundwater supplies. Although more expensive and controlled by regulatory agencies, groundwater injection, which forces excess stormwater down into subsurface water levels, can also be used to replenish groundwater aquifers. Natural percolation is a favored approach that provides assimilation of stormwater pollutants through an area's biomass (upper level of soils, roots, and plants); promotes filtration of pollutant particulates; and generally limits the capture of pollutants to within the upper 12 to 18 inches of soil.

Another means of recharging water is to use porous pavements, primarily on parking lots, but also on walkways and driveways. Pervious systems are typically concrete-paver blocks or

other materials that allow stormwater to seep through small gaps or holes, percolate into sub-base material, and infiltrate the underlying soils. In addition to porous pavement, other techniques can be used in the design of parking lots to provide some level of recharge. Planter islands

or peripheral recharge drains can be employed without investing in a porous parking surface.

Most jurisdictions require some level of stormwater best-management practices that typically require a level of treatment in quantity and quality reflecting predevelopment conditions. These are criteria for controlling and treating stormwater before it leaves the site. However, minimum standards are not sufficient for the development of a sustainable community. Total-water planning strategies should exceed legislated minimums; they should integrate and enhance water, wildlife habitat, and human conditions.

The reduction of piped infrastructure and increased use of open drainage channels, for example, provide multiple benefits locally and regionally for development projects. Pipes provide little, if any, treatment benefits for water quality. They also tend to increase flow rates and lead to concentrated discharge points into drainages or waterways that can cause downstream erosion and the introduction of concentrated pollutants.

WindMark Beach, on Florida's St. Joseph Bay, has boardwalks that encourage residents to enjoy the scenery without harming the area's natural resources.

COOPER, ROBERTSON & PARTNERS

63

Located in Santa Rosa Beach, Florida, the community of WaterColor is shaped by its site's natural edges—the Gulf of Mexico, Western Lake, a creek, marshes, and wetlands—and the abutting villages of Seaside and Seagrove.

An alternative technique is called daylighting, which involves the conversion of piped storm-water systems into bioswales—ecologically designed open drainage channels. Bioswales offer a flexible approach to treating and managing stormwater runoff for a relatively low cost. They are shallow, fairly wide channels that remove pollutants through vegetative filtration, soil absorption, and plant assimilation. The ability to remove stormwater pollutants is dependent on the length of time that water remains in contact with herbaceous vegetation and the soil surface within the swale. Bioswales are best suited for sites with minor elevation changes; they do not perform well in steep topography or dense soil environments.

Another promising approach in the treatment of waste or storm water is the constructed wetland, which is a biologically diverse ecosystem that utilizes natural processes to treat and clean runoff. An increasingly common bio-sensitive solution to water quality, constructed wetlands use filtration to remove sediments and pollutants from water. Constructed wetlands move waste or storm water through a gravel or sand medium on which plants are rooted. As water flows through the vegetation, it slows down and sediments and pollutants settle out. Sediment becomes trapped. Vegetation traps sediment and takes up pollutants, which have been converted to more soluble forms. Wetlands also harbor an abundance of micro-

organisms that assist in transforming and removing pollutants from water.

One benefit, when compared to a typical sewage treatment plant or conventional stormwater facilities, is that wetlands can be aesthetically pleasing by having a relatively natural-looking quality. Another advantage is that they can be constructed at a small scale and interspersed around or within a community, reducing the need for extensive piping systems. Treated water is recharged naturally into underlying groundwater or the natural drainage system. Constructed wetlands can also provide restoration opportunities for wildlife habitat. Wetland vegetation is then planted or allowed to establish naturally.

Holistic Development

Whether infill or greenfield, the primary determinants of community sustainability are location, form, and land-use interaction, which must be established during the initial visioning and programming of a project. All other high-performance practices and products only incrementally reduce the carbon footprint and ecological impact of a development. But by maintaining connectivity to employment centers, building close to transportation corridors, linking to regional green infrastructure, and developing around multi-use, compact cores, new developments can meet the growth needs of our communities and coexist harmoniously with the natural, social, and economic environment.

© JAY GRAHAM

The Costs and Benefits of Sustainable Development

Opposite: Kresge Foundation, Troy, Michigan. Below: The Student Resources Building at the University of California, Santa Barbara, uses sunshades and operable windows to reduce energy costs and a built-in weather station control system to coordinate indoor temperatures.

A COMMON PERCEPTION IN THE REAL ESTATE INDUSTRY is that sustainable development costs significantly more than conventional development. The fact is, with an extra investment of time, a competent team, and a thoughtful design process, sustainable development does not have to cost more than conventional development.

Some of the early attempts at sustainable development may have given sustainable practices a black eye because they suffered from the inevitable learning curve that arises when any new approach or technology is implemented. Out-of-control costs for these ill-fated projects were often the result of two shortcomings. First, developers who relied on checklists and certification programs often piled multiple increasingly expensive energy-saving or water-quality elements onto already designed projects. Often these costs broke the back of the project, resulting in a slide back to more conventional practices. Second, developers that incurred high additional costs most likely did not calculate and capture savings that could have helped offset those costs.

As more developers and builders gain experience with high-performance technologies, they find that green practices can be employed with minimal additional costs, which can be offset by other savings and benefits that add to overall profitability. With a little practice, many builders are finding that it is not difficult to apply alternative materials and sustainable practices in their conventional business model.

The key to developing an economically viable sustainable community is to adopt a whole systems approach early in the process. A whole systems approach looks at the interconnections between building systems, linking components of high-performance building and site design to each other so that dramatic efficiencies are realized. For example, the energy efficiency achieved through solar-oriented site design and building envelopes that allow natural airflow can lead to the downsizing of an HVAC system—and

OPPOSITE: © BARBARA KARANT/KARANT + ASSOCIATES, INC.; RIGHT: SASAKI

Broadway Crossing
in Seattle involves a
partnership between
a nonprofit housing
development corpora-
tion and Walgreens.
A 12,000-square-foot
(1,115-square-meter)
drugstore will occupy the
first floor and housing
for those earning less
than 60 percent of the
area median income will
comprise the rest of the
building.

major net savings. Developments that pursue whole systems thinking are highly engineered, responsive to site characteristics, and developed through alternative building models.

Getting a Handle on Costs

Experts agree that the following factors can posi-tively influence sustainable development costs:

■ early and decisive senior management commitment;

■ competency and experience of a multidisciplinary development team;

■ clarity of goals and objectives;

■ understanding of local and regional conditions;

■ appropriate cost/benefit methodology;

■ communication with and education of builders/contractors;

■ flexibility in programming;

■ sufficient time for planning and design; and

■ phasing of builder/contractor participation.

The single largest cost-saving strategy may be the early integration of sustainable goals and de-sign practices into the planning process. The ear-lier they are established and implemented, the higher the return on both soft- and hard-cost investments. Case studies demonstrate that costs can be significantly higher to achieve the same level of component efficiency when introduced more than halfway through the process.

It is also clear that the developers who have experience with sustainable development com-plete projects at a lower cost than those without experience. This means that first projects require both an intensive investment in research and a team that includes consultants seasoned in vari-ous aspects of sustainable development.

Avoiding surprises is another key to operating within a viable budget. Green building processes usually include some nonstandard line items. The following actions can help the development team avoid surprise costs.

JOHN STAMETS

DEVELOPING SUSTAINABLE PLANNED COMMUNITIES

The University of Ontario Institute of Technology in the city of Oshawa employs a borehole thermal energy storage system (BTESS), an underground series of loops that provide energy-efficient heating and cooling for the campus. This system, in conjunction with other energy-saving features, has cut heating costs by 40 percent and saved over 6 million gallons (22.7 million liters) of water per year.

■ **Increased planning and design time and budget**. Identifying the interrelationships between specific sustainable development practices and green building systems and future cost savings requires more time and intensity of effort on the front end. Changes or additions made after conceptual design traditionally have a much higher cost with a reduced return in savings and efficiencies. It is also important to retain consultants experienced in sustainable development, so that value and time can be gained from previous lessons learned.

■ **Inspection and documentation**. Regardless of good intentions, if careful testing, inspection, and documentation of innovative systems

are not included as part of the design and construction process, optimal performance may not be obtained. This is especially true with larger mixed-use or community-scale projects, in which multiple builders and literally hundreds of trades people are installing critical high-performance elements.

■ **Construction waste management**. The cost of landfill diversion and construction waste recycling should be identified early on and included in conceptual cost inventories.

■ **Increased contingency**. Incidental budgets are needed to cover potential cost overruns when using new technologies or less time-proven practices.

STEVEN EVANS

Steps for Identifying Sustainable First Costs

1. Integrate sustainable goals and performance objectives early in the development process.

2. Identify a preliminary program of sustainable elements that reflects the desires of the target market and the goals of the developer. Include a base case (conventional) solution for each component and products and practices that achieve two to three levels of increased sustainability performance.

3. Organize a costing team that includes planners, architects, landscape architects, construction managers, general contractors, and key subcontractors with appropriate experience and expertise. Bring in more than one builder and contractor, as each will have different experience.

4. Identify key product sources for high-performance green components, such as photovoltaic panels, low-VOC paints, and neighborhood electric vehicles.*

5. Facilitate two or three workshops to review each component proposed in the sustainability program. Estimate costs for the base case and the increased-performance alternatives. LCC analyses will be required for many components.

6. Resolve inconsistencies between sources. Consider retaining a certified value specialist or cost engineer.

7. Be flexible. Adapt the program as needed when new information becomes available through the design process.

*The U.S. Department of Energy's Energy Efficiency and Renewable Energy (EERE) website contains useful information on green components, systems, and practices (www.eere.energy.gov/buildings).

To reduce the use of fossil fuels to improve indoor air quality, the developers of 1400 on 5th, the largest green and affordable housing project in New York City, employed alternative energy sources, including geothermal heat pumps.

FULL SPECTRUM NEW YORK

Costing Methodologies

Some developers only assess first costs when considering a sustainable development, especially if the project is not being retained in ownership over the long term. But the first-costs approach, although essential to any financial analysis, can be misleading, because many sustainable practices often show their value through savings and environmental benefits over time.

That is where life-cycle costing (LCC) comes in. It aggregates costs and savings related to a green component over time and calculates a net present value on the component. A variation on LCC, and one gaining increasing attention, is life-cycle assessment (LCA), which takes a long-range view of all environmental costs that go into a

product, from raw materials to energy consumption, resource use, and emissions through the entire manufacturing process, maintenance, and disposal costs.

Developers of complex projects with multiple uses should not rely on any one of these methodologies entirely, but should investigate the relevance of these options based on their sell or hold strategies and the array of sustainable components being considered. Regardless of the technique used, more than just first costs should be considered. Some components have high first costs, such as tankless water heaters, but lower operating costs. Others have low first costs but high maintenance costs due to landscape and cleanout maintenance. Both tools can help reduce costs while achieving the environmental benefits of a robust green building program.

FIRST COSTS

First-costs analysis is the course most typically taken; it is easy and intuitive. By comparing the cost of a sustainable component or practice to the cost of its conventional counterpart, a cost difference can be identified. When completed for all of the sustainable components under consideration, a decision can be made on each component based on consistency with vision, business plan, and pro forma goals. Of course, the weakness of this approach, as noted above, is that it does not consider the life-cycle savings on the subject component.

70

OPPOSITE: PRAKASHPATEL.COM

The Phillip Merrill Center in Annapolis, Maryland, uses 90 percent less water than a conventional office of the same size.

Montgomery Park Business Center in Baltimore, Maryland, has a 20,000-square-foot (1,858-square-meter) green roof, which helped the developer to secure the Maryland Department of the Environment as a tenant.

KATRIN SCHOLZ-BARTH

One of the challenging aspects of cost analysis is identifying first-time costs. There is a scarcity of published cost information on green projects. The U.S. Green Building Council (USGBC), for example, does not require cost information on LEED certification applications and most developers hold real costs close to their chests. Besides, most cost summaries are of the final built project and do not provide comparison with more conventional alternatives. Unless a project is completely sustainable, individual green components are often intertwined with other upgrades or amenities, making it difficult to isolate items of a high-performance nature and their respective cost and added value.

One of the best sources of information on green building costs comes from case studies, available in a number of publications and on a variety of web pages. Although highly valuable, most case studies are limited in terms of providing a comprehensive cost and revenue database. They do, however, provide ideas for synergies, financing, cost recapture, and contact information for specific inquiries.

Because many green components are not standard, especially in high-velocity builder environments, extra detective work is often required. Multiple sources should be tapped, including

Basic Steps of a Life-Cycle Cost Analysis

1. Establish working criterion and parameters. Certain assumptions need to be established that frame the LLC process. A key decision is the length of the study period. For example, should it be 5, 10, or 30 years? The choice may correlate with a project hold, amortization, or product life expectancy period. The project time frame, frequency and intensity of maintenance, and the rate schedules for water and energy need to be projected.

2. Identify base case and alternatives to be evaluated. A base case that represents the least sustainable scenario is established against which to compare green alternatives. Two to three higher-performing products, practices, or combined packages are defined.

3. Identify investment requirements and ongoing costs. First costs and other capital investment costs are identified, including acquisition and interim replacement costs.
In addition, ongoing operations and maintenance costs are estimated, factoring into the equation the potential for energy and water cost increases, maintenance, and repair, as well as taxes, if applicable. Revenue components are also included at the appropriate time they occur, such as government incentives, tax rebates, and residual salvage value, if any.

4. Discount costs to net present value. Discounting addresses the fact that a dollar received or spent tomorrow is worth less than one spent today. It is a way of adjusting cash flows that occur over time on a common denominator—the present. Of course, the discount rate chosen can have a dramatic influence on the present value of future savings. The higher discount rate used for more risky development projects can make significant future savings seem insignificant, while the lower discount rates used on shorter-term projects give more impact to the future savings.

5. Calculate life-cycle costs for each alternative. Investment and replacement costs are combined and then adjusted for any residual value present at the end of the study period. Next, ongoing operations and maintenance costs are added, as well as energy and water costs. Incentives or rebates are also factored in. All costs (and revenues) have already been discounted to present-value dollars. The aggregation of these represents the total life-cycle cost of a product or practice.

6. Identify lowest life-cycle cost alternative. Typically, the criterion used to select the preferred alternative is the lowest life-cycle cost. Net savings can be calculated by subtracting the total cost of the preferred alternative from the base case. It may help to have already established a minimum acceptable return on investment to create a minimum threshold under which the time, uncertainty, and management investment are determined worthwhile.

architects, landscape architects, land planners, product suppliers, specialists in energy efficiency, renewable energy, and clean transportation solutions, as well as builders and contractors.

First-cost analyses require a significant investment in management time because cost assumptions must be validated. Product suppliers tend to be overly optimistic concerning installation costs, while builders and contractors (especially those with limited experience with the product) may be overly conservative. More than one builder or contractor should be brought in because each will have experience with different green products. Builders and contractors should be selected that have the most experience with green building products and techniques.

The Ecovillage at Currumbin, an ecologically sensitive mixed-use development in Queensland, Australia, achieved extraordinary sales pre-commitments in a market where parcels are usually marketed post-development. One of the Ecovillage's stated goals is to demonstrate the economic viability of sustainable development.

LANDMATTERS CURRUMBIN VALLEY PTY LTD

Each region has variations in availability of green products and the skilled labor needed to install them. PV contractors may be plentiful in Northern California, where local programs and incentives are strong, but they may have less experience in Salt Lake City, where such systems are less frequently installed. Such variations inevitably impact the cost of materials and installation.

LIFE-CYCLE COSTING

The true value of sustainable design is realized over time. Life-cycle costing (LCC) is a time-tested method of measuring efficiencies and savings over the life cycle of a product or building and making their value available to include in pro forma analysis. LCC allows future cost savings to be traded off against higher initial capital costs. The goal is to find the "sweet spot," where the best balance of investment and savings is achieved and the highest value is created.

Although it may be tempting to select green components with the lowest first costs, doing so does not optimize the value of long-term savings. A 2003 study, "The Costs and Financial Benefits of Green Buildings: A Report to California's Sustainable Building Task Force," by green-building financing expert Greg Kats demonstrated that, on average, a 2 percent increase in upfront costs, if carefully invested, would result in a life-cycle savings equal to 20 percent of total construction costs.

In an LCC analysis costs are usually separated into two categories—those that are one-time capital or investment costs and those that are ongoing maintenance and operations costs. These costs are projected over a fixed period and then discounted to a net present value to facilitate comparison. Incomes such as rebates, tax credits, and salvage values are included.

LCC is most effective in comparing several higher-performance products or practices to a base case, usually one using conventional development and building techniques. The process involves the identification of at least two alternative scenarios, each with an increasing level of efficiency or heightened environmental benefit. When these alternatives are compared to the base case, additional savings (or costs) accrued over a defined time period become visible. The primary goal is to identify which alternative has the lowest life-cycle cost. Often the costs of achieving higher and higher efficiencies turn out to be disproportionate to their savings. The comparison of several levels of efficiencies (shades of green) helps to identify the financial "sweet spot."

As an example, consider an analysis prepared by CTG, a sustainability consultant in Irvine, California, that examined the life-cycle costs of microturbines for generating power for an Orange County office complex. Five alternatives were tested: one base case using conventional power from the grid and four additional scenarios, each using an additional gas-powered microturbine unit. The alternative using the most turbines had the lowest consumption of energy (electric and gas) and highest energy cost savings, but it also had the highest capital and installation costs. The analysis showed that this choice

would generate the lowest net present value of power cost, although the payback period was the longest. This data allowed the developer to make an informed decision on what system to use by enabling him to weigh first-cost, life-cycle costs against the payback period for the installation of a higher-performance green technology.

Once the lowest life-cycle cost alternative is known, other financial measures such as total net savings, return on investment, internal rate of return, savings-to-investment ratio, and payback periods can all be calculated.

The U.S. Government Services Agency was looking to increase energy savings when it commissioned the design for the Internal Revenue Service Kansas City Service Center. Natural lighting is used throughout the building and rainwater is captured on the roof and reused for irrigation of fountain features.

© 2006 ASSASSI

A variety of computer programs are available to assist LCC analysis, most developed for government or military applications. Most of the programs are editable and can be used for private-sector projects. Often, modules are available that add tax and financial analysis capabilities. A certified value specialist or cost engineer may help to research costs and frame the outcome for easy inclusion into a project's cash flow or pro forma analysis.

Integrated Design Solutions and Cost Shifting

By linking green components, the additional costs of some sustainable practices can often be reduced, so that investment in higher efficiencies in one element leads to a reduction in the specification and the cost of another. Optimizing the interaction between individual components increases the opportunities for savings and efficiencies; so-called solution multipliers, or multiple savings, are possible downstream from an initial investment in a high performance com-

ponent. Specifying a smaller chiller in an office building, for example, frees up money to upgrade the building envelope, while the improved building envelope makes that smaller chiller feasible. Not to be confused with life-cycle costing, these are first-cost savings due to downstream reductions in development and building costs.

To illustrate the concept of whole-systems thinking and integrated design solutions, consider a strategy taken by Pulte Homes for residential development in Tucson, Arizona.

Pulte proposed a series of high-performance energy-conservation enhancements that increased costs by over $1,600 per home. Using a whole systems approach, the developer was able to produce cost savings of $1,500 per home by installing a right-sized air-conditioning system and avoiding the installation of roof vents, reducing the net cost of the chosen green elements to $100 per home.

Another example is the Crestwood Corporate Centre in Richmond, British Columbia, where the developer upgraded a building with low-E windows, increased natural light and ventilation,

© BARBARA KARANT/KARANT + ASSOCIATES, INC.

and increased insulation R-factor. Applying integrated design logic, the team reduced the building's chiller from 200 to 50 tons, a cost reduction that more than offset the higher shell costs. The end result was a green building that cost less to build than conventional construction.

Identifying these interrelationships and quantifying their savings is easier if "packages," or sets of linked components, are matched and priced in total. For instance, several alternative energy, stormwater, or mobility packages could be compared to each other for combined cost efficiency.

Implementing whole systems thinking requires a very different approach to the design and development process than conventional practices offer. Those who have used it

The Kresge Foundation's headquarters in Troy, Michigan, which involved the preservation of 19th-century farm buildings and the construction of an adjoining facility, has operable windows, geothermal wells, green roofs, and pervious paving.

© BARBARA KARANT/KARANT + ASSOCIATES, INC.

Sustainability at Stapleton

STAPLETON IS A 4,700-ACRE (1,902-hectare) master-planned community of 12,000 homes and apartments, 13 million square feet (1.2 million square meters) of retail and commercial development, and more than 1,100 acres (445 hectares) of parks and open space. Formerly Denver's main airport, the site is now home to the largest infill redevelopment project in the United States. Stapleton is located between downtown Denver and its successor, Denver International Airport.

Right: Stapleton's abundant trails and open space encourage walking and biking. Below: More than six million tons of concrete and asphalt runways from the former airport have been recycled for road base, alleys, sidewalks, curbs, and foundations at Stapleton. Roughly cut blocks of runway concrete called "Staplestone" are used for retention walls throughout the parks and open-space system.

After 70 years as the city's primary airport, Stapleton Airport reached obsolescence and closed in 1995. Following extensive community outreach, Stapleton's planners produced the Stapleton Development Plan, known as the "Green Book."

The plan outlines a clear dedication to affordable housing, traditional neighborhood design, environmental conservation, minority participation, and top-quality educational opportunities. It also reinforces Stapleton's role as a regional employment center, creating strong ties between the redevelopment site and the surrounding neighborhoods. During the creation of the final plan in 1998, the Stapleton Development Corporation selected Forest City Enterprises as the site's master developer. Construction began spring 2001 and buildout is estimated to take 20 years.

Conceived from the start as a sustainable community, Stapleton embraces the ideals of urban life: diverse and distinctive homes with walkable, tree-lined streets, neighborhood stores and nearby offices, schools, and parks. Its developers are integrating compact development with sustainable building practices as well as recycling site materials. The effort has paid off—Stapleton has won numerous awards for its sustainability plan, including the Stockholm Partnership for Sustainable Cities Award.

COMPACT, MIXED-USE DEVELOPMENT

Stapleton is a pedestrian-oriented community, with an overall density of more than 10 units per acre (25 units per hectare). Stapleton's land use plan calls for neighborhoods with a diverse selection of housing in close proximity to recreational, educational, retail, commercial, and transit opportunities. Emphasizing mixed-use zoning throughout, the integrated design promotes walking rather than automobile use. The proximity of homes, schools, and businesses to mass

LEFT: STEVE LARSON/FINEPRINT; ABOVE: JOHN ORDELHEID/360 MEDIA

transit, sidewalks, and bike paths will help reduce the potential for increased traffic congestion and related air quality issues.

SUSTAINABLE BUILDING PRACTICES

Beginning in 2006, all homes at Stapleton are part of the Environmental Protection Agency's Energy Star program. Independent, accredited home-energy raters must verify a home's energy efficiency before it can receive an Energy Star label. Prior to 2006, homes at Stapleton were required to meet the minimum level of the Built Green Colorado program administered by the Home Builders Association of Metro Denver.

PARKS AND OPEN SPACE

When completed, Stapleton will increase the amount of Denver City Parks by nearly 30 percent. Park and parkway design, including Stapleton's 80-acre (32-hectare) Central Park, have water-conserving landscapes. In addition to serving as a regional recreational resource for residents of Stapleton and the surrounding communities, the parks and open-space system also protects natural areas that support wildlife habitat and native plant communities. When the network of recreational trails is finished, it will complete the first loop of trails ever to surround a major U.S. city.

STORMWATER MANAGEMENT

Instead of running stormwater runoff through underground culverts, Stapleton uses an enhanced stormwater management system that sends runoff through constructed wetlands. The runoff that flows to Westerly and Sand creeks and the Platte River meets all required water quality guidelines.

RECYCLING

One of the goals of the Stapleton redevelopment project is to reuse some of the unique features of the old airport. Old airplane hangars and outbuildings have been recycled to house a variety of businesses, including Colorado Studios, a television and film complex. After the remaining terminal buildings were demolished, 50 percent of the old airport's concrete, rebar, and sheet metal were recycled. The 1,100 acres (445 hectares) of old runways have been crushed into material called "Staplestone," which is being used as road base as well as concrete aggregate for the site's roads, trails, and sidewalks, as well as in other projects around Denver. More than 200,000 tons (181,437 metric tons) of asphalt from parking lots and the commuter runway has been transported to the Rocky Mountain Arsenal National Wildlife Area, where the material has been used to create road base. The terminal's 5,000-car garage has become the Stapleton Transit Center, one of the busiest transportation hubs in the Denver metropolitan area. Even some of the old carpeting from the former terminal complex was recycled into carpet backing that is durable, cheap, and produces no offgassing, and thus no indoor air pollution.

EDUCATION

Education is at the core of all of the sustainability initiatives at Stapleton.

Forest City provides sustainability information through different venues such as community events, the "Sustainability at Stapleton" section of the *Front Porch* newsletter, and *New Leaf* and *New Leaf for Kids*—newsletters that feature activities to help residents and their children better understand the principles of sustainability. The 123-acre (50-hectare) Bluff Lake Natural Area serves as an outdoor classroom for children to study wetlands and observe wildlife such as bald eagles, great horned owls, foxes, and a variety of aquatic fowl.

GREEN RETAIL

Northfield Stapleton, a 1.2 million-square-foot (111,484-square-meter) retail center, was granted LEED Silver certification in October 2006. In addition to being one of the first built green retail centers in the country, Northfield Stapleton is the largest retail center ever to enroll in the Xcel Design Assistance Program (XDAP). Through XDAP, Xcel Energy, a public service company in Colorado, makes cash incentives available to tenants who follow the company's green building recommendations.

Stapleton uses an enhanced stormwater management system that sends runoff through constructed wetlands created within its open space.

STEVE LARSON/FINEPRINT

With less than a 1 percent cost premium, Liberty Property Trust achieved LEED Gold certification for The Plaza at PPL Center in Allentown, Pennsylvania.

successfully note that identifying the interrelationships between components that lead to overall cost reductions requires considerably more time and intensity of effort and special expertise on the front end. This might increase the investment in planning and design, and seemingly be more expensive overall, but these expenditures can be more than offset by future savings and value added benefits. Higher upfront design costs that result in lower downstream costs is an example of cost shifting—a hallmark of economically feasible sustainable development.

Putting It All Together

Any planned development has a tremendous number of variables. For a developer considering going green, or moving to a deeper shade of green, it may seem as if the variables multiply exponentially. With each choice of how green to go, the developer is seeking the highest value and the greatest profitability for the desired shade of green. Few communities can do everything to the highest level of sustainability. And at some point, the cost of higher performance becomes disproportionate to the added environmental benefit. How can a development team determine what makes the final cut? In selecting sustainability practices and products, it might be helpful to think of the choices on a continuum:

■ highest environmental benefit;

■ highest environmental benefit at lowest life-cycle cost (the "sweet spot");

■ lowest life-cycle cost;

■ lowest first cost; and

■ established end user preference/guarantee of recouping green premium.

For a complex, multifaceted real estate project, a developer would determine the spot on the continuum that best represents the development's goals and use it as a filter for making each decision. There is a band on the continuum that provides the opportunity for attaining the best balance between the total costs and the total benefits. This is where the greatest sustainable value is created.

In any sustainable community development there are multiple stakeholders—master developer, builder, homebuyer, and investor, as well as those who derive economic benefit from all the sustainable practices and products involved in creating the project. When a community is designed and planned in an integrated fashion and when sustainable practices and systems are incorporated all along the way, the stakeholders share in the premium that is created. A sustainable community, and the homes within it, are

better than just green. The whole works together and its value only grows over time.

Going for the green, in both sustainability and profitability terms, may be its own reward. In the future, however, sustainable design may not be optional. Legislation governing standards of energy and water efficiency, indoor air quality, and waste management is proliferating. At the moment, meeting or exceeding sustainable standards may give community developments a competitive edge in the market. However, before long, it is likely that sustainable practice will become a requirement, not an option. Integrated design and whole systems approaches are tools that allow developers to create a new generation of communities that are sustainable and profitable.

PETER AARON/ESTO

RICHARD FRANKO

5 Green Building Design

To mitigate site impact, the Zoomazium in Seattle was envisioned as a "room" in the forest. Deciduous trees provide seasonal solar protection, while evergreens provide shade and water retention year-round.

GREEN BUILDINGS DO NOT EXIST IN A VACUUM. From solar orientation to stormwater filtration and connections to public space and natural scenery, the sustainable design of buildings and neighborhoods must be interwoven. The guidelines established for individual buildings should be developed concurrently and in unison with every other aspect of a sustainable community, not after the lots and streets have been designed.

Consider the front porch. The location and orientation of the porch can enhance a neighborhood's social fabric, security, and aesthetic qualities. It can mediate the scale of a building and provide transitional public/private spaces for the residents. Porches can also offer solar shading and, if enclosed, capitalize on heat gain.

From the 40-story high rise to the single-family house, the individual building is where many development decisions involving energy, water, landscape, and materials are realized and enjoyed. Like natural systems, the buildings of the future will become more responsive to the environment and reflective of their bioregions. Making them truly green means we all benefit.

Setting Priorities

Sustainable building design is not simply an array of design features. It involves weighing options and making difficult trade-offs. Finding the optimum orientation for buildings and blocks is one of many such challenges. To optimize solar gain and daylighting, buildings are typically on an east-west axis, but it may be less disruptive to the land to build on a north-south axis. A building's orientation can save energy, but it may also clash with a floor plan that would activate the public realm or align homes in an orderly fashion. Early collaboration among development team members will help to resolve these potentially conflicting site and program demands. From engineers and landscape architects to daylighting experts and ecologists, a qualified design team not only helps set sustainability goals but helps save money if it is brought in early in the process.

Mechanical engineers, landscape architects, and civil engineers are especially important at the early stages of building design, when the site plan and orientation alternatives are discussed. The wind analyst or mechanical engineer will help with a detailed analysis of wind, solar, and psychometric profiles of the site and region. In a multifamily or single-family development, thermal energy modeling of typical units or houses can pinpoint optimal window locations, roof or solar overhangs, and large trees adjacent to

© ROBERT PISANO

All of the buildings at Teton Science School's new Jackson campus are intended to be used as educational tools exhibiting environmentally intelligent design. A demonstration photovoltaic system is tied into the power grid, permitting power to flow back into the grid at times of low on-site use.

buildings. To reduce costs, sample units in each orientation can be modeled. Initial site and soil analysis will help develop strategies and confirm feasibility and desired quantity for stormwater recharge within the building site or community. Cost consultants can help track any revisions to the typical capital costs and also quantify operational savings from resource-efficient strategies and unique systems. Standards and checklists set by green certification systems such as the U.S. Green Building Council's LEED™ are useful in monitoring and assessing achievements in sus-

tainable design. But it is important to remember that the most effective sustainable design solutions are integrated; one solution produces multiple benefits. Many solutions are site-specific and originate early in the design process.

In building design, the development team should not lose sight of the big goals:

- conserving energy and water resources and reducing carbon dioxide emissions;
- reducing the use of products that negatively impact human health and ecosystems;
- creating renewable energy on or off site to support community needs, including individual buildings;
- improving regional ecosystem health, including watershed performance, habitat health and connectivity, and water quality;
- creating environments that delight all the senses: sight, smell, touch, taste, and sound; and
- developing an authentic connection to natural systems.

The first two goals have been the bedrock of sustainability in the twentieth century; the last four are emerging as keys to green building in the twenty-first century.

Responding to Regional Conditions

Perhaps the most exciting element of sustainable design is the potential for buildings to leverage sun, wind, and water resources. That response is linked to the particulars of hydrology, topography, and climate that characterize a bioregion, a geographic area defined by its interconnected ecosystems rather than its political boundaries.

The character of a bioregion can be expressed in simple yet powerful ways by using materials, vegetation, and forms that work with its natural characteristics and resources. For instance, instead of funneling rainwater from the rooftop through the gutters and into a hidden stormwater collection system, special runnels in the structure and the landscape can display the

© JUAN HERNANDEZ

84

Clara Vista Townhomes: Green and Affordable

IN JANUARY 2006, Clara Vista Townhomes in Portland, Oregon, became the first LEED Silver–certified affordable housing project in the nation under the new LEED for Homes program. The project was developed by Hacienda Community Development Corporation, a nonprofit organization dedicated to improving the quality of life for low-income Hispanic families throughout Oregon.

Clara Vista is part of Hacienda's plan to transform Cully-Killingsworth, a 20-acre (8-hectare) neighborhood in northeast Portland, from a crime-ridden urban wasteland into a healthy community with hundreds of new housing units in close proximity to services and public transportation. The $8 million project is split over two sites and includes 44 three- and four-bedroom apartments. The units are rented to families earning between 30 and 60 percent of area median income.

Clara Vista's buildings reflect local vernacular styles and include solar hot water heating.

CARLTON HART ARCHITECTURE

Clara Vista's sustainable features include whole-house ventilation systems, on-site rainwater filtration, efficient hydronic space heating, abundant natural lighting, fluorescent lighting fixtures, fiber-cement siding, insulation, and Energy Star appliances. Each unit also features a rooftop solar water-heating system, which provides both heat and hot water. The project has natural drainage swales for stormwater management and low-flow plumbing fixtures in each unit.

Hacienda's commitment to green development practices stems from a desire to build homes that decrease the long-term burden of utility costs and create a safe, healthy environment for residents.

---

rainwater and celebrate its path. Consulting ecologists and civil engineers can help determine how the natural hydrology can drive the optimal design of such features.

Another important regional response in building design is the use of local materials. Bricks made from local clay, rammed earth walls from excavated soil, and wood from regional renewable timber stands or salvaged from nearby sources represent typical strategies. In the landscape, reinforcing local habitat, vegetation, and native hydrology such as a xeriscape in the Southwest or subtropical landscape in Miami help sustain the native climate. Designing for the thermal and solar profile of the region, such as the hot days and cool nights of desert climes or the more constant temperatures and overcast skies of the Pacific Northwest, can substantially reduce energy usage and costs and create an authentic aesthetic.

Precedents for building in harmony with nature include the adobe structures of the Southwest and timber longhouses of the Pacific Northwest. The goal of regionally based design is to use local materials, climate, and social patterns as inspiration for building form. The first objective is to take advantage of a location's opportunities; the second is to mitigate its challenges. Research into bioregion characteristics should address climate, water, vegetation and natural habitat.

Climate. Knowing how much sun, wind, rain, and snowfall an area receives can help in the design of key building components and the specification of appropriate materials and systems. This microclimatic information is not available

Above: The solar panels built into the roof of the Vista Montana apartments in Watsonville, California, are not visible from the street. Right: Beddington Zero Energy Development (BedZED) in South London has rooftop wind cowls that provide a natural ventilation solution.

TOP: CHARTER MAC; RIGHT: ZEDFACTORY.COM

on the Internet, and data from a source even as close as the local airport is often not specific enough. For most larger-scale developments, it is useful to invest in an on-site weather station, so that data can be collected for each season and modeled. A small weather station can be purchased for less than $2,000.

Water. Every development resides within a watershed that has unique characteristics. On some sites, it may be important to recharge as much water as possible into the soil; on others, it may be critical for surface water to feed into streams, where it can support circulation and habitat. Regions of the country with subsurface aquifers may require that a development team focus on water quality rather than the quantity of water infiltration.

Vegetation. Deciduous trees provide seasonal solar protection for a building, but evergreens provide shade and canopy water retention year round. Shade trees mitigate heat gain and glare, but they can also interfere with photovoltaic panels. While plants and trees play a large role in the shading of a building, the type of vegetation selected for a site can help reduce the need for irrigation and support the health of the soil and the organisms that live in it. Research should include soil structure and microorganisms as well as native plants.

Once an area's ecosystem, water resources, and natural habitat are understood, then individual site goals can be developed and prioritized. A site goal may be to use all rainwater once before recharging it into the ground, or to live within the annual rainfall quantity of the site. The latter would require calculation comparing local precipitation statistics to projected consumption needs of the planned development.

Conserving Resources

Energy and water are scarce resources that deserve careful consideration in every design decision, just as they do in daily life. According to Worldwatch Institute, buildings in the United States use 70 percent of available freshwater flows and 40 percent of available energy. Very basic green measures can reduce a building's consumption rate by 30 to 50 percent. This would be a great benefit to the environmental bottom line, not to mention the health and the pocketbooks of commercial building owners, homeowners, and tenants.

ENERGY

The first goal in creating a high-performance building is to reduce energy loads. This can be achieved in many ways. For instance, shading reduces heat gain in the summer and tightly sealed building envelopes decrease thermal transfer in the winter.

It is important to understand the typical, region-specific energy profile for each of the building types planned for a sustainable development. Occupant use patterns should also inform design decisions. For example, the per

capita requirement for heating and cooling a multifamily housing project in a mild climate can be quite low. The greatest use of energy in such a building is expended on the production of a domestic hot water. This user profile may point to solar water-heating system and low-flow showerheads as key energy-saving strategies. In contrast, the main source of energy consumption in the single-family cottages of a development in Colorado may be the heating and cooling systems. In this case, the quantity and quality of the insulation and windows may be top priorities.

The development team's mechanical engineer can analyze each of the building types to produce a typical energy profile for the designers. Once the areas of greatest energy use are identified, strategies for orientation, daylighting and fenestration, envelope design, and equipment selection can be determined and prioritized. With energy profiles in hand, the design team can sculpt the building form to respond to the sun, wind, and climate. Once again, the regional response and microclimate is critical: In the hot, dry Southwest, shading can dramatically reduce cooling loads during the day.

Building America, a website sponsored by the U.S. Department of Energy, provides research data for energy-efficient housing solutions specific to each climate region in the United States that can be implemented on a production basis. Using Building America protocols, buildings typically use 30 to 90 percent less energy than comparable code-compliant residential buildings in a given region. In some climates, new buildings can be designed to limit or even eliminate the need for refrigerant-based cooling systems by using operable windows, vents, and fan-driven fresh air systems. Hot, humid summers present the biggest challenge, but shading strategies, thermal stratification, and thermal mass can decrease the amount of refrigerated cooling required.

As residential building systems become more and more energy efficient, appliances and lighting become proportionally greater consumers of energy. All appliances, lighting, and HVAC equipment should be Energy Star® rated.

Rising and volatile energy prices make on-site energy generation increasingly attractive to ho-

meowners. Installation costs are going down and government incentives help to reduce first costs and reward ongoing energy generation.

When deciding whether to include renewable energy in a project, the following questions can help guide the team's decision-making process:

- What is the solar, wind, mini-hydro, or geothermal potential of the site?

- What are the regional resources? Is it more cost-effective to purchase green power from a local utility?

- What are the state and federal incentives available at the time of design and construction? These incentives can dramatically tip the balance for selecting strategies and must be reviewed for each project and location.

Portland State University's Stephen Epler Hall uses bioswales to funnel and disperse stormwater runoff.

© ECKERT & ECKERT

- Is the site located near a heat exporter, such as a waste treatment plant, power plant, or industrial site?

- Does the development include buildings with complementary energy profiles that would make the site prime for ground-coupled energy systems?

On-site energy production falls into four main categories.

Photovoltaics convert solar energy into electricity. Panels are adaptable to roofs, exterior walls, sun canopies, car shelters, and many other locations.

Wind turbines, though dependent on site and regional conditions, can be very effective. For example, Western Harbor, a sustainable mixed-use multifamily development in Malmö, Sweden, offsets 100 percent of its power requirements with one two-megawatt wind turbine, combined with photovoltaics, biogas, and solar hot water. The turbine is located offshore, where the wind conditions are better. In a location with limited wind resources, buying wind-generated energy from a "wind-rich" area is a sustainable alternative.

Geothermal systems tap into low and high levels of heat below the ground to provide heat-ing and cooling. In areas with high-temperature subsurface water, systems utilize the water for heating buildings. In most parts of the country, geothermal systems take advantage of the stable, 50- to 65-degree subsurface temperature that can help cool in the summer and heat in the winter. There are multiple systems that include closed horizontal loops, 300-foot-deep (91-meter-deep) vertical wells and injection systems that cycle groundwater.

Biomass is currently the largest source of renewable energy for large-scale energy production, and includes wood, crop residue, organic municipal waste, and biofuels. For individual buildings, systems range from wood-burning stoves to wood-pellet-burning boilers and combined heat and power (CHP) plants that burn biomass products to provide heat and electricity to communities. As biofuel research evolves, technology could become more common for community-level energy production.

WATER

Reducing the use of potable water is a goal easily understood by most homebuyers, and there are a number of strategies and products for achieving substantial savings in long-term water costs and in total potable water consumption.

The first and most basic strategy is to landscape with plants that need little or no water when established. Drought-tolerant and native plants are the best choices. If irrigation must be employed, the installation of "smart" controls can keep usage to a minimum. Irrigation is rarely needed over the long term for regionally appropriate landscapes. Water can be further conserved through the use of subsurface irrigation systems and soaker hoses, eliminating evaporation that occurs when water is expelled through the air via a sprinkler. In addition to water savings, there are aesthetic benefits, as well. Native plants and trees tend to blur the distinction between the individual lot and the larger natural setting. Educated builders and owners can have the satisfaction of contributing to the propagation of native plant species, some of which are threatened by invasive newcomers.

Minimizing impermeable surfaces can help to keep water out of gutters and storm pipes

Taylor 28 is a pedestrian-focused, mixed-use development near downtown Seattle in which underutilized roadway width is transferred to the public realm. Instead of discharging to the street, all stormwater runoff is collected and dispersed in a series of urban rain gardens.

legend

1 unit pavers
2 concrete curb with drainage slots
3 raingarden plantings
4 ponding zone
5 freeboard zone
6 overflow
7 mulch layer
8 raingarden soil
9 gravel filter
10 washed rock
11 perforated pipe sized to increase storage capacity
12 infiltration zone
13 edge restraint

© MITHUN

Top: The green roof at Seattle's Zoomazium provides habitat for birds and insects. Below: The Harrison Memorial roof garden evokes the marine environment of the Bremerton, Washington, community in form and use of materials.

while recharging aquifers. Permeable pavements can help meet groundwater recharge goals, and minimize discharge into storm drains and sewer pipes. A blanket of hardy plants provides natural filtration as well as a more beautiful site. Increasingly, this blanket is being extended to the building itself, in the form of green roofs and walls. To offset some potable water use and deliver long-term savings to the household, rainwater

can be captured before it is recharged into the ground or redirected to municipal stormwater systems. Rain collection barrels can be placed at downspouts, and underground tanks can store large volumes of water to be pumped out for re-

use in irrigation systems, toilets, and other functions deemed appropriate by local jurisdictions.

Treating blackwater and graywater on site can provide dramatic savings in water usage. This is a more complicated undertaking and will need a consultant to design and specify the correct system. The consultant should have a track record of designing, installing, and building fully permitted systems. Biological or mechanical membrane filtration systems, which are expected to become increasingly popular due to the growing need to reclaim water worldwide, can provide a tertiary level of treatment of the water for use in irrigation or toilets. However, regulations are specific to each state, county, or city and must be examined closely by the consultant. Other combined water treatment options include subsurface flow constructed wetlands (SFCW) systems, which treat effluent to a tertiary level before recharging the water through conventional drainfields. This option can serve a community or a single-family home, provided enough room is available for the treatment system, which includes a gravel substrate and above-ground plantings that help break down the effluent.

The efficacy of reclamation systems is dependent upon the amount of water being treated, the cost of water, and the maintenance required.

TOP: © RYAN HAWK; LEFT: © 2007 EDAW/PHOTOGRAPHY BY DIXI CARILLO

90

© 2002 DIXI CARILLO

Some systems necessitate a full-time operator, while others require monthly maintenance. Reclaiming potable water is also a viable means of reducing consumption. There are ways to use potable water more than once. Showers, sinks, and washing machines are the most common collection points for graywater, and unlike rainwater, the supply is available all year round.

In conjunction with reclamation and treatment strategies and systems, developers and builders need to research and invest in efficient plumbing components and fixtures. Building codes and financial incentives from licensing agencies have also improved the appeal of installing such fixtures in both single-family homes and multifamily dwellings. Dual-flush toilets, low-flow showerheads, and water-efficient washing machines are also ways to reduce usage. However, net savings are worth little if the user is dissatisfied. A balance between user comfort and resource conservation is the key to successful water-saving appliance applications.

While the specification of field-tested and user-friendly low-flow plumbing fixtures and appliances is growing, it is essential to research post-occupancy reports on different fixtures before purchase to avoid user dissatisfaction. For example, poorly designed low-flow models may require more than one flush, but a toilet with properly designed bowl geometry and surface materials can provide better performance. The

Xeriscapes, such as this one in Civano in Tucson, Arizona, use low-water plantings and require a water conservation plan.

GREEN BUILDING DESIGN

These low-growing rooftop plants spread to form dense vegetation once the entire roof is covered. Maintenance is needed only once a year.

most water-efficient toilets are composting models, which require removal of digested bio-solids from a holding tank that is typically one floor below the lowest toilet; this system is best suited to users willing to carryout regular maintenance.

Like low-flow toilets, the first generation of waterless urinals had some problems, including sediment accumulation and odor, but newer units, when properly located and installed, offer no-flow performance.

Optimizing the Building Envelope

Some of the most significant challenges in sustainable design and construction involve the building envelope: the roof, walls, floors, and all the openings in them. Moisture barriers and insulation, for example, interconnect with structural elements in increasingly complex and efficient ways. They are all critical to energy efficiency, healthy interior environments, and the long-term durability of buildings.

The building envelope does more than keep moisture out of the structure. Its design can contribute greatly to the sustainable performance of the building by taking into account the specific climate in which the building is located. Region-based systems address vapor diffusion, air transport of vapor, moisture migration, and dew point. Different climates require different solutions. In the case of envelope design, one size does not fit all.

While fenestration can optimize daylighting, it also affects the interior temperature of the building. Unless heat gain or loss is managed—through building orientation, for example—any ben-

Guidelines for Wise Water Use

REDUCE USE OF POTABLE WATER
- low- or no-flow fixtures
- appropriate plants for the region
- smart controls for irrigation

RECLAIM USED WATER
- graywater treatment and reuse
- blackwater treatment and reuse or recharge

CAPTURE RAINWATER
- from roofs
- from hardscapes
- in greenscape areas

WATER TERMS MADE SIMPLE
- **Potable water:** drinkable water
- **Stormwater:** general rainwater and runoff from sites
- **Blackwater:** toilet water
- **Graywater:** sinks, showers, laundry, etc.
- **Combined water:** blackwater and graywater
- **Rainwater:** roof runoff
- **Reclaimed water:** treated water

efits secured by maximizing daylight will be for naught. Shades and louvers can counteract the need for additional heating and cooling systems, and can also offset lighting costs in some cases.

The use of computer-assisted thermal modeling can be invaluable when making decisions about the building envelope. This type of program can help determine the best locations for windows and skylights as well as operable

KATRIN SCHOLZ-BARTH

LANDDESIGN

Left: A bioretention pond in front of the sales center in the Sanctuary outside of Charlotte, North Carolina, is designed to treat stormwater runoff from the roof. Below: Cisterns can be used to collect rainwater and reintroduce it into the landscaping.

© 2002 DIXI CARILLO

windows, if natural cooling is an option. Variable heat sources, such as computers and people, can be incorporated into the plan to create a model for cooling systems. Such a tool helps the design team determine fenestration and orientation.

Windows are a critical part of the envelope; their size and placement can add a great deal to a structure's energy and natural cooling performance. In colder climates, windows represent 25 percent of the heating load. In warmer climates, up to 50 percent of the cooling load can be from solar gain and thermal transmission of windows. In a hot, sun-filled climate like that of Tucson, Arizona, with heavy cooling loads, the priority is to limit solar heat gain while preserving daylight and good visibility. This can be done with a window that has a low solar heat-gain coefficient (SHGC), a high percentage of visible light transmittance, and a low U-factor to reduce thermal transmission. At a minimum, windows specified for projects in such a climate should be double-glazed, with a U-factor below 0.30, with spectrally selective low-E coatings, inert gas fill, and low air leakage.

If the project is in Boston, however, window selection is focused on issues of heating load and heat flow through the window is paramount. The ideal window in this region has a low U-factor to reduce heat transmission through the glass, and a variable SHGC to allow sunshine in during the winter and keep it out during the summer. The traditional method to achieve this goal is using exterior awnings in the summer and storm windows in the winter.

To help the design team specify the best windows for a project, there are web-based resources for window selection, including the following.

Efficient Windows Collaborative (EWC) offers tools to assess relative performance in different U.S. cities of multiple windows and glazing types. It also includes code data, by state, and links. The website is a joint venture of the Center for Sustainable Building Research at the University of Minnesota, the Alliance to Save Energy, and the Lawrence Berkeley National Laboratory. It has a window selection tool and guide for energy modeling with shading and façade strategies.

Energy Star, a joint program of the U.S. Department of Energy and the U.S. Environmental Protection Agency, rates equipment, windows, appliances, lighting, and construction practices in terms of energy reduction. To achieve a goal higher than 15 percent above baseline, products must exceed Energy Star minimums. To put these standards into perspective, the PassivHaus protocols, a far more rigorous construction standard in Germany, require windows that perform twice as well as those that receive an Energy Star label.

National Fenestration Rating Council, a non-profit organization that establishes criteria and performs tests to rate and label windows, doors, skylights, and related attachment elements. Its ratings are the industry standard basis of comparison for energy performance.

Operable windows are an essential part of the green building tool kit; they can provide natural cooling, occupant control, and enhanced connection to the outdoors. They need to be carefully used in areas with security, noise, and particulate issues. Natural cooling with operable windows should be combined with the introduction of tempered outdoor air to provide better indoor air quality year round.

According to Lawrence Berkeley Laboratories, windows are responsible for over 4 percent of the total energy use in the United States due to heat loss. To help reduce that loss the development team or builder should consider windows with low-energy transmission rates (U-factor). Emerging technologies include dynamic windows, or windows that adapt to daily and seasonal changes to optimize solar harvesting. Integrated façades—walls that combine operable windows and shading with features like heat-chimney double walls and solar reflectors—can control and redirect much of the daylight that hits the building envelope.

Selecting Green Materials

The construction of buildings and landscapes involves thousands of materials and chemical

Green Roofs and Walls

GREEN ROOFS AND WALLS create a living surface on the building envelope. They have been used for centuries in traditional construction, from turf roofing in rural Norway to vine-covered walls in the courtyards of Mediterranean villages. Recent advances combine high-tech systems with selective and strategic planting to create buildings that function well ecologically, economically, and aesthetically.

Green roofs and walls help to reduce dust and sequester carbon dioxide, improving air quality.

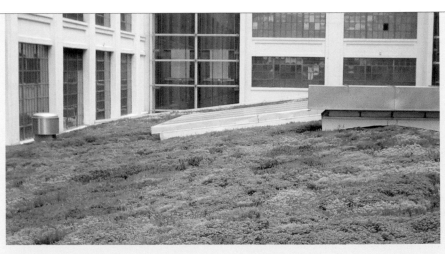

Green walls can be constructed in different ways. In some cases, trellises or mesh screens may be used as armatures for vine or plant growth. In other instances, vines may grow directly on exterior walls. Green walls can be a valuable design element, especially in higher-density areas, where vegetation and natural habitat is limited.

Installed on flat or sloped surfaces, green roofs require a more complex construction assembly than a green wall, but offer many benefits. Greens also cost more than a standard system. Depending upon the type,

KATRIN SCHOLZ-BARTH

the green roof assembly above the building insulation can add approximately $7 to $21 per square foot to the cost of a basic roof and $2 to $17 per square foot to the cost of a higher-grade roof. Depending upon the planting medium depth and the seismic region, there will be a cost impact on the building structure.

BASIC CONSTRUCTION

For the commercial and institutional markets, roofing manufacturers design and warrant assemblies with a variety of moisture retention and root barrier options. These systems can be installed on a variety of pitches and

across large areas. The vegetated roof at the Ford Motor Company plant in Rouge River, Michigan, for example, is 454,000 square feet (42,118 square meters), or about ten acres (four hectares).

For the residential market both prefabricated commercial assemblies and simpler contractor-built systems can be used. The Northwest Ecobuilding Guild offers information on residential projects and assembly types.

As with every aspect of sustainable design and construction, green roofs require a collaborative, whole-systems approach. Landscape architects design the planting systems, working with experienced contrac-

compounds. Each one has a different lifecycle, with unique origins, chemical composition, and reuse or landfill options. The ideal material is locally sourced and locally processed, free of toxic emissions, and reusable or biodegradable.

As in other design decisions for green buildings, the pros and cons of each product must be weighed against one another. For instance, substituting fly ash in a concrete mix is an excellent example of the reuse of an industrial byproduct, but the creation of fly ash through the combustion of coal releases carbon dioxide into the atmosphere. Incorporating sustainable materials such as bamboo into a building takes advantage of a rapidly renewable material, yet if it is shipped to the job site from Asia, it will not score well for low embodied energy. A high-quality metal roof that will last 40 years may be a better choice than a split-cedar roof that will last 10 years and is locally grown and renewable.

Fortunately, the green building materials market is rapidly expanding. Unfortunately, "greenwashing," inflated claims for the environmental benefits of materials, is also more prevalent, so it is important that the development team take a critical look at sources. When choosing sustainable materials and products, it is important to consider several criteria.

Low emissions. Select materials that produce little offgassing during or after installation.

Reduced material use. Eliminate extraneous materials and finishes. Interior and exterior surfaces that do not need to be stripped and resealed periodically will reduce chemical use over the life of the building.

tors and plant suppliers. Architects address roof assembly and water runoff issues, while the structural engineers accommodate any additional loads. The vegetation must be selected to work with the local climate. Irrigation and deeper soil may be required to survive dry periods. Many installations use succulents like sedums and plants that can withstand sun and wind. A typical green roof cross-section, starting at the top layer, encompasses vegetation varying with location and rainfall patterns; growing medium of varying depths and containing organic or inorganic material, depending on whether cultivation is extensive (two to six inches deep) or intensive (more than six inches deep); filter fabric; drainage; waterproofing and root repellant (optional); water retention (optional) and thermal insulation; vapor control; and structural substrate.

Green roofs have multiple benefits, including the following:

Reduced cooling and heating loads. Green roof assemblies can reduce heat gain and loss, sometimes to a surprising degree. An industrial plant in Frankfurt that was obliged to install a vegetated roof due to the city's aggressive green building program recovered the investment in less than three years through savings in heating and cooling costs and the reduction of associated industrial equipment.

Long-lasting roof membranes. By decreasing exposure to ultraviolet light and temperature extremes, vegetated surfaces can increase the lifespan of a roof and reduce typical replacement costs.

Sound insulation. Even a 4.7-inch-deep (11.9-centimeter-deep) substrate layer, less than the depth of most green roofs, can reduce sound transmittance by as much as 40 decibels.

Rainwater detention and treatment. Rainwater is slowed and detained at varying rates (depending upon the depth and type of substrate) to provide stormwater retention, treatment, and evapotranspiration. Between 25 and 90 percent of the water can be retained, depending upon the season and system.

Diminished heat-island effect. Local microclimate temperatures can be reduced by eliminating dark-colored, heat-absorbing surfaces.

Improved air quality. Green roofs and walls help to reduce dust and sequester carbon dioxide, improving air quality.

Increased habitat. Landscaped roofs create habitat for insects, birds, butterflies, and other wildlife. In some regions, with the appropriate soils, native plants can be used.

Community aesthetics. Green roofs can enhance the appearance of a building and a community.

Municipal incentives. In some jurisdictions, green roofs can help with design approvals by making it permissible to add floor area or reduce stormwater fees.

Rating system goals. Green roofs are eligible for LEED rating system in the categories of "Urban Heat Island" and "Reduce Energy Consumption."

After the system is installed, the building staff or homeowner will need to learn maintenance and weeding procedures for sustaining the qualities and benefits of the roof.

The State of Indiana Forensic Health Sciences Laboratories was designed and constructed to meet LEED certification requirements. Ten percent of its materials have recycled content, 20 percent are locally manufactured, and 50 percent are locally harvested.

Below: Rainwater collection, photovoltaic roof panels, composting toilets, passive solar orientation, daylighting, and natural ventilation are some of the sustainable strategies employed in the design of IslandWood's Learning Studio on Bainbridge Island, Washington.

Recycled and recyclable content. Use products with post-consumer recycled content and ensure that construction waste is recyclable.

Salvage. Seek materials reclaimed from demolition. Contractors can perform selective deconstruction of a building to save or recycle key components of the structure.

Low embodied energy. Consider how much energy is required to manufacture and ship materials. Make local sourcing a priority.

Habitat impact. Determine whether or not the extraction or harvesting of the material destroys or degrades native habitat.

Lifecycle impacts. Research product lifecycle assessments. They weigh multiple environmental impacts in the extraction, harvesting, manufacturing, and use of materials.

Weighing Material Choices

Structural materials are very important to sustainable design because of the large quantity of material involved. With wood and steel, it is necessary to consider tradeoffs that include

ABOVE: RATIO ARCHITECTS, INC.; RIGHT: © MITHUN

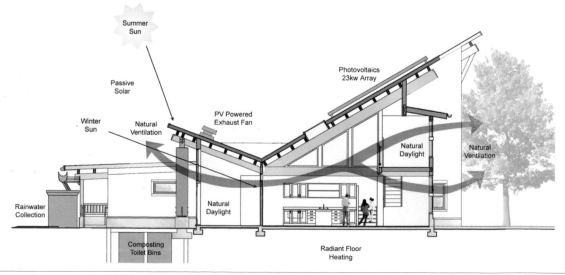

renewability, embodied energy, durability, and recyclability.

A typical choice for builders is between wood and steel framing. Both have merits, but the selection should be based on regional factors for manufacture and harvesting. Wood is inherently renewable, often locally available, and can be sustainably harvested. Steel, on the other hand, consumes more energy in its manufacture; because steel conducts heat so well, its use in exterior walls creates the need for more insulation. However, steel is stable over time, with no shrinkage or moisture content changes, and it is extremely durable as well as recyclable. Much of the steel on the market today has recycled content. As the costs of steel-based structural systems become more and more competitive with wood, developers and design teams should weigh a number of factors (local climate, sourcing possibilities, and construction practices) and investigate prefabricated systems.

There has been extensive discussion and debate over polyvinyl chloride (PVC), a petroleum-based material typically used in siding,

Sunshades complement energy reduction strategies by helping to reduce summer heat gain.

© ECKERT & ECKERT

flooring, windows, and other building materials. While it performs as well as other materials on a life-cycle assessment basis and is believed to be functionally inert, the toxic materials used in its manufacture keep the debate alive. There are lower-impact choices for sheet flooring.

Useful Resources: Sustainable Construction Materials

A NUMBER OF WEBSITE DATABASES and analytical tools can assist in locating and specifying sustainable construction materials. Industry certification groups like Green Label and Floor Score test for a limited range of chemicals, so it is important to research multiple sources. Third-party analysis and certification can help.

■ **The Environmental Impact Estimator**, developed by the Athena Institute, lets building teams assess the environmental implications of a variety of building types. Databases are being expanded in North America. The BEES (Building for Environmental and Economic Sustainability) life-cycle assessment software program is a material selection resource from the National Institute of Standards and Technology. It offers evaluations of more than 200 products. Performance scores are calculated from a number of environmental impacts, from global warming to indoor air quality, and include global cost factors such as acidification, eutrophication, fossil-fuel depletion, and habitat alteration. A note about BEES: Although it is supported by the U.S. Environmental Protection Agency's Environmentally Preferable Purchasing program and is based on consensus standards, the user should be aware that manufacturers supply much of the data on which the scores are based.

■ **The Building Green program**, produced by *Environmental Building News*, has a specification directory called GreenSpec (www. buildinggreen.com). Products are organized into the categories established by the Construction Specifications Institute, and the information is available with the purchase of a subscription or annual directory.

■ **Greenguard Environmental Institute** certifies specific products for indoor air quality, testing for VOCs, aldehydes, styrene, and other substances identified as carcinogens and reproductive toxins under national and international standards.

■ **The PHAROS** is an emerging protocol that offers material analyses from the Healthy Building Network.

Several software programs are available to aid in the selection of materials based on impacts to the environment, including:

■ **SimaPro 6.0**, a life-cycle assessment software package, is a modeling tool for products developed by PRe in the Netherlands.

Concrete is a less controversial choice, but still requires careful consideration. Concrete is very durable, and can be broken down and reused for site work and other purposes. It has substantial thermal mass, absorbing and retaining heat throughout the day, and the capability for cooling at night.

Common cement is very energy-intensive to produce. But fly ash from coal-burning power plants, and blast-furnace slag from steel plants (both waste products) are being substituted for a percentage of cement. The result has high compressive strength and significant cost savings. Cement plants, using local supplies, can mix the material to the structural engineer's specifications.

In addition to fly ash, members of the design team can find many local sources for materials, as well as salvaging and recycling opportunities, through sustainable design and building trade shows held in their region. Local chapters of pro-

fessional organizations—the American Society of Landscape Architects and American Institute of Architects—also offer information about local and national sources of sustainable materials.

Ensuring Indoor Air Quality

High indoor air quality is achieved in a number of ways, beginning with the shape and character of the space itself and its relationship to the outdoors. Natural daylighting and ventilation, key components of green design, go hand in hand with these overall design factors. Not coincidentally, they represent health benefits for the user as well as energy savings for the owner. Well-designed mechanical and natural ventilation systems increase the introduction of fresh air into the interior environment, thereby diluting and exhausting unhealthy emissions that can become trapped there. Filtration of circulating air is critical to remove particulates, and a regu-

LEED: A National Green Building Standard

THE UNITED STATES GREEN BUILDING Council (USGBC), a national nonprofit, developed the Leadership in Energy and Environmental Design (LEED) system to rate new and existing buildings according to their environmental attributes and sustainable features. Current LEED certification programs exist for New Construction, Existing Buildings, Commercial Interiors, and Core and Shell, alongside pilot programs for Homes, Schools, and Neighborhood Developments. LEED for New Construction (LEED-NC) is the most widely used and includes a list of 34 potential performance-based credits worth up to 69 points, as well as seven prerequisite criteria, divided into six categories:

■ Sustainable Sites
■ Water Efficiency
■ Energy and Atmosphere
■ Materials and Resources
■ Indoor Environmental Quality
■ Innovation and Design Process.

LEED allows the project team to choose the most effective and appropriate sustainable building measures for a given location and/or project. Points are tallied to determine the appropriate level of LEED certification. Depending on the criteria met, four levels of LEED certification are possible—Certified, Silver, Gold, and Platinum—and indicate increasingly sustainable building practices.

In recent years, LEED has become the most recognized national standard for green buildings and seen tremendous growth. Total LEED construction starts in 2000 had an estimated value of $792 million. From 2000 through 2003, while the value of all U.S. construction starts declined by almost 50 percent, the value of green building projects continued to rise. In 2006, LEED construction starts were valued at over $7.2 billion. Currently, there are over 4,600 LEED-registered and more than 600 LEED-certified buildings in the country. States and municipalities across the country have adopted LEED-based ordinances for public buildings and, more recently, for large private construction.

THE COST OF ATTAINING LEED CERTIFICATION

Despite a general perception that green building is expensive, studies have increasingly found minimal first-cost investments to achieve LEED certification. For a particular project, the cost of achieving LEED will depend on many factors, including project type, location, and team experience. Higher levels of certification (and sustainability) often require a greater first-cost investment. In general, early integration of sustainable building strategies and LEED into the design process is essential for developing green buildings at a low cost. Since many sustainable design and building practices are new to developers, costs tend to decrease with experience in green construction. For instance, the city of Portland, Oregon's first three completed LEED Silver buildings were finished in 1995, 1997, and 2000. They incurred cost premiums of 2 percent, 1 percent, and 0 percent, respectively.

Researchers, architects, and developers wanting to know how much it costs to build green or achieve LEED, have run into a number of challenges. Until recently, little data had been collected on conventional

lar maintenance schedule will keep filters from becoming clogged.

But material choices, especially those with surfaces exposed inside the building, are very important. Some of the material components that are currently considered negative elements in the environment include persistent bioaccumulative toxics; persistent organic pollutants; volatile organic compounds; semivolatile organic compounds; and heavy metals (mercury, lead, cadmium). While these substances pose hazards to humans and animals, they are especially dangerous when confined to an indoor environment in the form of gases or particulates. Although interior finish and furnishings industries are offering more and more greener alternatives, a number of these compounds can be found in standard carpets and carpet pads, industrial wood products, paints, and stains, and sealants.

Awnings reduce exterior solar gain and glare.

© ECKERT & ECKERT

buildings to determine what the project would cost as a green design. When available, these data are typically based on modeling and detailed cost estimates.

The 2004 Davis Langdon study, "Costing Green: A Comprehensive Cost Database and Budgeting Methodology," compared construction costs for 63 green and non-green buildings and found no statistical difference in the cost per square foot. These results held true when sustainably designed buildings were compared only to buildings within their category, such as schools, libraries, and laboratories.

While they provide an important context for understanding the cost of building green, studies such as these, which compare the costs of similar buildings in different locations built at different times for different purposes, do not provide a specific answer to the question of how much it costs to "green" a project.

Two recent Capital E studies—"The Costs and Financial Benefits of Green Buildings" conducted in 2003 and "Greening America's Schools: Costs and Benefits" in 2006—have attempted to fill this knowledge gap by assembling financial data on

58 green buildings—mostly schools and office projects—constructed between 1995 and 2006. Using actual construction costs and models developed by the architects of specific sustainable projects, these reports found "green premiums" ranging from 0 percent (no additional cost compared to a conventional design) to more than 6 percent for two LEED Platinum buildings. The average green premium was found to be about 2 percent of total construction costs.

THE BENEFITS OF BUILDING GREEN

Building green, high-performance designs results in financial benefits over the lifetime of a project. Over the long term, an investment in a green feature or system can produce a "green premium" that is 20 times greater than the initial cost. "Greening America's Schools" found that building "green" would save an average school $100,000 each year—enough to hire two full-time teachers. For K–12 schools, building green involves an initial cost of $3 per square foot ($32 per square meter) and provides $9 per square foot ($97 per square meter) in benefits from energy savings alone

over 20 years. Green design emphasizes the creation of healthy, comfortable spaces and can lead to financial benefits in the form of improved worker productivity, student test scores, and long-term earnings for individuals and businesses. For a typical green school, the present value of 20 years of increased student earnings associated with increased test scores is $49 per square foot ($527 per square meter).

While many green-building benefits are difficult to quantify, including state and corporate competitiveness, recycling, and emissions impacts, they nonetheless provide real benefits to owners, occupants, and surrounding communities. It has become clear that building green is not only good for the environment, but a prudent financial choice.

Gregory H. Kats, founding principal of Capital E, is an expert on clean energy and sustainable development strategies.

99

Some of these compounds are also found in pesticides and many cleaning products. Educational programs about green cleaning products and pest management for building maintenance staff and occupants is important for the long-term sustainability of a healthy indoor environment.

Typical flooring materials and the adhesives and sealants used for fabrication and installation have long been targeted for replacement with more sustainable and healthy alternatives. Carpeting, in particular, has been the subject of much scrutiny. Because the typical installation is multilayered and has a relatively short life span, it can be a burden on the waste stream. The foams, plastics, and synthetic fabrics in carpet and backing materials traditionally embodied a large amount of energy. And the adhesives that hold them together typically contain a number of compounds that can offgas into the environment, threatening the short-term comfort and long-term health of building occupants. On the plus side, carpet manufacturers are developing lower-emission adhesives, backings, and yarns. Some manufacturers are also using more sustainable production practices and offering products with recyclable content that can be sent back to the mill when replaced. The development team can use products with the Carpet and Rug Institute's Green Label and Green Label Plus, which measure emissions for carpeting, cushions, and adhesives.

Hardwood flooring has always been a good choice for indoor air quality. Finishes and sealants can be an issue, but there are now a number of water-based and low-VOC products available. Forest Stewardship Council–certified hardwoods cost no more than other hardwood choices. As an alternative to conventional hardwoods, bamboo flooring is attractive and very durable. It is also rapidly renewable and well priced. The only drawback is that bamboo is likely to be grown in Pacific Rim countries, which means its delivery to the U.S. market has a higher embodied energy component.

"Natural" flooring options include cork and linoleum, and they are sustainable and low emitting. But even linoleum, which has a base of renewable linseed oil, emits some low-level volatile compounds.

Along with walls and ceilings, smooth bare concrete should be considered for floors in sustainable construction where concrete is used in the structure. However, it is important that sealants be chosen for durability, traction, and low emittance.

System-Wide Strategies

The future of sustainable design lies in systems: local and global production and distribution of materials. At the individual building level, green

10 WAYS TO GREEN A BUILDING™
ac martin partners, inc

1. North/South Orientation min. heat gain & max. daylighting
2. Overhangs on South Elevation prevent solar gain at its worst
3. High Performance Glass tuned to each elevation's exposure 5% Improvement
4. Abundant Fresh Air per Floor diurnal use of microclimate to heat/cool 20% Improvement
5. Open Offices on Perimeter provide natural light to majority
6. Sustainable Materials and recycling of construction debris
7. Central & Transit Friendly Site Energy savings & a morale boost
8. Extensive Photovoltaic Installation provides building's own electricity
9. Planned Tenant Recycling Program built-in systems improve usage rates
10. Computerized Lighting System supplements daylight only as needed 10% Improvement

AC MARTIN PARTNERS, INC.

Percent of Available Outdoor Light Filling the Indoors: the Daylight Factor

This plan of the building shows daylight factors measured after the building was constructed, for comparison with initial estimates and model studies.

- ☐ 10.0-12.0
- ☐ 8.0-10.0
- ☐ 6.0-8.0
- ☐ 4.0-6.0
- ☐ 2.0-4.0
- ■ 0.0-2.0

MAIN FLOOR PLAN
YESLER COMMUNITY CENTER

MITHŪN

This Yesler Community Center plan shows the daylight factor measured after the building's construction and is used for comparison with initial estimates and model studies.

design involves interlocking systems for heating, cooling, ventilation, wall construction, and the building envelope. In the current market, a high-performing residential building has a well-insulated and detailed envelope, insulated windows, high-efficiency lighting and appliances, and low-flow fixtures. A building with a higher level of environmental performance would offset power needs with rooftop photovoltaics to generate electricity and solar panels to heat water.

Ten years from now, every new building should have an efficient envelope and optimum orientation. Looking ahead 25 years, it is likely that the installation of renewable energy systems will be considered essential. Every new project, no matter the budget, can achieve the goal of reducing impacts on the regional ecosystem. Developers should focus first on the decisions that will affect the building for the next 100 years: solar orientation, high-performing envelopes, durable materials, ventilation-friendly footprints, engaging community spaces, low-emitting materials, and habitat connections. As the budget allows, high-performance equipment—renewable energy generators, reclaimed-water systems, green roofs and walls—will drive the building toward a higher level of sustainability.

Luckily, these goals are closely aligned with creating places that are attractive to the market. Homebuyers are increasingly aware of the threats of environmental destruction and waste, and hold sustainability in high value. They demand houses that are built with the health of occupants in mind and anticipate the long-term benefits and stable value of resource-efficient buildings.

When the development team is midway through a building project, the decisions can seem endless and the scientific data supporting environmental effectiveness lacking in rigor or consistency. This is when the team needs to take a step back, remember the primary goals of the sustainable community, and make the best choices based on the data available. Information is much more widely available than it was a decade ago, and that availability will continue to grow. "Cradle to cradle" materials, and the market for them, will continue to evolve, making the development of regenerative buildings more affordable. In the meantime, designing with the primary elements of water, wind, sunlight, energy, and native habitat provides a richer design palette and a more integrated connection between natural resources and the built environment.

© MITHUN

GREEN BUILDING DESIGN

DANIEL K. SLONE

6 Maintaining Sustainability

The redevelopment of Denver's Stapleton airport into a mixed-use community included the restoration of Westerly Creek, which had been buried under a former airport runway. The creek is now a thriving watershed and wildlife sanctuary.

© JAY GRAHAM

ALTHOUGH SUSTAINABLE DEVELOPMENT on a community scale is still in its infancy in the United States, the state of the art is advancing rapidly. The industry has absorbed many lessons from some of the early attempts to incorporate sustainable development practices into neighborhood and community-scale development. One significant lesson learned is the need to approach development in a much more holistic, integrated manner, as discussed in previous chapters. Another important lesson learned is the need to put mechanisms in place to maintain a community's green and sustainable features over time. Observers can point to some highly visible large-scale communities that publicly embraced ambitious green agendas in their earliest stages of development, only to see those good intentions squandered in the implementation process or when ownership was transferred. This chapter discusses tools and strategies for ensuring that a development's sustainable features are maintained as the community evolves and matures.

Open Space Conveyances

The presence of parks, greenways, and other recreational open spaces on a community master plan does not guarantee their implementation or continued existence. Such spaces and related programs may be changed in subsequent rezoning actions. Homeowner associations may fall on hard times and convey these amenities for development. Three sets of tools, used together or separately, are available to address these possibilities: restricted conveyances; codes, covenants and restrictions (CC&Rs); and conservation and open-space easements. A fourth tool, the conveyance of an open space to a nonprofit stewardship organization, is becoming increasingly popular among developers.

Restricted conveyances are deeds in which the grantor imposes restrictions on the conveyed property, retaining the ability to enforce those restrictions. For example, a property owner who wants to be certain that a property will be developed in a sustainable manner may include restrictions in the deed that require the buyer to pursue and implement a green agenda. In their most extreme form, these deeds may include language automatically returning property to the grantor if the restrictions are violated. More commonly, such deeds give the grantor the right to seek specific enforcement or damages. Only the grantor has the authority to allow the developer to seek any variance from these restrictions. Restrictions and easements can be either "appurtenant" or "in gross," depending on the grantor's

102

Codes, covenants, and restrictions can protect green infrastructure and open space.

TOM FOX/SWA GROUP

intent. They are appurtenant when they "run with the land," meaning that the benefits and burdens of the land are passed along from owner to owner. Restrictions or easements are considered in gross if an individual or entity holds them; they are not enforceable by those who succeed the original grantee. In general, appurtenant restrictions and easements are more likely to endure because they do not disappear with the death or dissolution of their holder.

CC&Rs, another set of tools for maintaining sustainability, are often a combination of restrictions, easements, and detailed rules of use that can be imposed on a piece of property at any

time by recording the appropriate document. They are enforceable against subsequent owners by those who impose them, but they can also allow enforcement by third parties. These kinds of documents are often used to establish a rational program across property planned for conveyance to multiple owners. CC&Rs may create rights enforceable by one neighbor against another. They are often used to establish enforceable contract rights for regulatory agencies in addition to their normal regulatory powers. Wetlands or wildlife habitat, for example, can be protected from development with CC&Rs. The CC&Rs can also identify programs or structures that are allowed. These documents are frequently used to protect ongoing sustainability programs, with enforcement rights conveyed to nonprofit third parties. In the absence of a specific, benefited property or a state statute creating the right for enforcement without regard to ownership, care must be exercised to make sure that rights will exist over time. CC&Rs can be very difficult to alter because all of the beneficiaries must agree to any proposed change.

Conservation or open space easements, for example, involve the actual conveyance of a portion of the property rights to a third party for the long-range protection of a property. A seller might also retain a portion of property rights as an easement when conveying the ownership of the property to a third party. These easements are the mechanism most commonly used for granting local and national organizations enforceable restrictions on property uses. Typically, they bar the property owner from altering the natural, open, scenic, or ecological features of the land. In some states, statutes make it clear that certain grantees of these easements (usually private conservation organizations) do not need fee ownership of any adjoining property in order for the easements to be perpetual, but in other states the absence of such ownership may limit the term of the enforceability. Governmental entities may also receive conservation easements. In order for the restric-

tions imposed through the easements to be released or modified by a private owner or public agency, the beneficiaries must agree.

Easements can be affirmative or negative. An affirmative easement gives the easement holder certain benefits, such as the right to cross property to access another property or to install and maintain utility lines on a property. Easements can also be negative, giving the holder some positive right such as access to air, light, or a view that are expressed as a set of prohibitions on the actions that can take place on the subject property. Some courts do not recognize negative easements and treat them instead as negative restrictions that run with the land and are indistinguishable from the restrictions that might be imposed in through CC&Rs. Often holders or beneficiaries of conservation or open-space land protection agreements argue that these interests are easements rather than restrictions because some courts impose fewer requirements to uphold easements than to uphold restrictions.

Beneficiaries of CC&Rs or easements can include the seller, purchasers of other parcels within a community, adjoining landowners, existing nonprofit organizations, newly created nonprofits, or local or state government entities. Some forms of these restrictions can result in reduced property taxes for the remainder owner. For example, if the owner of a 100-acre (40-hectare) property on which 50 single-family

Above: Qingpu District, a western suburb of Shanghai, China, is rapidly becoming an international economic center. The municipality is taking pains to protect its older town centers and natural waterways. Below: The Irvine Company worked closely with nonprofit environmental organizations and government agencies to protect and perpetuate biological diversity at Shady Canyon in Orange County, California.

ABOVE: SWECO FFNS ARCHITECTS; LEFT: TOM FOX/SWA GROUP

Cabrini Apartments' sustainable strategies—promoting energy efficiency and the management of resources—were developed jointly at an early stage by the owners, the developer, the public, and a multidisciplinary team of professionals.

STEVE KEATING

units can be developed gives away the right to develop 90 percent of the units through the gift of an open space easement, then the property should be assessed for a substantially lower amount for real estate tax purposes. Organizations may refuse to accept gifts of the benefit of restrictions or easements unless they are accomplished by a fund or ongoing funding source sufficient to cover the costs of administering the property. For example, a developer may want to donate 1,000 acres (405 hectares) of wetlands and adjoining habitat to a conservation group. This gift may have significant tax benefits for the developer. However, the group may re-

fuse to accept the gift unless the developer also provides them with cash or a future source of cash to pay insurance costs associated with the property and the costs of posting and managing the property.

Whether styled as rights retained by the grantor, restrictions imposed for the mutual benefit of some group of future owners, or an easement held by a national, state, or local group, the restrictions imposed on properties can cover a wide range of land use issues. They can require preservation, prohibiting the subdivision of property and the construction of structures on a property. They can allow the sustainable continuation of activities (e.g., farming or silviculture) or authorize and set the rules for restoration of natural systems (e.g., streams, prairies, or forests) or the creation of new systems (e.g., wetlands). They can address restrictions of use, preclude or regulate activities such as hunting and the use of all-terrain vehicles, or constrain where development is allowed. They can regulate how development occurs, specifying the green building standards to be utilized. They can prescribe these standards or cross-reference other standards such as the U.S. Green Building Council's LEED standards. They can provide extensive detail for the use and occupancy of land, both open spaces and developed areas.

Another important tool for the preservation of open spaces is the conveyance of fee simple title to a nonprofit steward. Many variations on this theme are possible, often dictated by the significance of the preserved property as open space, prime farmland, historic resource, or critical wildlife habitat. Typically, recipients are national institutions such as the Nature Conservancy, Conservation Trust Fund, American Farmland Trust Fund, and the Trust for Public Lands, or local nonprofits. Conveyance of ownership to these organizations is made subject to those rights the conveying developer wants to retain. Consequently, the developer may retain the right to use the land for recreational purposes, diffusion of stormwater or wastewater, or similar undertakings. Some developers have found that the agendas of these organizations are too limiting for their purposes, and they have found it beneficial to create new, locally based nonprofits to own and manage their open spaces. A national

106

Preserving the Landscape through Conservation Easements

HOMESTEAD PRESERVE is being developed as an 11,500-acre (4,654-hectare) conservation-based community surrounding

Homestead Preserve's Old Dairy barn will be preserved and will serve as a community meeting place.

the historic Homestead Resort in Hot Springs, Virginia. Shortly after acquiring the land in 2002, developer Celebration Associates conveyed 9,250 acres (3,743 hectares) of critical Appalachian mountain habitat to The Nature Conservancy, creating the Warm Springs Mountain Preserve. After more than two years of environment assessment and master planning of the remaining acreage, Celebration Associates placed an additional 935 acres (378 hectares) into permanent conservation easement with the Virginia Outdoors Foundation. These easements protect pristine ridge tops, sensitive waterways, wetlands, and forested wildlife corridors from any and all development in perpetuity.

No more than 450 homes will be built on lots ranging from one-half to 13 acres (.2 to 5.3 hectares). Platted building envelopes of up to 15,000 square feet (1,394 square meters) have been located on each home

site so that visibility from adjacent properties, Bath County's main highway, and from the Homestead Resort, is minimized. Wherever possible, private roads are being constructed along existing trails and forest roadways to minimize tree removal. The Homestead Preserve Pattern Book specifies four architectural styles for residences and

establishes green design and construction practices for all buildings within the development, as well as appropriate landscaping options. As a result of these combined efforts at Homestead Preserve, no more than 325 acres (131 hectares), or less than 3 percent of the total acreage, will ever be disturbed by development.

HOMESTEAD PRESERVE

stewardship organization may be willing to pay a substantial amount for an appropriate property, while others may only be willing to take property that comes with an endowment or some arranged stream of income to pay for management. Certain gift conveyances of easements or fee ownership may generate federal income tax deductions for charitable gifts or state income tax credits. These tax benefits may be critical to the economic viability of the open space preservation plan.

The same mechanisms used to convey stewardship of expansive open spaces can also be used for the preservation of contiguous parcels or common areas within new communities. A development with large residential lots may im-

pose easements or restrictions on parcels being conveyed to private owners. For example, a local zoning or subdivision code may require that lots be a minimum of ten acres (four hectares) each. This size lot falls within the classic range of "too big to mow, too small to farm." If roads are designed to place the lots with their short ends facing one another and the building footprints are pulled to the front one-half acre, then a section of 20 lots would create a contiguous, undeveloped 190 acres (77 hectares). This area could be conveyed to the homeowners but subject to an easement to continue farm operations or forest management or recreation, for example, on the undeveloped area.

The construction of Nordheim Court at the University of Washington restored a predevelopment wetland, providing necessary habitat for native plants and animals.

© DOUG J. SCOTT

When this approach to preserving open space over private property is utilized, issues sometimes arise regarding liability to the property owner for acts of the farmer. This issue is best addressed by insurance, which can be maintained by the homeowners association. Another issue is security for the crops from vandalism or theft, although the likelihood of significant impact from such activities is low. A more serious issue is the overspray from pesticides or herbicides used for crop maintenance, which can be a problem when sustainable communities attract people with heightened chemical sensitivities looking for a healthy-living alternative.

Keeping Green Infrastructure Green

Green infrastructure—both natural systems and engineered landscapes —sometimes requires different mechanisms for oversight, maintenance, and repair than conventional development.

The maintenance requirements of green stormwater infrastructure, for example, are different than those for a conventional development's curb-and-gutter conveyance to storm sewers and discharge into streams. In conventional projects, most residential stormwater either sheet-flows over driveways and yards or is conveyed via roof gutters connected into a storm drain. While there may be maintenance agreements for stormwater ponds in conventional subdivisions or commercial areas, there are few inspections after construction unless a problem becomes noticeable. In the case of a sustainable development, stormwater control may be achieved through a combination of pervious surfaces, swales, constructed wetlands, low-impact design (biofiltration and infiltration), and green roofs. Effective functioning of the system depends on the maintenance and operation of components, which are often installed on private property. Even though many minor components should not need inspecting unless problems become evident, a green stormwater system will likely need more oversight for proper functioning than a conventional system. The best mechanism to obtain access for inspection and maintenances is through the easements and requirements of the CC&R. The property owners association can even provide the maintenance as a paid service.

Similarly, construction of future phases of a system can be ensured through zoning requirements and the CC&Rs. This approach can be utilized to address the continued installation and maintenance of other green infrastructure as well. For example, CC&Rs can prohibit the use of potable water or groundwater in irrigation systems, requiring instead use of graywater or rain-barrel water harvesting.

Development projects often base their phasing plans and their density projections on assumptions regarding infrastructure performance—that is, how effective infrastructure will be in fulfilling its purpose, whether that is moving water or moving traffic. If these assumptions include the high efficiencies that accompany sustainable projects and those elements are not implemented or maintained, future plans can be jeopardized. The developer may not be able to build as many units in the next phase because the wastewater infrastructure in the prior phase was not installed as anticipated. However, problems can be avoided through the use of CC&Rs to require waterless urinals, two-button toilets, and low-flow faucets in residential, commercial, and civic buildings. Architectural guidelines can ensure that these features are installed initially, but inspections are necessary for long-term compliance. Reduced electrical needs can be similarly addressed. The developer's design guidelines can require that energy-efficient measures be utilized and maintained. The property owner association can be the appropriate vehicle for long-term maintenance of alternative energy sources such as district heating or cooling, photovoltaic streetlights, or windmills for moving stormwater.

The private party steps necessary to keep green infrastructure green may sometimes depend on the willingness of public agencies and monopoly utility providers to participate in green infrastructure programs. Some local agencies and publicly regulated utilities may have mandates that require them to utilize green infrastructure. Developers should be aware of and take advantage of the financial benefits available to third parties from green infrastructure. Maintaining a

green stormwater system, for example, may allow a municipality to claim credits for nutrient reductions in a state nutrient-trading program that may allow later expansion of its sanitary sewer without the purchase of additional credits. Utilities' capital costs for stormwater, wastewater, potable water, and provision of electricity may also be reduced by aggressive maintenance of the green infrastructure. For example, if a project is energy efficient or uses distributed alternative energy sources, the power company may avoid the costs of expanding generation facilities or extending new electrical distribution networks as well as the costs of maintaining these facilities and networks.

Green infrastructure affects and is affected by other systems in a sustainable community, so its maintenance needs to be part of a holistic vision. Narrow roads, tree-lined streets, environmentally responsible landscaping programs, and a mix of uses all influence the amount and quality of stormwater, paved heat islands, fertilizer usage, and vehicular trips. To ensure the continuation of such beneficial elements through multiple

The Santaluz community in southern California preserved natural drainage courses, minimizing the need for storm drains.

TOM FOX/SWA GROUP

109

When the city of Vista, California, redeveloped its downtown, a flood control channel was rebuilt and turned into a riverwalk and park.

phases of a community it is important to stipulate design guidelines contractually in the sale of sections of community-scale development projects and through cross-development agreements within projects. Cross-development agreements provide for the owners of different parcels to have mutual cross-easements and to share common maintenance expenses for components such as parking lots and infrastructure. These agreements can be enforced through the CC&Rs.

In some cases, the use and maintenance of green infrastructure can be negotiated with a municipality through a development agreement, which provides the developer with certain vested rights and outlines agreed-upon approaches to utilities over all or a portion of a development's buildout. Similarly, the documents created in the course of securing some publicly assisted financing and identifying community development areas can address both the nature of the infrastructure systems and their ongoing maintenance.

Green Building Compliance

Ensuring that individual buildings comply with the developer's green standards is another area of concern. While initial compliance is often addressed through a development's design guidelines, many changes to a building's green features may occur over time that do not trigger design review. For example, energy-efficient windows might be replaced with cheaper alternatives, permeable pavement may be resurfaced with an impermeable surface, and dozens of other key green components might be compromised over time. A building permit might be necessary for some changes, but such permits are often ignored by do-it-yourselfers and building officials can only enforce requirements already in the local codes or imposed through zoning. If a building was green as a result of a voluntary program, officials cannot require it to remain green. Although organizations like the U.S. Green Building Council plan to implement recommissioning and recertification programs in the future, their current focus is on initial certification. Moreover, it seems unlikely that developers would be willing to require compliance with recertification through their CC&Rs and other documents before such programs can be assessed. In the end, even sustainably designed civic buildings may be compromised once they are turned over to the homeowner association

RBF CONSULTING

Using native landscaping is ideal, as is keeping out invasive plant species.

(e.g., recreation or meeting halls) or local government (e.g., libraries or schools).

For a community-scale development project that is constructed over a number of years, erosion of building sustainability compliance can have significant consequences. For instance, if low-flow water usage devices are replaced with standard toilets, available water and wastewater capacities will be reduced and the long-term development consequences, such as use of infrastructure capacity, increased. If energy efficiency is not maintained, expensive power lines and generation facilities will likely be required for later phases of the buildout, increasing development costs.

Developers can take a number of steps to prevent the erosion of sustainability. Continuous education on environmental and economic benefits is a good strategy. Deed restrictions can require owners to maintain resource-efficient technologies through buildout or beyond. A committee of green experts can be established to approve changes that might reduce building sustainability if done inappropriately. Enforcement might require a seller to obtain a certificate of building compliance from the property owners association before a sale is transacted, thus, putting pressure on owners to comply with green standards. This sort of approach would be implemented through the CC&Rs.

A developer may use similar mechanisms to protect a project's "upgradeability." For example, a development team may want to install photovoltaic panels on a building in a later phase of its green program, so the developer will need to ensure that surrounding uses do not inappropriately shade the building. Protection of solar access can also be provided through easements.

Operational Sustainability

Operational sustainability is critical to the long-term health of a community. Indoor air quality and energy efficiency can be compromised if residents and cleaning crews use hazardous chemicals or replace energy-efficient light bulbs with conventional sources. If permeable parking lot surfaces are not swept, the voids fill and lose their effectiveness. If indigenous plants are replaced with high-maintenance exotic shrubs, landscaping will be substantially less sustainable. When treated lumber, VOC paints, herbicides, pesticides, and hazardous cleaning materials creep into the daily operations of a sustainable community a condition of entropy is set in motion.

Operational sustainability is shaped by the choices made when a building or community is being planned and constructed. For example, in order to ensure that HVAC equipment can be replaced in the most sustainable manner, the equipment must be installed in such a way that it can be removed without knocking out walls or having to cut the equipment into pieces. Similarly, the ability to avoid annual repainting or to respond to graffiti in an inexpensive, rapid fashion is dictated by the choice of materials and finishes on exterior walls. These missteps can be minimized by

TOM FOX/SWA GROUP

Coffee Creek: Nurturing Nature

FROM SITE PREPARATION and building materials to wetlands restoration and energy-efficient systems, the 675-acre (272-hectare) Coffee Creek Center seeks to integrate the natural and the built into a seamless whole. The planned community is located 50 miles (80 kilometers) southeast of Chicago in Chesterton, Indiana.

To restore and preserve approximately 180 acres of sensitive watershed surrounding the creek flowing through the center of the property, Coffee Creek Center's developer, Lake Erie Land Company, donated the land as a park, along with an amphitheater, walking trails, and water amenities, to a nonprofit organization established by Northwest Indiana's leading environmental groups. The goal of the Coffee Creek Watershed Conservancy is to identify, maintain, and enhance the biodiversity that resides within the watershed corridor.

Coffee Creek Center in Chesterton, Indiana, has a 167-acre (68-hectare) conservation easement that includes a native prairie, a restored stream, and extensive walking trails.

KEVIN WARREN

Lake Erie Land Company also restored the creek and substantial areas of prairie vegetation within the park. While the nonprofit makes ongoing management decisions on the watershed conservation property, the developer retained several rights for itself and community members: Residents are guaranteed access to the trails and amphitheater; and the developer is free to construct a wetlands mitigation bank on the property and to construct and maintain a stormwater system that infiltrates the water collected in the surrounding community's curb-and-gutter system.

The homeowner and commercial owner associations contribute to the maintenance of the park and have enforcement rights, if appropriate standards are not met. The developer's rights were addressed in the restricted deed of conveyance. A set of restrictive CC&Rs covers the watershed park to ensure that the property remains undeveloped. An agreement between the property owner associations and the park owner provides details of ongoing maintenance procedures for the park.

producing a life-cycle analysis during a development's initial design process, which will identify the sustainable performance of materials and methods that can be used to provide maintenance and operational guidelines to residents, cleaning crews, and maintenance staff. However, very few projects complete this sort of analysis on a development-wide basis, though an increasing number of owners do it for specific projects like a pool or a community building.

Sustainable operations are not as simple as choosing between timber and a plasticized wood product for decks or fences. In setting the standards for operations, numerous program agendas must be balanced against one another. The sustainable landscape program may call for seasonal grasses, but the project's marketing and sales staff wants something brighter and more flowery for big open-house events. Some residents may love the feel of the timber playground

equipment, but the steel-and-plastic equipment may be safer, have fewer toxicity issues, and provide better accessibility. Avoiding pesticides may result in increased plant replacement costs. Providing bags and receptacles for dog waste may improve runoff quality, but at significant cost to the homeowners association.

Similarly, maintenance of infrastructure must factor in the performance targets of the infrastructure itself as well as any new opportunities for sustainable practices. Stormwater facilities can be designed with sediment forebays, for example, to allow removal of sediments without destruction of the wetlands vegetation. The program analysis should identify a beneficial use for the silt harvested from the basins. Similarly, the sludge generated from a green wastewater treatment facility could be transferred to a landfill or it could be used to generate methane gas for power or methanol for use in ethanol production.

CHRISTAIN SCHULZ/AFUSIO

112

Sustainable operations are vital to continuing green building programs. They require the institutionalization of sustainability goals and ethics in the operations staff. The programs are often more obvious to the public than the sustainable materials or designs themselves, and, therefore, have high value for branding the developer's approach to sustainability and educating the public on important sustainability programs.

Sustainable Economics

Maintenance costs in any development project, sustainable or not, are always a concern. Any neighborhood or community-scale development must take them into account. Communities that include significant park area or open space and other environmentally sensitive features incorporated into the parks have even more reason to be concerned about maintenance costs. High maintenance costs related to sustainable practices and features can lead to higher homeowner association fees and thereby erode affordability. Some sustainability experts present the triple bottom line of sustainability (i.e., environmental sustainability, social sustainability, and economic sustainability) as a three-legged stool. In this instance, one leg (environmental) of the stool undermines another leg (social).

Executed correctly, many programs for sustainable operations can cost less than their conventional counterparts. Less electricity is purchased, less potable water is utilized, fewer chemicals are purchased, and less waste generates reduced disposal costs. Sometimes these reduced costs come at the price of some increased capital outlay, so financial structuring is required to make sure that the entity enjoying the reduced costs either pays the capital costs or is providing some pass-through for repayment before or as it harvests the operational cost benefits.

Similarly, some sustainable maintenance programs can turn what would normally be a cost into a source of revenue to be applied against other maintenance costs. For example, common areas can be farmed or held as forests for sustainable lumber production. Not only does this avoid maintenance costs for the common areas, it may generate revenue. Received directly, however, such revenues may have tax consequences for a homeowners association, so developers need to be sure to understand the most appropriate structure, particularly in projects where nonprofit entities may be brought in to operate such programs. In order for these types of opportunities to be fully realized, working common areas or easement areas over private properties must be contiguous and of adequate size for utilization.

Another potential source of revenue for maintaining sustainability is the capture of certain credits available for environmental characteristics associated with the preserved portions of the project or even the operation of green infrastructure. A development project may generate credits that can be sold when it sets aside wetlands, streams, or endangered-species habitat. Additional credits may be generated through the construction of new wetlands or the restoration

Swales in the mixed-income neighborhood of Salishan in Tacoma, Washington, filter storm-water runoff and protect the water quality in the T Street Gulch that passes through the center of the site.

TORTI GALLAS AND PARTNERS

Funding for the maintenance of open-space amenities, especially those that are overseen by a third party, may come from homeowners association dues.

of environmentally compromised waterways. Setting aside areas as carbon sinks or inserting best management practices for nonpoint-source water quality credits may create new sources of revenue for operations. Use of wastewater as reuse water may produce funds from the sale of the water as well as revenues from credits created through the reduction of nitrogen and phosphorous in the receiving waters. Developers must consider not just the availability of the programs, but also both the source of capital to take advantage of the programs and who will receive the benefit of the revenues.

No developer plans to continue paying a development's operating costs after buildout. Exit strategies typically depend on when one or more commercial or residential property owner associations can take on operational costs. While the creation documents for these associations can assign them the burden of continuing and funding sustainability programs, at some point the association takes over control of its documents and can eliminate such requirements. The CC&Rs can also require continuation of the sustainable operations, but they may still rely on the association for funding and may require repeated trips to

court for enforcement. A better strategy, if available, is to link a desirable benefit such as continued use of an open space, riverfront, or other amenity area with the property owner association's continuation of funding for the sustainable operations. Homeowners will lose access to the amenity if the association stops paying operation costs. This strategy works best when the amenity area has been conveyed to a third party.

Some developers reduce or avoid maintenance costs by transferring ownership of project areas—such as roads, parks, water, sewer, and stormwater facilities—to local or state agencies or to quasi-governmental entities such as community development districts. These entities may or may not be willing to maintain operations in a sustainable manner. Sometimes the obligation to continue programs can be imposed in the transfer. Typically, the public entities will make any obligations subject to available funding. Developers can retain for themselves and successor associations the right to enforce certain standards or to maintain certain features themselves. Some tax increment financing and community development districts allow the creation of new public entities that have the ability

SWA GROUP/TOM FOX

not only to cover the capital costs of infrastructure but also to pay for ongoing maintenance costs. Some states limit these entities to raising money for capital costs.

One mechanism for bridging some of the gaps in financing is the creation of third-party, non-profit stewardship organizations. Just as in connection with the conveyance of environmentally sensitive lands to these types of entities, third parties can be established to provide certain sustainable maintenance functions directly, implement green educational programs, and suggest changes as new sustainable technologies become available. These entities can be funded by charges imposed in the founding documents on resale of property within the community, donations, and developer contributions.

Operational sustainability is a key aspect of a project's green profile. Ensuring long-term funding for sustainability programs is often challenging. This difficulty highlights the importance of establishing and adhering to the holistic vision that drives all aspects of a design.

Disaster and Replacement Strategies

Another important maintenance issue is how well a sustainable community and its individual parts weather catastrophic events. Landscaping may be lost to wildfire or locusts. A flash flood may take out the constructed wetlands used to polish stormwater and fill swales with sediments. Windmills, photovoltaics, and green buildings may be located in regions susceptible to lightening, hail, snow, hurricanes, tornadoes, or earthquakes. Of course, up-to-date insurance policies are important to maintain, and reserves should be set aside in case coverage proves inadequate. But the best way to prepare for nature's wrath is by designing a resilient development that can not only protect occupants but survive a weather event in reasonably good condition, with repairs that are fairly easy and economical to make.

Sustainable design, however, should include assessment for how best to prepare the constructed environment for catastrophic events. Any time a structure must be replaced, there is sure to be waste from an environmental perspective as well as an economic one. Consequently, anticipating the most likely events and designing accordingly

can be an important sustainable undertaking. Locating buildings outside of floodplains, designing constructed wetlands with space for overflow relief, and providing protective covers for sensitive equipment are all a part of ensuring sustainability.

If components cannot be protected adequately, then designing for their ready replacement is important. For example, maintaining a protected nursery of relatively mature trees and plants allows quick, inexpensive replacement. Perhaps most important, however, is planning to make the best of a bad situation. Guidelines should be in place that outline how construction debris resulting from a storm event will be recycled, trees downed in a windstorm will be utilized and replaced, disrupted wildlife habitat will be provided with food and shelter, and reconstruction plans will embrace advances in green technologies. In addition, plans should be in place to provide for the safety and recovery of people and

Above: This regional flood control channel in Irvine, California, comprises soil cement, cellular concrete mats, and pinned prefabricated concrete blocks and meets local jurisdictional agency requirements. Left: In 1998, Caltrans, California's Department of Transportation, began a court-mandated program to test various best-management practices by retrofitting existing drainage systems. The program uses extended detention basins, infiltration devices, wet basins, biofilters, and media filters.

RBF CONSULTING

Portland's South Waterfront District: Green from the Ground Up

THE SOUTH WATERFRONT DISTRICT in Portland, Oregon, is a 130-acre (53-hectare) redevelopment project on a former industrial site along the Willamette River. The new district was initiated by the Portland Development Commission (PDC) and is being developed through public/private partnerships.

The South Waterfront District is planned to maximize urban density while creating a high quality of life for residents and regenerating the natural environment. By its scheduled completion in 2012, the South Waterfront will be home to over 10,000 new residents and extensive commercial, educational, retail, and recreational facilities. The master plan links the new district to Portland's downtown via an extension of the city's popular streetcar system and to uphill residential neighborhoods and a university campus by a new aerial tram. Two city parks and a riverfront greenway will bring important natural amenities to the formerly abandoned area. Through a series of master planning, green building, and restoration ecology techniques, PDC and its developers aim to make the South Waterfront a national model for sustainable development.

Portland developer Homer Williams, credited with transforming the city's Pearl District into the creative destination it is today, and Gerding Edlen, developer of the sustainably designed Brewery Blocks project in the Pearl, are lead developers for the South Waterfront. The developers are collaborating with the city of Portland, the PDC, and the Oregon Health and Science University (OHSU) on the first phase of the development, the 38-acre (15.4-hectare) River Blocks central district.

Now underway, the River Blocks central district is anchored by a new OHSU facility and five residential towers with condominium and apartment units for 3,000 residents. The OHSU Center for Health and Wellness brings state-of-the-art academic, clinical, and research facilities to the district, as well as daycare and fitness centers that will be open to the South Waterfront community. The plan calls for a 250-room hotel and conference facility and extensive retail.

The integrated environmental and planning techniques used at River Blocks will set the standards for future phases of development at South Waterfront. All of the buildings are being designed and built to meet at least LEED Silver certification for environmental performance. The development is planned and designed to meet broad sustainability goals informed by the Natural Step approach to development and by the lessons learned by Gerding Edlen at Brewery Blocks. The project goals are as follows.

LIVABILITY

The mix of uses and multiple transportation options—pedestrian-friendly streets, bike paths, buses, streetcars, Flexcars, and an aerial tram—improve livability while reducing car usage. Building site lines, river pathways, and green open space connect human inhabitants to their natural environment.

REDUCE USE OF NATURAL RESOURCES

Building materials are locally sourced, have recycled content, and are designed to be recyclable whenever possible to reduce impact on the environment. A high percentage of the wood specified for the project will come from Forest Stewardship Council–certified forests, and innovative eco-friendly materials will be used. Ninety-five percent of the construction waste generated on site is being recycled. Water conservation measures are expected to reduce use of potable water

---

If alternative energy sources, such as this photovoltaic farm, are located in areas susceptible to hurricanes or earthquakes, insurance to cover any losses is critical.

© 2007 EDAW/PHOTOGRAPHY BY DIXI CARILLO

pets. Attention should also be paid to maintaining and restoring the natural systems that may bear the brunt of storm events, to reduce structural damage. Barrier islands, coastal wetlands, sand dunes, and stands of trees can mitigate storm impacts. And their replacement may help avoid future damage.

Sustaining Species and Amenities

Human habitation inevitably changes the natural environment, including the very attributes that brought people to an area in the first place. Over time, these changes can be profound. Feral invasive species travel the ditches, roads, and clearings made for new communities. Planted flowers and vines move from yards to woods. Plants providing food and shelter for indigenous wildlife are often replaced with species having aesthetic traits only. Dogs roam the woods, killing small animals in their path. Cats prey on songbirds. Riparian zones along streams and lakes are cut down. Piers intrude into waterways. Preserved creeks are remade into culverts for mosquito control.

In order to protect desired community features, not only must strategies be developed from the beginning and education continued unabated, but steps must be taken to ensure continued imple-

minimize negative impact on indoor air quality. Natural ventilation systems and an innovative chilled-beam system at the OHSU facility augment conventional air conditioning. Building management will provide condominium residents and retail tenants convenient access to green cleaning products.

USE ONLY WHAT'S NEEDED

In all aspects of building and management, River Blocks will use natural resources only when and where needed. Low-flow plumbing, efficient lighting and appliances, and variable controls will respond precisely and efficiently to need. Individual metering in each residential unit will encourage conservation.

The first phase of Portland's new South Waterfront District will feature five new LEED Silver condominium towers.

A sophisticated marketing center on the South Waterfront site highlights the development's urban lifestyle qualities and its connection to nature. River Blocks is attracting homebuyers and renters from the education and research sectors, and many empty-nesters who are moving to the city for the first time. Twenty percent of the living units at River Blocks are reserved as affordable housing.

by 50 percent. Conservation will significantly reduce the demand for energy.

MAXIMIZE "FREE" RENEWABLE RESOURCES

Solar orientation and solar technology are integral to the design of South Waterfront buildings. The OHSU facility has an on-site microturbine plant that generates electricity. Rainwater is captured and restored to the site through green roofs and integrated landscaping. Wastewater is treated and reused for toilets and landscaping. Green roofs on the site will naturally cool the environment. Bioswales will provide aesthetic enhancements and mitigate stormwater runoff.

ENSURE A CLEAN AND COMFORTABLE INDOOR ENVIRONMENT

Materials and building components are selected for performance as well as occupant health. Choices such as high-performance windows and shading devices modulate solar heat. Low-VOC paints and materials

GERDING EDLEN

mentation. Existing or newly created nonprofits may provide oversight, but they must be active participants in the education of residents and other users. For large-scale community developments, an environmental manager should be hired by the developer—and later, the property owners association—to supervise educational programs and the implementation of the design, maintenance, and operations of a green program.

An environmental manager, whether a full-time employee or a consultant, should

- serve as a resource for residents and the development team on sustainability programs;
- monitor and respond to private "creep" of debris into common areas;
- implement controls of feral and domestic animals;

- oversee planting and shelter programs to mitigate impacts on indigenous wildlife;
- supervise restoration of desired habitats;
- design programs to reduce impacts from overuse of natural resources, trails, and other recreational activities;
- supervise forest-management programs;
- remove invasive species and enforce prohibitions on the introduction of invasives; and
- manage programs for beneficial use of common areas.

These operational programs should help preserve the amenities, setting, and wildlife that attract people to a development in the first place.

Code Flexibility

When developers "hardwire" their codes by incorporating them into the CC&Rs, there is a tendency to create absolutely rigidly unchangeable documents. CC&Rs can be more difficult to change than zoning or other statutes. While zoning changes require a majority of a political board or council to approve, every member of a community may need to approve CC&R changes. A restriction may call for nothing but "natural" materials to be used in a development's structures, accidentally precluding an excellent photovoltaic device designed to mimic a natural material. A restriction may require that all landscaping be indigenous, not only precluding a developed hybrid like the new American elm but also many nonindigenous plants that have been successfully utilized in a region for more than a century. Design, architectural, landscaping, and sustainability codes should be crafted to provide prescriptive information, like a list of acceptable plants; they should also provide the standards that led to each restriction, such as "is tolerant of the range of local climate conditions and normal plant diseases and bugs within the region." If a new approach, material, or process meets the standard, it should be reviewed further and approved, if appropriate.

Codes and programs should be flexible enough to accommodate both continuous learning and new strategies when old ones fail or conditions change. They should be able to adapt to philo-

Pringle Creek Community: Guided by Principles

PRINGLE CREEK COMMUNITY was conceived in the early 2000s as an exemplar of an affordable and ecologically sensitive master-planned community. When completed in 2009, the 275-acre (111-hectare) development in Salem, Oregon, will contain more than 150 dwelling units, as well as a mix of commercial uses, community amenities, and open spaces.

Pringle Creek Community will contain approximately 150 residential units of different types, sizes, and prices. Commercial uses and a farmers market will be located in the town center, while paths and bikeways will be found throughout the community.

In 2004, Sustainable Fairview Associates (SFA), a group of local investors, purchased the site from the state of Oregon. The parcel came with special challenges, as it contained the Fairview Training Center, a former institution for the developmentally disabled that was closed by the state in 2000. SFA, working in conjunction with local residents and Salem officials, determined that the site should be used to create an ecologically sound mixed-use community. In 2005, SFA sold 32 acres (13 hectares) to Salem-based developer Sustainable Development, Inc., to implement the first phase of the community. Sustainable Development, Inc., set to work dismantling some of the existing buildings and recycling the materials by donating or selling them to area builders. Other extant structures, such as a carpentry shop built in 1938, will be retained and renovated.

Pringle Creek's master plan, overseen by A.C. Nielsen Development Services, is guided by six principles that integrate environmental and societal concerns:

Build efficiencies by building green. New and existing community buildings will be constructed or redeveloped to the U.S. Green Building Council's LEED standards. Some single-family houses are planned for "net-zero" energy consumption—the homes will produce as much energy as they consume for heating, cooling, and electrical needs.

Celebrate the natural environment. Developers have preserved 80 percent of the trees on the site and adjoining wetlands are being protected and enhanced. In order to protect the community's namesake, runoff is being diverted away from nearby Pringle Creek. Narrow "green streets" allow most of the rainwater to infiltrate the soil and recharge the aquifer. Only 10 percent of the normal runoff from roofs, sidewalks, and patios will enter the creek. The porous asphalt of the green streets absorbs rain and drains it to the soil below. Bioswales alongside the roads will be planted with grasses, bushes, and moss that absorb water and filter pollutants.

Encourage social diversity. To ensure accessibility at a variety of income levels, developers

OPSIS ARCHITECTURE

sophical changes, such as a shift from preservation to restoration, and incorporate emerging technologies and applications.

As its greenness begins to fade and new technologies or approaches emerge, a project must be able to adapt to and adopt them. The developer's intent to create a sustainable community must become the occupants' intent. And residents must be educated by the developer to enable the project to become more sustainable over time, not less.

Adaptability

Sustainable development is as much about embracing a holistic approach as it is about incorporating a checklist of green features. An integrated whole-systems design process will result in sustainable systems that are less expensive to operate and maintain and a community that can evolve and adapt to change. To maintain a sustainable community, operations must be conducted so that they do not undermine green programs over time. Tools such as restricted conveyances, conveyances to nonprofit stewards, CC&Rs, and conservation easements should be employed to ensure that open spaces remain accessible and in good condition, green programs continue uninterrupted, and infrastructure is maintained. Adaptability should be built into the programs, codes, and structures of communities in such a way that sustainability becomes second nature.

are building housing of different types and sizes. The master plan provides for quality construction priced for those with moderate incomes, especially the elderly and disabled. The affordable housing component features smaller houses that will support a lower cost of living through energy efficient design.

Cottages will be clustered around a common green.

Activate the local economy. Local developers, architects, builders, tradesmen, and subcontractors will be used whenever possible. Commercial activity will be initiated and carried out without municipal government subsidies. The town center will feature retail shops and office buildings, with an emphasis on tenants from the region. A covered, open-air pavilion and farmers market are planned.

Conserve and reuse natural materials. Builders will conserve and recycle construction material whenever possible on site. As a result of this effort, several buildings have been relocated or recycled and over 200 tons of concrete and 100 tons of wood and steel have been recycled. Construction equipment will run on biodiesel fuel from the local cooperative station and new homes will be built using 100 percent Forest Stewardship Council–certified lumber. In addition to reusing site materials, the community will

make the most of natural energy sources. Geothermal energy will be used to heat and cool buildings in the village center. Rainwater will be captured and stored to irrigate community gardens and green space.

Smart transportation and movement. Pringle Creek residents will have access to an on-site car-sharing program and all housing will be within walking distance of a future transit center. Residents can also use the on-site biodiesel cooperative station that

is run on solar power. The community will include green corridors and path systems for walking, jogging, and biking. The trail system will provide convenient walking paths to a variety of destinations on the site. The street system will be fully interconnected with sidewalks on both sides.

Pringle Creek Community broke ground in May 2006.

RAMSAY WORDEN ARCHITECTS

119

122

132

152

7 | Case Studies

162

172

182

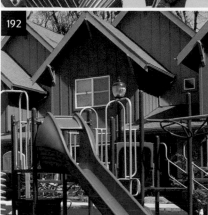

192

202

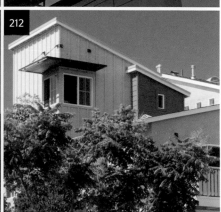

212

Brewery Blocks

PORTLAND, OREGON

BREWERY BLOCKS IS A PEDESTRIAN-FRIENDLY, mixed-use neighborhood on the site of a former brewery in Portland's Pearl District. The project brings together commercial, residential, and retail space in a live/work/play environment that draws visitors from throughout the region. New high-performance buildings designed in harmony with restored historic structures give the community its sense of place. The master plan is guided by principles of environmental sustainability and historic preservation and all of the buildings—new and old—have been designed to meet the U.S. Green Building Council's (USGBC) LEED standards.

Developed by Gerding Edlen Development, a Portland-based firm with experience in energy-efficient buildings and suburban commercial projects, the 4.6-acre (1.86-hectare) Brewery Blocks site includes a solar demonstration project, several green roofs, a chilled-water plant, a 94 percent construction-debris recycling rate, operable windows in both the residential and commercial properties,

SPECIAL FEATURES

- Transit-oriented urban infill neighborhood
- Redevelopment of former brewery
- LEED-certified buildings
- Central chiller plant
- Solar design
- Green roofs
- Recycling and salvage of existing buildings and materials
- Recycling of construction waste

The Louisa apartment tower has a landscaped roof. The former brewery's restored tower is visible in the background.

GREGG GALBRAITH/RED STUDIO, INC.

123

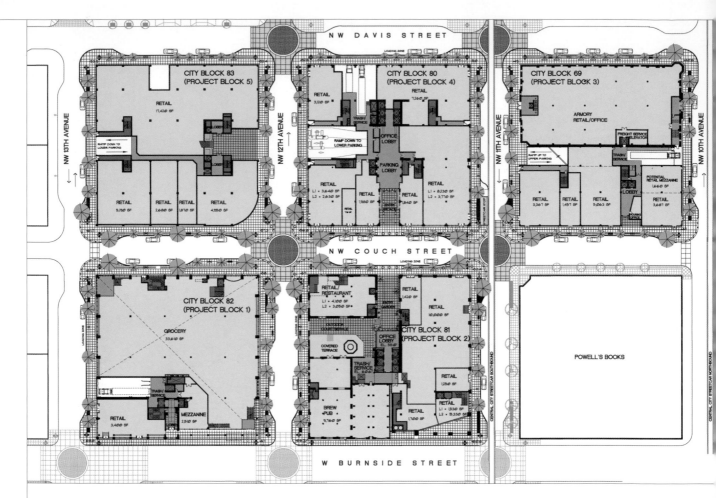

NW DAVIS STREET

CITY BLOCK 83
(PROJECT BLOCK 5)

CITY BLOCK 80
(PROJECT BLOCK 4)

CITY BLOCK 69
(PROJECT BLOCK 3)

NW COUCH STREET

CITY BLOCK 82
(PROJECT BLOCK 1)

CITY BLOCK 81
(PROJECT BLOCK 2)

POWELL'S BOOKS

W BURNSIDE STREET

Brewery Blocks site plan.

and many resource-efficient design and material choices.

Since its conception in the late 1990s, during an industry downturn, the project has become a symbol of successful redevelopment and place making in Portland. Commercial rents at Brewery Blocks are well above the city average and the project's environmentally friendly Henry condominiums sold out nine months before construction was completed. Thirty-five hundred people now live and work in an urban neighborhood that prior to 1999 had several hundred residents.

Site and Context

Brewery Blocks was initiated in 1999, when senior partner Bob Gerding was completing a speculative commercial building one block north of the Blitz-Weinhard Brewhouse. Then run by Stroh's, the 100-year-old facility was functioning, but was no longer in sync with the neighborhood. The Pearl District was evolving. Former warehouse and industrial buildings had attracted tech-

nology and design firms, artists, galleries, and loft dwellers. The railroad yards at the northern edge of the district were being transformed into high-rise residential towers. Just a few blocks to the south was one of the city's biggest tourist draws, Powell's World of Books. Gerding saw an opportunity to connect these destination points with a bustling, mixed-use neighborhood.

Two historic properties distinguished the Brewery Blocks site: an 1898 National Guard Armory-turned-warehouse; and the 1906 Blitz-Weinhard compound, a local icon with small-scale masonry buildings, red-brick smokestack, and malt vats. Little existed beyond these buildings to distinguish the five-block area, except for an old Chevrolet car dealership with remnants of an art deco past. It was, in Gerding's mind, an area waiting for its next use.

Gerding's initial call to Stroh's in 1998 did not receive a positive response, but a year later the beer maker was ready to sell. Gerding Edlen optioned the property and began a two-year-long planning process.

Development Process

The Brewery Blocks site was zoned EX, a City of Portland designation that allows for a broad range of uses consistent with Gerding Edlen's development strategy. City officials were eager to see the long-underutilized area redeveloped. They encouraged the team to move forward with its plans.

The partners began to build their team soon after optioning the site in 1999. They drew on local talent that shared the firm's values and a penchant for innovation. The original team included GBD Architects, two local contractors, engineers, an energy modeler, a sustainability/LEED expert, and a historic preservation specialist. Gerding Edlen enlisted the team early on to participate in an integrated visioning and development process. As Edlen puts it, "We wanted to create an atmosphere where people could explore, and where we could be open to the big dumb idea." The principles of the master plan emerged from these early creative discussions, as did the project's strong retail component. "We knew that the project's success rested on our ability to create a walkable retail environment," says Edlen.

Gerding Edlen and their team immersed themselves in an intense visioning, learning, and planning process. "For all practical purposes we took ourselves out of the market," says Edlen. Key members of the team traveled to San Francisco, Vancouver, and Seattle to study successful retail models and streetscape designs. They embarked on an intensive course of environmental self-education, studying sustainable principles, researching innovative technologies, digging for public incentives, and attending LEED training sessions.

In 2000, Gerding Edlen hosted its first "eco-charrette," focusing the team on the environmental goals of the project. "It was a good start," recalls Wilde. "But we were still learning." The team made some early decisions that would became essential to the project—for example, taking a rigorous approach to energy efficiency and demolition waste recycling. The group also decided to incorporate measures like operable windows and light shelves in commercial buildings. Other ideas went by the wayside, including an ambitious plan for photovoltaics and the use of an old malt vat for stormwater storage. "At first, I think we wore somewhat rose-colored glasses," observes Wilde. "We thought that just by deciding to do great things, we would get them done. Our competency was an evolutionary process." To better watch over their goals and take advantage of grant opportunities for sustainability,

Brewery Blocks buildings were designed and built to be deconstructed for easy recycling and reuse at the end of their useful lives. A Whole Foods Market occupies part of block one.

Wilde asked a staff member to step into the role of sustainability coordinator. She tracked the firm's environmental progress, managed communications with environmental and LEED consultants, and tracked grant opportunities.

While Wilde and his project team steered the planning and public permitting processes, Edlen and Gerding were pounding the pavement to secure financing. This was, despite strong public-sector enthusiasm, no easy feat. Portland was in a real estate downcycle. As one member of the team put it, "People in the development community thought we would have our heads handed to us." Notes Edlen, "This kind of

Brewery Blocks, located at the former site of the Blitz-Weinhard Brewery, is a five-block mixed-use project in Portland's Pearl District.

BRUCE FORSTER/VIEWFINDERSNW

the general mix of retail, residential, and commercial stayed fairly constant, plans for specific uses on each block had to remain flexible. The final Brewery Blocks master plan is the result of ongoing adaptation and response to market conditions.

Master Plan

Five blocks make up the Brewery Blocks neighborhood, which runs along the east-west axis of Couch Street. The Gerding Edlen master plan takes advantage of the site's location and its proximity to public transportation—Portland's free downtown trolley rolls through the Blocks—to make this a connected, transit-friendly development. Brewery Blocks sidewalks flow easily into surrounding blocks, connecting the project seamlessly to surrounding Pearl District streets.

Brewery Blocks' operable windows bring in fresh air, save electricity, and connect occupants to life on the street.

The project team developed seven guiding principles to inform the Brewery Blocks' master plan and design:

- create a live/work/play environment, with a balanced mix of uses;
- activate the street with retail;
- design in sympathy with the Pearl District's eclectic, industrial architecture and make each block unique;
- develop a pedestrian-friendly environment with a strong transit orientation;
- preserve and celebrate historic buildings;
- locate parking underground; and
- pursue sustainable practices.

mixed use was still very new and the economy was bad. Investors thought the numbers just wouldn't work."

The tide turned in early 2000, when local investor Peter Scott agreed to invest 50 percent in equity toward the $19.5 million site cost. This soon attracted an additional $50 million in private local equity and loan financing. The City of Portland provided a $6 million low-interest loan to support construction of the underground garage and $2 million in grant money for streetscape improvements. City funds were contingent on LEED certification.

Brewery Blocks is located near five transit stops.

Gerding Edlen developed Brewery Blocks in two phases between 2000 and 2006. Securing Whole Foods as a retail anchor was the team's first major success. While

BRUCE FORSTER/VIEWFINDERSNW

The master plan was guided in part by the unique characteristic of the "Portland block." The city's 40,000-square-foot (3,716-square-meter blocks) lend themselves to compact, human-scale development, but make aboveground parking solutions difficult. Therefore, the team's master plan mantra: parking underground.

The Brewery Blocks community is anchored by its two historic properties, the Blitz-Weinhard Brewhouse and the Armory. New buildings and infrastructure are located around these buildings in a compatible but assertive manner. The Armory shares its block with the 15-story Henry condominiums and the Brewery connects to a ten-story commercial building. Gerding Edlen located a 1,300-car garage under the more expendable blocks 4 and 1, and half of block 2. Block 1 also hosts the 25,000 gallon (94,635 liter) central chiller plant. The 1929 façade of the Chevrolet dealership has been partially restored.

"We were really lucky to have such a big area to work on. It enabled us to maximize uses and take advantage of scale opportunities," says senior partner Mark Edlen. A total of 1.7 million square feet (157,935 square meters) were developed at the Brewery Blocks: 600,000 square feet (55,742 square meters) of leasable commercial space, 200,000 square feet (18,581 square meters) of retail, and 500,000 square feet (46,452 square meters) of rental and for-sale housing. Every block is supported by ground-level retail. In addition to Whole Foods, the project's other retail anchor is the landmark Powell's Books. The soon-to-be completed Portland Center Stage at the Armory will be its cultural heart.

From the sleek Louisa tower to the carefully restored Armory, each block reflects and responds to the unique character of the Pearl District. As requested by the developer, GBD Architects took an eclectic approach to design, assigning lead architects with distinct sensibilities to each block. Buildings are bold and "big-boned" in keeping with the industrial origins of the neighborhood.

The physical and iconic heart of the Brewery Blocks is the former brewery. Gerding Edlen and its architects restored the compound and incorporated its masonry forms, chimney, and giant vats as place-makers. The brewery is joined to a ten-story office building via a central seismic core and mechanical system and a steel grid structure that joins the buildings above ground. The brewmaster's tasting room has been reinterpreted as a restaurant and bar that opens to a shared courtyard.

Four new buildings compose the contemporary architecture at the Brewery Blocks: the 15-story Henry condominium tower that shares a block with the Armory; the

Louisa apartment tower, the M Financial building, and the office tower that adjoins the brewery. An assemblage of large windows, balconies, and moss-green concrete cladding distinguishes the Henry. M Financial is distinguished by its golden brick and integrated solar panels. A setback above the building's third floor makes room for several green roofs and natural light. The 16-story Louisa is the project's most polished building, with its sleek gray exterior.

A central chiller, located near the Whole Foods Market, serves the entire five-block project.

Gerding Edlen preserved the 1929 façade of the Chevrolet dealership and made use of the building's concrete base to build up a new four-story structure within the existing walls. Steel "exoskeleton" braces the delicate art deco walls and stabilizes the new floors within. Whole Foods and telecommunications facilities occupy the space. The 25,000-square-foot (2,323-square-meter) district chilled-water plant on the rooftop suggests industrial and warehouse buildings common to the district.

The new buildings and their historic neighbors are tied together with vibrant retail and street-level architecture. Gerding Edlen took advantage of the "Portland blocks" to provide large, open retail spaces with generous windows and high street visibility. Wide sidewalks, street furniture, plantings, and outdoor dining support the pedestrian-friendly outdoor environment.

BRUCE FORSTER/VIEWFINDERSNW

Green Design and Construction

Gerding Edlen's environmental sustainability is connected to the firm's long-term view of development and a commitment to local community. "You can't think about sustainability without thinking about how people live and work, and about place making," says the firm's green champion and senior project manager Dennis Wilde.

Their charge to the Brewery Blocks team was simple: "Let's do as much green as we can and still survive financially." The Brewery Blocks presented opportunities well beyond previous projects. Because Gerding Edlen had control over the Brewery Blocks, notes Wilde, "We decided to pursue a more comprehensive and fully integrated environmental agenda."

The original brewhouse now contains office and retail space.

That approach incorporated the Natural Step, a framework grounded in natural science that encourages systems thinking and helps corporations to profitably integrate environmental considerations into strategic decisions and daily operations.

The firm's environmental goals and strategies evolved during the course of the project. In 2000, Gerding Edlen committed to using LEED as its green-building performance tool. "We needed a yardstick. LEED had just been released

and it seemed to be a good way to keep ourselves honest, to make sure we weren't greenwashing ourselves," says Wilde. In committing to LEED, Gerding Edlen committed to taking a proactive approach to green site development, water conservation, energy efficiency, indoor air quality, and materials, and to certification of every building.

Architects worked closely with sustainable design specialists to incorporate solar design features into the project and to take advantage of natural light. Energy modeling was incorporated into every building's design process. Design elements often have multiple functions; for example, balconies on the Henry and Louisa provide solar shading, architectural distinction, and connection to the outdoors. Operable windows in commercial buildings bring in fresh air, save energy, and connect occupants to life on the street. Every building is designed to meet LEED certification standards. The Henry has already achieved LEED Gold.

Construction of the environmentally innovative buildings was an ongoing learning experience for Gerding. Hoffman and RH coordinated with the design team to meet LEED guidelines and with green technical specialists to install green roofs, solar arrays, and innovative heating

GREGG GALBRAITH/RED STUDIO, INC.

128

and cooling systems, and they oversaw the installation of hundreds of new green finish products at the Henry and Louisa. Intricate seismic support systems for the historic buildings required a nimble technical response. The buildings also required sensitive disassembly, cleaning, and reinforcement under the watchful eye of Gerding Edlen's historic preservation consultant. Further, the buildings were designed for easy dismantling and recycling at the end of their useful lives.

Gerding Edlen provided green guidelines to all commercial and retail tenants, and made features such as light monitors and HVAC shut-off valves available at no cost. The developer's management company provides free refills on green cleaning products. Fifty percent of the energy that Gerding Edlen purchases for its tenants comes from green, renewable sources.

Marketing

Gerding Edlen envisioned Brewery Blocks as a development that would attract the wave of architects, filmmakers, ad agencies, software companies, and telecommunications companies who were defining the new Pearl District. The Brewery Blocks would be a place where these creative people could live, work, and play. Gerding Edlen knew early on that retail would be the cornerstone of the project's success, so the firm targeted high-end national retailers and local entrepreneurs with appeal to cultural creative urban dwellers. Five full blocks of ground-level retail offered new opportunities to companies that had shied away from crowded downtown storefronts. Companies such as Diesel, Anthropologie, Adidas, and Sur La Table that had previously not entered the Portland market were drawn to the 10,000-square-foot-plus (929-square-meter-plus) spaces and street visibility. Local entrepreneurs like the Henry Tavern and Finn Clothing, and regional favorite Peet's Coffee were among the first to set up shop.

The project drew early attention from ad agencies, architecture firms, and IT companies, but as the project progressed, more established downtown firms also showed interest. "The Blocks got a reputation as being an up-and-coming project and the younger partners in downtown firms lobbied to have their firms move here," observes internal commercial broker Scott Eaton.

Gerding Edlen relied on existing relationships and word-of-mouth to build its market, and the tenacity and imagination of its broker team. "To tell you the truth," says Edlen, "we were not very sophisticated with our materials and we learned along the way. We analyzed the market. We anticipated needs and responded quickly. We built relationships." This low-flash, nimble-footed approach worked well for the company. Tenants and buyers alike were drawn to the project's innovative concept, the firm's reputation, and the quality of the proposed designs.

The Henry stands as the project's most dramatic success. The condominium building sold out nine months before construction was completed, at a square-foot price of $348—the highest in Portland. Similarly, the Louisa apartment building—built to condominium standards and considered the project's most tricky component—rented out within a few months of opening.

The project's unique historic buildings posed the biggest marketing challenge. Who would rent a three-story brewery with a brewmaster's room and big vat? Ultimately, GBD Architects adopted the space for its expanding staff. The Armory proved an even greater challenge. Gerding Edlen's search for compatible tenants for the five-story vaulted space included several sports clubs and REI. Ultimately, the Portland Development Commission approached the firm to make the Armory a cultural center. It soon will be home to Portland Center Stage and community cultural facilities.

Experience Gained

Gerding Edlen's venture into mixed-use development was exceptionally successful. Astute market assessment, a deep connection to the community and its values, and a nimble response to shifts in the market were key factors. The developer rounded out expertise in retail and commercial development by bringing experienced brokers onto the team.

The developer went far beyond its previous experience in energy efficiency to embrace sustainable planning, design, and construction. The project's environmental achievements can be attributed to an integrated team approach coupled with a process of continuous learning. Senior partners set the tone and encouraged innovation. A supportive public atmosphere at the state and city levels and targeted sustainability grants, tax credits, and incentive programs enabled the team to undertake significant green innovation that would otherwise not have been possible.

Ongoing exploration of best practices, including visits to similar projects in the United States and Europe, expanded team expertise into uncharted terrain. In general, LEED certification proved to be a useful tool for tracking green progress, while the Natural Step provided broader philosophical guidance. However, the evolving nature of

USGBC standards at the time of the project made application in a mixed-use context challenging. The LEED New Construction and Core and Shell standards worked well for office and multifamily properties, but were problematic for retail space.

The developer estimates that high-performance green features account for 1 percent of total project cost. Much of the investment, however, is being recovered through operation savings, tax incentives, and grants. Soft costs associated with LEED certification, including team education, eco-charrettes, energy modeling consulting services, and extra design services, ranged from $200,000 to $350,000 per building. Dedicating a full-time sustainability coordinator to the project enabled Gerding Edlen to track LEED progress, effectively coordinate with sustainability consultants, and secure public incentives and grants.

The Louisa tower's green roof serves as a deck for residents and helps keep surrounding air temperatures cooler than a traditional roof.

As expertise and confidence in the team's capacity to carry out green innovation grew, team members moved away from LEED "point chasing" to green choices that brought the most environmental value—and, in most cases, lead to LEED points. Green roofs, however, were not well integrated with other water conservation strategies on the site, resulting in limited success.

Because most national retailers make build-out and purchasing decisions at the corporate level, the team found it difficult to apply green tenant guidelines. Nevertheless, local managers showed interest in the guidelines and in eco-friendly purchasing. Homebuyer and home renter response to environmental quality and amenities proved to be enthusiastic, while commercial tenant response was green-neutral.

As a result of the positive experience with Brewery Blocks, Gerding Edlen has committed to meeting LEED standards for all of its projects and to go beyond standard green building practice. The firm is now exploring how its work can contribute to a restorative ecology and economy and give energy back to the grid. Environmental quality worked hand in hand with place making, convenience, and design quality to distinguish Brewery Blocks from competitors in the Portland market. Rents and sales prices in the community are among the highest in the city.

GREGG GALBRAITH/RED STUDIO, INC.

Brewery Blocks

LAND USE INFORMATION

Site area (acres/hectares)	4.6/1.86
Office net rentable area (sq f/sq m)	538,425/50,021
Retail gross leasable area (sq f/sq m)	160,000/14,864
Residential units	365
Structured parking spaces	1,300

RESIDENTIAL INFORMATION

Unit Type	Unit Size (sq f/sq m)	Number Units	Range of Initial Sales Prices/Rents
Condominiums	755–2675/70–249	123	$269,000–$1,080,000
Apartments	641–1506/60–140	242	$1,200–$4,000/month

OFFICE INFORMATION

	Block 1	Block 2	Block 4
Net rentable area (sq f/sq m)	97,197/9,030	188,530/17,515	252,698/23,476
Number of Tenants	4	16	10
Average Tenant Size (sq f/sq m)	36,758/3,415	13,747/1,277	27,185/2,526

RETAIL INFORMATION

Tenant Classification	Number of Stores	Total Gross Leaseable Area (sq f/sq m)
Grocery Store	1	46,921/4,359
Food service	6	29,686/2,758
Clothing and accessories	7	30,615/2,844
Shoes	1	1,589/148
Home furnishings	1	13,576/1,261
Hobby, specialty, gifts	4	33,804/3,140
Banks	2	3,809/354

DEVELOPMENT COST INFORMATION

Site Acquisition Cost	**$19,750,000**
Site Improvements (all blocks)	
Excavating/grading	—
Sewer/water/drainage	$324,194
Paving/curbs/sidewalks	$591,077
Landscape irrigation	$380,243
Fees/general conditions	$868,358
Other	
Demolition	$38,535
Street Signals/Lights	$1,335,122
	$3,537,529
Garage Work—All Blocks	
Shoring/Excavation	$5,965,770
Concrete	$11,252,034
Masonry	$163,929

Steel	$384,943
Weatherproofing	$413,633
Doors/Windows	$97,481
Finishes	$495,516
Specialties	$81,178
Mechanical	$1,477,816
Electrical	$1,666,898
Fees/general conditions	$2,699,115
	$24,698,313
Construction Costs	
Block 1	$29,313,074
Block 2	$56,850,589
Block 3	$49,896,872
Block 4	$52,309,412
Block 5	$51,030,353
Total Development Costs	**$287,386,140**

DEVELOPMENT SCHEDULE

Site acquired	1999
Planning started	1999
Construction started	2000
Residential sales started	2004
Commercial leasing started	2001
Project completion	
Blocks 1, 2 and 4	2003
Blocks 3 and 5	2006

DEVELOPMENT TEAM

Developer
Gerding Edlen Development
Portland, Oregon
www.gerdingedlen.com

Architect
GBD Architects, Inc.
Portland, Oregon
www.gbd-architects.com

General Contractors
R&H Construction Company (Block 1)
Portland, Oregon
www.rhconst.com

Hoffman Construction (Blocks 2, 3, and 4)
Portland, Oregon
www.hoffmancorp.com

Mechanical/Electrical/ Plumbing Engineers
Glumac International (Blocks 1, 2, and 4, full design)
Portland, Oregon
www.glumac.com

Mechanical and Plumbing Design/Build Contractors
Kinetics (The Henry)
Portland, Oregon

Total Mechanical (The Louisa)
Portland, Oregon
www.totalmechanical.com

Electrical Design/Build Contractors
Cherry City Electric (The Henry)
Salem, Oregon
www.cherrycityelectric.com

Dynaletric (The Louisa)
Portland, Oregon
www.dyna-portland.com

Sustainability Consultant
Brightworks
Portland, Oregon
www.brightworks.net

Daybreak

SOUTH JORDAN, UTAH

DAYBREAK, AT 4,126 ACRES (1,670 hectares), is the largest master planned community in Utah history and the first large-scale project guided by new urbanism principles. Developed by London-based mining company Rio Tinto, through its subsidiary Kennecott Land, the project is located 20 miles (32 kilometers) south of Salt Lake City. Groundbreaking for an information center and model home complex took place in early 2004. When finished in 2017, Daybreak will have at least 13,500 residential units, a lively mix of uses, and a commercial core (9.1 million square feet/845,418 square meters of retail/commercial) oriented toward transit systems.

The development incorporates about 1,250 acres (506 hectares) of open space, which in turn facilitates 100 percent stormwater retention. All homes are Energy Star® certified. Phase one of the development includes an elementary school and community center that are LEED Silver certified, deriving their heating and cooling needs from ground-source heat pumps.

SPECIAL FEATURES

- Reuse of former mining land
- Significant portion of land area preserved as open space and parks
- 100 percent retention of stormwater on site
- Low-water landscaping and use of recycled water for open space irrigation
- LEED-certified school and community center
- On-site construction waste recycling program

Daybreak contains a variety
of housing types at various
levels of affordability. Houses
are typically sited close to
the street and have porches
and parking in the rear.

ED ROSENBERGER

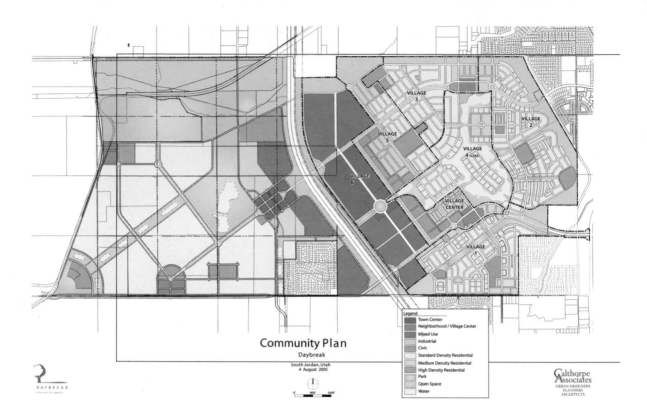

Community Plan
Daybreak

South Jordan, Utah
4 August 2005

Legend
- Town Center
- Neighborhood / Village Center
- Mixed Use
- Industrial
- Civic
- Standard Density Residential
- Medium Density Residential
- High Density Residential
- Park
- Open Space
- Water

Calthorpe Associates
URBAN DESIGNERS
PLANNERS
ARCHITECTS

Kennecott Land is the first land developer in the United States to obtain International Organization for Standardization (ISO) 14001 certification, which puts into play a system for incrementally ratcheting up performance vis-à-vis the environment. For example, the company's goal for construction waste recycling was 77 percent in 2005 and will increase 2 percent annually with an ultimate aim of 100 percent construction recycling. If rigorously pursued, this system, combined with an unusually strong corporate commitment to sustainability, could shift a sprawl-happy regional paradigm and produce results that are radical even in an international context.

Daybreak site plan.

The Site

The Salt Lake Valley is sits between the Oquirrh Mountains to the west and Wasatch Mountains to the east. The Great Salt Lake spreads to the northwest. Eastern portions of the valley are largely built out. Copper mining operations pivot around Bingham Canyon, one of the world's largest open pits.

In 1989, Rio Tinto, one of the world's largest mining companies, bought Kennecott Utah Copper and took ownership of 93,000 acres (37,636 hectares) on the west-

ern side of the Oquirrh Mountains. More than half of the land is in the mountains and is still actively mined for copper. Another 40,000 acres (16,187 hectares) lies in the western foothills in an undeveloped area that for over a hundred years has served as a buffer between development and mining operations. In 2001, Kennecott Land was created to manage and develop the non-mining land owned by Rio Tinto.

The 4,126-acre (1,670-hectare) Daybreak site is located on the eastern edge of the buffer area at the foot of the mountains and within the city limits of South Jordan (population 41,000). Historically, much of the site has been used for farming. However, a small portion of the tract (13 percent) sits on the former site of evaporation ponds used in conjunction with mining operations in Bingham Canyon. The ponds were used for evaporation until 1965 and for periodic storage of runoff water until 1987. Studies in the early 1990s concluded that there were elevated levels of heavy metals in the soil where the holding ponds had been located. Kennecott Copper entered a voluntary cleanup agreement with the Environmental Protection Agency to remediate the evaporation ponds. Ten years later, Kennecott Land decided to go beyond standard industry practice and spent tens of millions of dollars to remove the remaining pond sediment from the site in order to develop an 85-acre (34-hectare) lake and housing on the east side of Daybreak.

The Daybreak site has one serious handicap from a sustainability perspective: Its location 20 miles (32 kilometers) south of downtown Salt Lake City, the regional employment center, would generate more car trips and exacerbate regional air quality problems. These environmental ramifications will be partially mitigated in the longer term as Daybreak attracts local employment generators and by a light rail extension planned for the area in 2010.

The rail system will abut a north-south highway scheduled to bisect Daybreak after 2010. Several parallel arteries, providing access to Salt Lake City, are already in place: Utah 111 along the development's western border, the Bangerter Highway immediately east, and Interstate 15 about 2.5 miles (4 kilometers) east.

Development Process

In the early 1990s, Kennecott Utah Copper (KUC), a subsidiary of Rio Tinto, hired the Florida planning firm of Glatting Jackson to select a parcel from its holdings for possible development. Two factors drove the selection of Daybreak. First, roads, water, and sewer system were nearby. Second, Glatting Jackson thought the relatively youthful market in South Jordan might accept a master-planned community based on the principles of traditional neighborhood design.

Meanwhile, Rio Tinto was going through a sea change. After decades of conflict with communities close to its mining units, the corporation had joined the Global Mining Initiative, which subsequently launched the Mining, Minerals, and Sustainable Development project to shift the industry onto a sustainable trajectory. Rio Tinto also realized another historical practice—"disposing" of excess lands—was antiquated and misguided. In April of 2001, the company split Kennecott Land from KUC and charged the former with transforming 40,000 acres (16,187 hectares) of developable land into a profitable business founded on sustainable principles.

Peter McMahon, previously a financial officer based in Brisbane, Australia, transferred to Utah as president of the new subsidiary. He put an organization together, wrote a business plan, and hired Calthorpe & Associates of Berkeley, California, to produce a master plan with design guidelines. By early 2003, the project was ready to proceed. Rio Tinto had agreed to fund Daybreak. Nearly one-third of the project (1,238 acres/501 hectares) would be set aside as open space.

The Daybreak elementary school is one of the project's several LEED-certified buildings.

ED ROSENBERGER

(The agreement also established a "Planned Community" zone for mixed-use development.)

Each Daybreak phase is organized around a village of 1,000 to 1,200 residential units. Development will progress village by village, moving westward across the Mountain View Corridor (the major north-south freeway that is proposed for 2015), which will bisect the property in approximately 2010. Construction of a major town center should commence between 2012 and 2014.

Sustainability as a Core Value

When Rio Tinto decided to reorient its global businesses around sustainable practices, it was a long-term

Daybreak's 85-acre (34-hectare) artificial Oquirrh Lake, which is open to non-motorized boats. Two vehicular bridges link the surrounding land to a residential island and two wood-and-steel pedestrian bridges connect to bike paths.

imperative. The company wanted to foster better relationships with neighboring communities, which meant focusing on the benefits of investing in sustainability to drive long-term shareholder value. McMahon explains: "We have 8 to 10 more Daybreaks to go. Our sustainable practices are an investment in the future. Given worldwide trends on sustainability and our desire to have other lands entitled, it's about long-term value creation—a different business model."

Rio Tinto sees that advantage in reduced expenses for litigation and environmental cleanup, greater operational efficiencies, and an optimized chance for future entitlements. The company began to institutionalize its green commitment by adopting the Brundtland Commission's definition of sustainability—a project is sustainable "if it meets the needs of the present without compromis-

ing the ability of future generations to meet their own needs"—and then customizing it: Sustainable development should balance a healthy environment, social well-being, and a healthy economy.

Next, Rio Tinto tied management bonuses to sustainability performance and issued mandates to business units to establish sustainable development focal areas along with annual metrics for evaluating progress. Kennecott Land selected air quality, economic development, environmental education, energy/greenhouse gases, open space, transportation, waste generation/recycling, and water. Business units were also required to obtain ISO-14001 certification by establishing systems that reduce environmental risk and lead to annual improvements in performance. Kennecott Land was the first business unit to complete the process.

Its drive toward incremental improvement is built top-down into Rio Tinto's operating structure. Kennecott Land pushes this ethic through builder and trade units

ED ROSENBERGER

The Daybreak entrance. Located 20 minutes south of Salt Lake City, Daybreak is the largest master-planned community in Utah.

by codifying its green requirements in design guidelines. The 180-page Daybreak manual delineates construction requirements ranging from streetscape features to indoor air and light quality, building materials, landscaping, and garage location. Before a builder can apply for a certificate of occupancy, a developer inspection is required.

Master Plan

After Kennecott Land took over Daybreak, McMahon faced a conundrum. On the one hand, he wanted to establish the company as the most sustainable developer in the United States and believed strong market conditions supported that ambition. On the other hand, he didn't want to compromise profits by introducing communities that were too compact for the market. Salt Lake City is founded on 10-acre (4-hectare) blocks and exceptionally wide streets. In outlying areas today, most lots run one-third to one acre.

McMahon selected Peter Calthorpe as master planner because of his emphasis on building strong neighborhoods and communities. All of the Calthorpe designs are guided by three goals: create an environment with as many transportation and social options as possible (pedestrian- and bicycle-friendly streets and schools, jobs, and religious institutions close to homes); provide housing options for diverse populations; and integrate existing natural features and topography, weaving open space throughout and providing recreational opportunities.

Calthorpe saw tight development as a key tool for achieving those goals at Daybreak, but the developer insisted on a compromise: Daybreak would fall between national averages for new urbanist communities and what was typical of an exurban development in Utah. If the market adjusted, the developer would ask the city of South

Jordan to increase entitlements from the present 3.3 units per gross acre (8.15 per gross hectare) to 5.0 units per gross acre (12.35 per gross hectare), which equates to 8.5 units per acre (21 units per hectare) net of open space and roads.

Daybreak's east side, which totals 2,231 acres (903 hectares), comprises seven villages and a town center that pinwheel around a lake. Gridded streets with sidewalks and greenbelts support internal pedestrian circulation. Subtle shifts in design differentiate one village from the next; each village is focused around a neighborhood center, which is within a one-quarter mile walking radius of the village. The neighborhood centers will feature civic uses such as a library, church or daycare center, along with small amounts of higher-density multifamily housing. Affordability and diversity are built into Daybreak by virtue of price, product type (traditional single-family detached, townhouses, green courts, mansions, carriage homes, and apartments), and amenities (senior center, library, gymnasium, and programmed and unprogrammed green spaces.) In 2002, Envision Utah, a public/private partnership that advocates for smart growth, gave Kennecott Land its top award for the planning and design of Daybreak.

As the development moves west, similar development patterns emerge that continue to respond to the market place. Kennecott Land believes that residential growth from Daybreak and surrounding areas will support a mixed-use, lifestyle-oriented town center akin to Santana Row in San Jose, California, and Birkdale Village outside Charlotte, North Carolina—two successful urban villages built in suburban settings.

In an attempt to speed extension of the Utah Transit Authority's Mid Jordan rail line, Kennecott organized area stakeholders into a lobby that successfully worked toward accelerating the environmental impact statement process. Funding for construction of the line was agreed to by the legislature through an increase in sales tax. To decrease commuter time, the developer is beginning to work on a Village Center that will promote local job creation. Another relatively short-term possibility is the location of a major university center or health care facility at Daybreak.

Landscape Design

Utah law mandates that all new developments detain stormwater from a ten-year, 24-hour storm event. But Kennecott made an early commitment to retain all of its runoff—up to a 100-year storm event. Infiltration basins are located in open space throughout Daybreak; in fact,

Nearly one-third of the site is reserved for parks and open space, such as this soccer field.

the need for basins drove the location and size of some parks. A sediment trap at the fore of each basin captures the first flush of water, heavy with sediment. Gravel galleries underneath promote percolation and prevent mosquito breeding. The developer assumed this would add to development costs. However, localizing infiltration paid for itself by reducing capital costs (fewer conveyance structures, reinforced concrete pipes) and impact fees (South Jordan charges developers for discharging into the municipal stormwater system). It also reduces maintenance costs (sedimentation removal) for South Jordan, which will eventually own the system.

In addition to the basins, the developer felt Daybreak needed a major amenity and opted for an 85-acre (34-hectare) lake with a surrounding trail system, because of its appeal to a broad demographic spectrum. Stormwater flows into adjacent wetlands. Both wetlands and lake (a

synthetic liner will reduce percolation losses) are designed to attract desirable migratory birds and other wildlife, such as deer and fox. Kennecott will fill and maintain lake levels with existing water rights that flow from Lake Utah.

More than 900 acres (364 hectares) of open space will be landscaped with native/low-water plants, a strategy that could cut irrigation in half compared to a typical Utah development.

Green Building Design and Construction

In phase one, builders purchased finished lots and constructed product subject to criteria set forth in the design manual. All phase-one houses were designed and built with four-sided architecture and constructed with a combination of fiber-cement board, brick, rock, or stucco. Houses are sited close to the street and typically have porches. Car access may be from an alley or the street.

Builders are currently required to recycle their construction waste. A private vendor operates the recycling program, collecting materials from large bins on site. Accepted materials include metal, concrete, dirt, wood, tin, carpet, wire, sheetrock, plastic, and vinyl. Between 2004 and 2006, the builders and contractors recycled more than half of all the construction waste they generated and, in 2006, achieved a recycling rate of 76.8 percent.

The average housing unit (home plus lot) uses 10 percent less water than the average unit in the Jordan Valley Water Conservancy District. This is due to smaller lot sizes with less grass, water-saving appliances, drip irrigation systems, and drought-tolerant plantings. Kennecott is investigating other options, such as diverting graywater from sinks into cisterns for lawn irrigation and stormwater retention on the lot level—an ambitious goal, which would offer another source for cistern filling.

All Daybreak homes must be Energy Star certified; Kennecott anticipates that Daybreak will be the largest Energy Star community in the country. The program permits builders to select from a menu of options such as passive solar design and orientation, materials with high insulating factors, energy-efficient appliances, and instantaneous hot water heaters, in order to achieve a target that is at least 15 percent more efficient than the state's energy code. In addition to a monetary benefit for the homeowner, the 500 homes that were already occupied in Daybreak at the end of 2005 generated approximately 3,000 tons fewer greenhouse gases than what non-Energy Star homes emit. At the completion of Daybreak, Kennecott expects the 14,000 housing units will generate approximately 55,000 tons per year less of greenhouse gases than an equivalent number of non-Energy Star homes. This savings is equivalent to removing 12,000 passenger cars from the road. Achieving this result costs an additional $2,000 to $3,000 per unit. The developer is also investigating alternative means of energy production, such as photovoltaic systems and wind turbines.

Kennecott has installed ground-source heat pumps in Daybreak's information pavilion, elementary school, and community center as another way of reducing carbon dioxide equivalents and energy consumption. The technology uses the earth's stable temperatures (55 degrees Fahrenheit at a depth of 300 feet/12.78 Celsius at a depth of 91.44 meters) much the same way an aboveground heat pump uses air temperature. Closed-loop pipes, containing an exchange fluid, such as water and/or antifreeze, are driven 250 to 300 feet (76 to 91 meters) into the earth. The circulating fluid stabilizes the differential between ambient air temperature and ground temperature. Costs for the ground-source systems were comparable to conventional systems largely because they require less space in the building envelope. The developer hopes to use ground-source heat pumps in other elements of the community.

The information pavilion uses passive solar design to moderate internal temperatures. Windows have low-emissivity glass. Eaves limit sun exposure in the summer but permit heat gain in the winter. Also, the framing system for the building was constructed from lumber reclaimed from dry docks in the Pacific Northwest. Gardens, demonstrating native and waterwise plants, surround the pavilion. Stormwater is captured and infiltrated on site for irrigation. On-street parking reduces the need for paved surfaces, stormwater runoff, and the heat island effect. The information pavilion is built to LEED standards.

To reduce energy consumption, the elementary school incorporates natural daylighting (windows and clerestories, both exterior and interior); high-performance glass and shading devices; energy efficient lighting; and motion-based switching. Low-VOC products were specified for all paints, sealants, and adhesives.

The average price for houses in year one was approximately 13 percent higher than homes of a similar size elsewhere in the area. Most of this is attributable to Energy Star certification, four-sided architecture, recessed garage designs, and community amenities. The

All Daybreak homes are Energy Star–certified and use less water than standard houses due to smaller lot sizes with less grass, drip irrigation systems, and drought-tolerant plantings.

ED ROSENBERGER

developer plans to reduce the four-sided requirement, except on corner lots and areas of high impact, and explore ways of moving the garage closer to the house without negatively impacting aesthetics.

Marketing

Market studies conducted through the 1990s established that 65 percent of Salt Lake Valley residents were Latter Day Saints, a market that, on the whole, places a high value on homeownership and education. The developer expected buyers to come from the greater South Jordan area. But many are relocating from the east side of the valley and from out of state. Empty nesters are a growing niche and the company plans to target more products to them.

Initially, the development team marketed Daybreak in a factual manner (i.e., large lake; homes spanning a wide range of prices), but shifted to a more emotional strategy aimed at selling a quality lifestyle and collective experience. Advertising and marketing pieces emphasize the South Jordan school district, which is rated number two in the nation, and the joint use nature of the first elementary school and community center. (This concept will be repeated adaptively as additional schools are built. Prospective future partners are a library, daycare center, and community swimming pools.)

Marketing materials, on the other hand, soft-pedal environmental features, because the developer fears that it would label Daybreak as an expensive community. When the topic does come up, the sales team focuses on Energy Star certification and the value created through utility savings.

In the first 18 months that Daybreak was open, the developer sold 785 lots and 825 homes, becoming the second largest seller in the valley. Higher lot prices, new building plans, more architectural control, and the Energy Star requirement are translating into a premium on Daybreak houses. However, buyers are apparently willing to pay more in order to live in a community with a sense of place, a large range of amenities, and new schools.

The developer installed ground-source heat pumps in the Daybreak information pavilion, as another way of reducing Carbon Dioxide Equivalents (CDEs) and energy consumption. The center also uses passive solar design and lumber reclaimed from the dry docks of the Pacific Northwest.

ED ROSENBERGER

Daybreak

LAND USE INFORMATION

Total site area:	4,126 acres/1,670 hectares
Residential units:	13,667
Total office space:	5,185,000 sq f/481,702 sq m
Total retail space:	2,390,000 sq f/222,038 sq m
Total industrial space:	1,500,000 sq f/139,355 sq m

LAND USE PLAN

	Acres/Hectares	Percentage of Site
Residential	1,380/558	33
Retail	159/64	4
Office/industrial	86/35	2
Roads/parking	746/302	18
Open space	1,250/506	30
Other (civic)	505/204	13
Total	**4,126/1,670**	**100**

RESIDENTIAL UNIT INFORMATION

Unit Type	Unit Size (sq f/sq m)	Number Units Planned	Range of Initial Sales Prices
Single-family detached	1,300–4,000/ 121–372	8,803	$160,000–$450,000
Single-family attached	900–3,000/ 84–279	2,883	$132,000–$167,000
Active adult	–	911	–
Mixed use	–	490	–
Apartments	–	580	–

DEVELOPMENT COSTS (AT BUILDOUT)

Site Acquisition Cost	Historical cost basis
Site Improvement Cost	$574,000,000
Soft Costs*	$49,000,000
Total Development Cost	**$623,000,000**

*Excludes allocated corporate overhead costs.

DEVELOPMENT SCHEDULE

Planning started		April 2001
Construction started		June 2003
Completion (projected)		
Village1	2006	1,061 lots
Village II	2007	1,481 lots
Village III–VIII	2008–2017	11,125 lots
Estimated project completion		2017

DEVELOPMENT TEAM

Developer
Kennecott Land Company
Murray, Utah
www.kennecottland.com

Land Planner
Calthorpe Associates
Berkeley, CA
www.calthorpe.com

Experience Gained

Kennecott has a unique business model of long-term value creation. Given environmental stresses in the United States and increasing regulation from local authorities, it represents an evolutionary step forward. The same could be said for the company's definition of sustainability as a balance of environmental stewardship, community, and financial viability.

Kennecott took the time, even in the midst of setting up an organization and launching its first land development project, to pursue ISO certification. This was an enormous challenge, consuming significant staff time, but it gives the company a unique profile in the development industry and sets the stage for slow, steady improvement in environmental performance.

Kennecott wants to be the nation's premier sustainable developer—in a market that, on the whole, places less value on compactness and environmental sensibility than many others in the country. This has led the developer to stress the aspects of its sustainable development efforts that have a broad market appeal. However, if prospective homebuyers and residents are not engaged as partners in the vision, they are less likely to help optimize sustainability indicators, especially those related to resource conservation. Also, a blurred vision can undermine sales and ambitions to be an industry leader.

In the first village, the developer established a fine grain builder lot mix on each block. The idea was to optimize architectural diversity. However, it led to a number of problems. For example, one builder excavated its site for a foundation and placed the dirt on a lot owned by someone else, slowing the latter's progress. In the future, the developer plans to sell entire blocks to each builder and use design guidelines to promote streetscape aesthetics.

Glenwood Park

ATLANTA, GEORGIA

WHEN COMPLETED, THE 28-ACRE (11-hectare) Glenwood Park will bring shops, restaurants, offices, and a wide variety of housing to an urban area with a history of industrial use. The environmentally responsible, new urbanist neighborhood, located two miles from downtown Atlanta, is the first venture for Green Street Properties LLC. Charles Brewer, founder and former CEO of MindSpring, teamed with former Post Properties executive Katherine Kelley and environmental pioneer Walter Brown to create the Green Street team. Driven by shared ethical values, the team has created a sustainable community committed to traditional neighborhood design, walkability, mixture of residential and commercial uses, and environmentally responsible practices.

Glenwood Park is certified by Atlanta's EarthCraft™ Communities, a regionally focused independent program run by the Greater Atlanta Home Builders Association, due to its infill site selection, natural water management, responsible planning and design, preservation landscaping, community involvement, and green building methods.

SPECIAL FEATURES

- Urban infill site
- Compact, mixed-use neighborhood
- EarthCraft™ community
- Construction materials and waste recycling
- Graywater irrigation system
- Rainwater harvesting and reclamation
- Pervious parking surfaces

Public green spaces, pedestrian-oriented areas, recreational facilities, and shops and restaurants all reinforce a sense of community.

LOREN HEYNS/DREAMST JDIO

143

Glenwood site plan.

SINGLE FAMILY HOMES

TOWNHOUSES

SHOPS/ OFFICES/ RESTAURANTS/
MULTI-FAMILY RESIDENCES

Development Philosophy

Brewer ran his Internet company on nine core values, including honesty, frugality, and having fun. After MindSpring Enterprises merged with EarthLink, he left the company and sold his stock. With the ability to fund any of his passions he turned to a new interest—neighborhood development. Brewer was hooked after reading *Suburban Nation*, an eye-opening critique of sprawl in the United States. He held onto his previous core values and launched Green Street Properties, a real estate development company dedicated to creating healthy, livable communities.

This rendering shows the prominence of the project's primary open space and namesake, Glenwood Park. Commercial uses are allocated to the site's perimeter and residential uses are near the park.

Green Street Properties' passion for cities, walkable neighborhoods, and environmental protection is rooted in all aspects of their business. Prior to embarking on Glenwood Park, the management team adopted a statement of Development Principles and Core Values and Beliefs. The principles include:

- recognize the influence of the built environment on our lives, behavior, society, and the natural environment;

- practice the principles of good urbanism, employing diversity, walkability, and a mix of uses to create community;

- learn how to live sustainably, rather than acting as consumers and destroyers of nature;

- apply design, building, and management practices that emphasize environmental sustainability;

- support the economic bottom line (the real estate development world will not follow or recreate an example that does not make good money); and

- create loveable and memorable places.

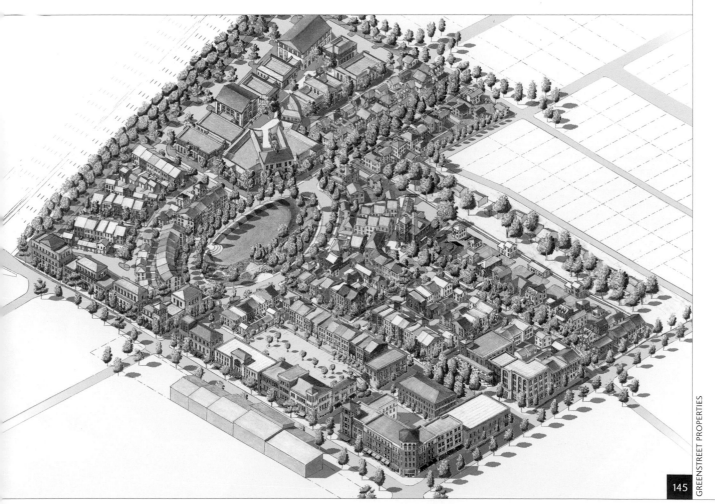

These principles grew out of the Core Values and Beliefs which describe how every employee of Green Street Properties aspires to treat each other, their customers, and their business associates. These include:

- respect the individual and believe that individuals who are treated with respect and given responsibility respond by giving their best;

- require complete honesty and integrity;

- make commitments with care, and then live up to them;

- work should be fun (being a good business person does not mean being stuffy and boring);

- be frugal (guard and conserve the company's resources with at least the same vigilance applied to personal resources);

- give your best effort;

- understand the mission, goals, and expectations;

- practice the Golden Rule; and

- own problems and be responsive.

Glenwood Park offers an alternative for those who are dissatisfied with the choices provided by conventional development. The development pragmatically accommodates cars, but is designed for people. Sidewalks emphasize pedestrian comfort and safety. And the walks are not long, since it is "a neighborhood of footsteps, not miles."

The new urbanist mix of retail stores, residential elements, office space, and civic buildings satisfies commercial needs not met in surrounding neighborhoods and creates diverse employment opportunities. Offices help to maintain a vibrant, active, daytime environment and the range of places to live—from small condominiums to detached single-family homes—enable many employees to live down the street from where they work. Public green spaces, pedestrian-oriented spaces, recreational facilities, shops and restaurants all reinforce a sense of neighborhood and bring the community together.

Glenwood Park's site plan and construction and management procedures emphasize resource efficiency and environmental protection and restoration. Elements of nature are incorporated throughout the project, making them a part of people's daily experience. The development was designed to allow a great deal of flexibility, enabling the community to gracefully change over many decades and allow the unplanned to blossom.

LOREN HEYNS/DREAMSTUDIO

Site and Context

The site has a long history of industrial use. Most recently, it hosted a concrete recycling facility. Small remnants of industrial land exist nearby, but Glenwood Park is predominantly surrounded by century-old, single-family neighborhoods such as Grant Park to the west and Ormewood Park and East Atlanta to the east. These communities suffered a sharp economic decline in the 1960s, but property values have been escalating in recent years. The northern edge of the property is lined by Interstate 20, which has a ramp onto Bill Kennedy Way that runs along the west edge of the site. Most of Glenwood Park is located to the east of this road, but it includes a 100-foot-wide (30-meter-long) strip of land to the west as well. Glenwood Park is directly on an active bus route that goes to downtown Atlanta and is less than a mile from two Metropolitan Atlanta Rapid Transit Authority rail stops. The development also sits on the proposed route of Atlanta's Beltway, a 22-mile (35-kilometer) transit loop mingled with green space and trails.

Master Plan

More than 30 people were invited to a design charrette for Glenwood Park in December 2001. Dover, Kohl & Partners of Miami and Tunnell-Spangler-Walsh & Partners of Atlanta led the participants, who included local neighborhood groups, design professionals, and key acquaintances of the design team. The charrette made substantial contributions toward the New Urbanist master plan.

Green Street Properties commitment to urbanism is seen in its investment in the public realm. Narrow, tree-lined streets, wide sidewalks, and rear garages keep pedestrians safe. Benches line storefront retail and a small public park, Brasfield Square. The entire community sits around an oval-shaped park featuring a playground, pond, and grassy field. The pond is encircled by trails and viewing decks and also filters stormwater. Native vegetation surrounding the water provides habitat for wildlife.

The variety of housing styles makes each home distinctive. Sizes range from 610-square-foot (57-square-meter) condominiums to 4,800-square-foot (446-square-meter) detached single-family homes.

Single-family homes, brownstone-style townhouses, and condominiums are artfully blended throughout the community. The variety of housing styles, designed by four architecture firms, makes each home distinctive. Sizes range from 610-square-foot (56-square-meter) condominiums to 4,800-square-foot (446-square-meter) detached single-family homes.

Fifty condominiums are located above street-facing retail in four buildings surrounding the town center. The one- and two-bedroom units feature bamboo floors, nine- and ten-foot ceilings, granite countertops, walls lined with expansive windows, and juliet balconies. These homes overlook Glenwood Park's main street retail shops and Brasfield Square. Other condominiums were built as stacked flats, providing the appearance of a four-level

townhome. Residents of upper-level units enter a door at street level and walk up a set of stairs to their unit. Brownstone townhomes surround the mixed-use town center and intermingle with streets of single-family homes. Most of the eastern edge of the property is bordered by single-family homes with wooded backyards. An additional condominium building is planned for the northwest corner of the property, located next to the pool and close to the central park.

Amenities such as the playground, pool, and dog park are technically for private use. The developers, however, chose to open all of the facilities to the public to avoid the perception of a "gated community."

LOREN HEYNS/DREAMSTUDIO

Green Building Design and Construction

Green Street Properties chose three builders—Capstone Partners, Hedgewood Properties, and Whitehall Homes—for their skill and prior green-building experience. Each builder fashioned its own home designs based on Glenwood Park's architectural guidelines. Every home in the community meets the EarthCraft guidelines, and the EarthCraft Communities program has certified the development. Environmental design elements include:

- construction and waste recycling;

- pervious pavement in parking areas;

- water-efficient landscaping;

- rainwater harvesting and reclamation;

- graywater irrigation system;

- recycled wood-fiber exterior trim;

- porch decking made from reclaimed waste wood and recycled plastic;

- prefinished and low-VOC flooring and low- or no-VOC and bio-resistant paints; energy-efficient insulation, including spray foam, sealed and conditioned crawlspace, air sealing, and high-performance windows;

- tankless water heaters;

- programmable thermostats and lighting control systems;

- Energy Star® lighting fixtures and appliances;

- high-performance HVAC systems; and

- energy recovery ventilators.

Glenwood Park's environmental practices are paying off in many ways, both for the development itself and the Atlanta area at large. The developer has recycled 60,000 cubic yards (45,873 cubic meters) of concrete, 800,000 pounds (362,873 kilograms) of granite rubble blocks, 250,000 pounds (113,398 kilograms) of metal, and 40,000 cubic yards (30,582 cubic meters) of wood chips; reduced the quantity of construction waste sent to landfill by 30 cubic yards (23 cubic meters) per home; saved approximately 100 acres (40 hectares) of land in an unbuilt part of the region by building at a density that is four times greater than normal subdivision development; and planted over 1,000 trees and thousands of other plants,

flowers, and shrubs. In ongoing efforts: approximately 35,000 gallons (132,489 liters) of water are harvested each week using a combination of stormwater and well water; the amount of stormwater runoff from the site is reduced by two-thirds; the amount of miles driven by Glenwood

Park residents when compared to normal driving patterns in other parts of the region totals 1,627,500 fewer miles (2,619,207 kilometers) per year; and 1.3 megawatts of energy are saved per year.

Permitting Process

Site engineering was completed and site development permits were acquired in 2002. Green Street Properties encountered three major challenges during the permitting process. The project's narrow streets and tight corners were the first test for the new urbanist plan. A series of lengthy discussions with city officials produced a new city ordinance allowing specific dimensions for qualifying "traditional neighborhood developments." The second obstacle involved stormwater retention and sewer treatment. All permitting authorities supported the developer's plan to fix existing sewers (including a broken sewer line) and create a stormwater retention park, however, jurisdictional confusion and uncertainty over water rights significantly delayed permission. Ultimately, all proposed changes to sewer lines, drainage ditches, and stormwater filtration were approved.

Glenwood Park partnered with Southern Living magazine to build The Idea House, which contains recycled and sustainably harvested materials, a tankless hot water heater, Energy Star® appliances and high-efficiency HVAC systems. The house is open to the public, with proceeds from tour entry fees to benefit EarthShare Georgia, an environmental fundraising organization.

LOREN HEYNS/DREAMSTUDIO

Finally, the developers encountered problems when they presented their main street design for Bill Kennedy Way to the Georgia Department of Transportation. Eventually, the developers convinced the department to transfer possession of Bill Kennedy Way to the City of Atlanta, which supported the addition of trees and on-street parking.

In January 2003, Glenwood Park held its groundbreaking ceremony and began construction. Nearly 40,000 cubic yards (30,582 cubic meters) of concrete required demolition and burial, several sewer lines needed to be rebuilt, and improperly placed fill needed to be relocated. During this process the construction team surprisingly discovered more than 40,000 cubic yards (30,582 cubic meters) of wood chips underground. The chips—enough to cover a football field 36 feet deep—were donated to an Alabama power plant, which used the material as fuel. The team also encountered 13 underground storage tanks. Fortunately, none of the tanks created major contamination problems.

Marketing

The mix of office, retail, and a wide range of residential options creates a diverse community at Glenwood Park. Buyers with various incomes, ethnic backgrounds, and ages are attracted to the project, including young profes-

sionals, singles, couples, families with young children, and baby boomers. The project was even popular within the development team; about a dozen members have purchased homes in the community.

Green Street Properties relied mostly on word of mouth and free press to market the neighborhood. At times, print ads were placed in an Atlanta monthly paper, and pieces were broadcasted on National Public Radio. The Glenwood Park website continues to receive a high volume of traffic. Floor plans, photographs, community maps, press releases, and resident resources entice prospective buyers to visit the project. The large central park was constructed early in the development process because it serves as both a stormwater retention facility and a recreational amenity. This park gave potential buyers a tangible sense of what the neighborhood would be like at buildout. It was completed just in time for an Earth Day celebration that drew several hundred people to the site.

Priced to be accessible to buyers across a range of income levels, condominium units are selling from $140,000 to $350,000, townhomes from $350,000 to $610,000, and single-family homes from $405,000 to $950,000. Most of the units that have been built are sold. While the majority of buyers at Glenwood

Glenwood Park was built to accommodate cars, but pedestrians are the priority. Sidewalks support pedestrian comfort and safety.

149

LOREN HEYNS/DREAMSTUDIO

LOREN HEYNS/DREAMSTUDIO

Park are aware and supportive of the environmentally responsible elements of the community, they are not willing to pay a "green premium" to live there. Initial sales prices are market rate, if not slightly lower due to the up-and-coming nature of the broader downtown area.

The community surrounds an oval-shaped park featuring a playground, pond, and grassy field. Amenities such as the playground, pool, and dog park are technically for private use, but the developers chose to open all of the facilities to the public to avoid the perception of a gated community.

Glenwood Park's retail tenants are selected for their neighborhood value—to serve the needs of the residents and the surrounding communities as well. To date, these include a coffeehouse, a wine bar and bookstore (focusing on cooking, art, and design), a Latin restaurant, and a salon.

The rich public realm created at Glenwood Park spurred residents to organize their own community events. While much of the neighborhood was still under construction, owners were organizing charity events, ball games, and barbecues. When the development is completed, the Glenwood Park Community Association will manage the community. Residents currently gather once a month on an informal basis in private homes or at local establishments. The association will formally govern Glenwood Park's shared community spaces, such as the main park and Brasfield Square.

Experience Gained

Glenwood Park is still under construction, however, it is far enough along to have established a sense of place. Sales are strong, leasing is drawing high-quality tenants, and the Atlanta building industry, community residents, tenants, and neighbors are praising the new neighborhood. Glenwood Park has received a number of awards and honors since groundbreaking.

Green Street Properties attributes its success to a handful of key factors. Glenwood Park was completely financed by a small group of insiders. Because no bank debt was used, the developer was able to quickly make decisions without financial pressure to pursue more conventional paths. The talented and diverse project team maintained a good working relationship with local government and neighbors supported the project from the earliest stages.

Glenwood Park

LAND USE INFORMATION

Site area: acres/hectares:	28/11
Percentage of office space completed:	100
Percentage of retail space completed (2006):	71
Average tenant size (square feet/square meters):	2,394/222

LAND USE PLAN

Office net rentable area (square feet/square meters):	21,000/1951
Retail gross leasable area (square feet/tk square meters):	50,850/4,724
Residential units:	328

RESIDENTIAL INFORMATION

Unit Type	Unit Size (sq f/sq m)	Number Units Planned (2006)	Range of Initial Sales Prices
Single Family	2,120–4,800/ 197–446	99	$405,800–950,000
Townhouse	2,070–3,285/ 192–305	91	$358,900–610,000
Condominium	610–2,197/ 57–204	138	$140,500–352,365

DEVELOPMENT COSTS

Site Acquisition Cost	**$5,608,000**
Site Improvement Cost	
Excavation/grading	$1,500,000
Sewer/water/drainage	$3,600,000
Paving/curbs/sidewalks	$2,600,000
Landscaping/irrigation	$1,141,000
Fees/general conditions	$132,000
Other	$980,000
	$9,953,000
Construction Cost	
Superstructure	$50,000
HVAC	$50,000
Electrical	$75,000
Plumbing/sprinklers	$200,000
Finishes	$115,000
Graphics/specialties	$115,000
Fees/general conditions	$650,000
Other	$535,000
	$1,790,000
Soft Costs	
Architecture/engineering	$1,250,000
Marketing	$939,000
Legal/accounting	$280,000
Taxes/insurance	$430,000
Title fees	$120,000
Construction interest and fees	$585,000
Other	$250,000
Total	$3,854,000
Total Development Cost	**$21,205,000**

DEVELOPMENT SCHEDULE

Site purchased	November 2001
Planning started	December 2001
Construction started	January 2003
Residential sales started	January 2004
Project completion	
Phase I	December 2006
Phase II	estimated December 2007

DEVELOPMENT TEAM

Developer
Green Street Properties
Atlanta, Georgia
www.greenstreetproperties.com

The Meddin Company
(retail development)
Atlanta, Georgia
www.meddin.com

Builders
Hedgewood Properties
Atlanta, Georgia
www.hedgewoodhomes.com

Whitehall Homes
Atlanta, Georgia
www.whitehallhomesatlanta.com

Capstone Partners, Inc.
Atlanta, Georgia
www.capstonepartnersinc.com

Architects
Stevens & Wilkinson
Stang & Newdow, Inc.
Atlanta, Georgia
www.sw-sn.com

Surber Barber Choate &
Hertlein Architects, Inc.
Atlanta, Georgia
www.sbcharch.com

Smith Dalia Architects
Atlanta, Georgia
www.smithdalia.com

Historical Concepts
Peachtree City, Georgia
www.historicalconcepts.com

Master Planning Assistance
Dover Kohl & Partners
Coral Gables, Florida
www.doverkohl.com

Landscape Architects
Hughes Good O'Leary and Ryan
Atlanta, Georgia
www.hgor.com

Tunnell Spangler
Walsh & Associates
Atlanta, Georgia
www.tunspan.com

Engineers
Long Engineering
Atlanta, Georgia
www.longeng.com

QORE Property Sciences
Duluth, Georgia
www.qore.net

Bennett & Pless, Inc.
Atlanta, Georgia
404.325.2000

Contractors
John W. Wilson Grading
Fayetteville, Georgia

Fortune Johnson
Atlanta, Georgia
www.fortune-johnson.com

Merit Construction
Knoxville, Tennessee
www.meritconstruction.com

Brunning & Stang
Atlanta, Georgia
www.brunningandstang.com

Greenwich Millennium Village

LONDON, UNITED KINGDOM

LOCATED ON THE THAMES RIVER in East London and launched in 1999, Greenwich Millennium Village (GMV) encompasses 63.8 acres (25.8 hectares) and represents a £689 million public/private investment. It is part of a larger 325-acre (131.5-hectare), multibillion-pound project, transforming Greenwich Peninsula from one of the most contaminated sites in Great Britain to a mixed-use community and leisure destination.

SPECIAL FEATURES

- Affordability
- Brownfield redevelopment
- On-site cogeneration plant
- Passive solar design
- Green building features
- Extensive use of recycled materials
- Water savings
- Recycling of construction waste

GMV's passive solar architecture in combination with state-of-the-art construction techniques, high-grade insulation, and efficient appliances are forecast to reduce energy consumption by 80 percent. An on-site cogeneration plant—one of the first in Britain for a multifamily housing project—supplies electrical and heating needs. Other sustainable features include clustered, high-density development that reduces automobile dependency;

Residences are a mix of one-
and two-story condominiums,
one- to four-bedroom townhouses, and live/work units.
Each cluster of buildings surrounds a landscaped courtyard.

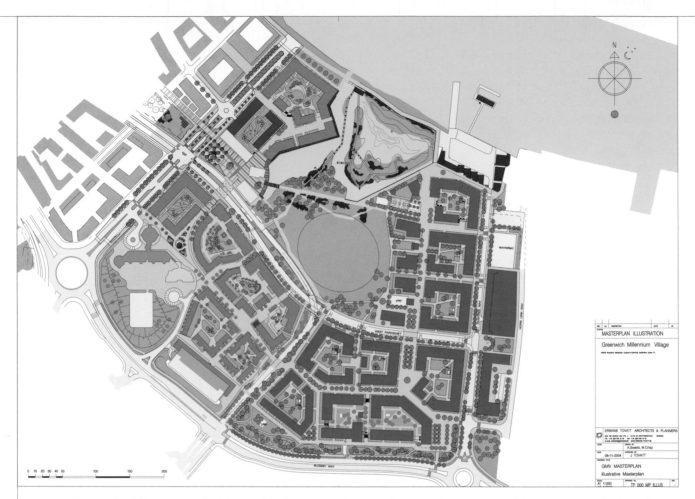

use of green building materials; 14 acres (5.7 hectares) of open space; and a program to reduce construction waste.

When finished in 2013, GMV will have 2,956 residential units (30 percent of them will be affordable), 70,396 square feet (6,540 square meters) of office space, and 25,000 square feet (2,323 square meters) of retail. Civic components include parks, a primary school, a health clinic, a member-operated yacht club, and a community center.

Greenwich Millennium Village site plan.

Site and Context

London grew from an outpost of the Roman Empire to a commercial hub during medieval times by virtue of its location on the Thames River. Peaking at 8.6 million in 1939, the population then declined due to the German blitz, a postwar reconstruction policy that favored construction of new utopian cities, and the advent of containerized shipping, which rendered obsolete a vast maritime infrastructure of docks and warehouses. This left East London in a state of physical and economic deterioration. Consequently, from 1981 to 1998, the British government invested billions of pounds

sterling in redevelopment of the area. Rail and subway lines were extended into the Docklands. A high-rise commercial hub arose on the north side of the Thames at Canary Wharf. And thousands of new housing units bolstered the residential base.

One area—a peninsula on the south side of the Thames within the borough of Greenwich—lagged behind this development curve. Originally a marsh, the peninsula had been used for agriculture and later as a landfill. Toward the end of the nineteenth century, British Gas purchased 300 acres (121.4 hectares) on which it constructed a shipyard, chemical plants, and gas refineries. Due to those operations, hydrocarbons and heavy metals accumulated over a period of one hundred years. After the decline of the Docklands, British Gas attempted to redevelop the property but failed. Finally, London's last large tract of undeveloped waterfront, which happens to be close to Canary Wharf, went on the market.

English Partnerships (EP), a government agency responsible for regeneration and brownfield development, studied the parcel. There were two major problems, both costly to overcome. The first was environmental remediation. The second was the parcel's insular nature: it was hemmed in by a highway on the southwest and by the Thames on the northwest, north, and northeast. Successful redevelopment would require a network of transportation linkages.

In the final analysis, one imperative may have superseded all others: Britain needed a place to stage its official celebration of the millennium. After purchasing the property in 1996, EP contracted with the architecture firm Richard Rogers Partnership to develop a conceptual plan. Designers sketched a mixed-use urban quarter with a business district at the head of the peninsula; a 1.24-mile-long (two-kilometer-long) parkland spine; and housing on either side. The focal point for millennium happenings would be a domed exhibition hall, the Millennium Dome, within the business district. The master plan also called for the construction of a 63.8-acre (25.8-hectare) model village at the base of the peninsula.

The site, now Greenwich Millennium Village, is a trapezoid bisected by West Parkside. It is bounded by the Thames to the northeast and by three perimeter roads: Pear Tree Way, Bugsbys Way, and John Harrison Way. Beyond Pear Tree Way, to the north, there is a member-operated yacht club and the Thames. To the south of Bugsbys Way is a commercial zone, featuring a 14-screen cinema and big-box retail. There, Sainsbury's has constructed a flagship grocery that uses 50 percent less energy than other stores. Across John Harrison Way to the northwest is the 198-acre (80-hectare) Meridian Delta Ltd. project, which will feature 10,000 high-rise residential units, 3,693,700 square feet (343,156 square meters) of office space, 362,812 square feet (33,706 square meters) of retail, and 48 acres (19.4 hectares) of open space. Another component is the O2 riverfront entertainment district, which will be operated by Anschutz Entertainment Group; it centers on the Millennium Dome, now being revamped as a 23,000-seat multipurpose arena.

The four-acre (1.6-hectare) Ecology Park consists of two lakes surrounded by marsh and woodlands. It provides habitat for many species, including warblers, swifts, and skylarks.

Greenwich Millennium Village rises above the shore of the Thames River in East London. The Millennium Dome exhibition hall is visible on the right.

Located at the base of the peninsula, GMV serves, in effect, as a gateway for what—in 15 to 20 years—will be an urban quarter of about 40,000 people. The village is connected to the rest of the peninsula, to the borough of Greenwich, and to London by highways, a new station on the Jubilee line of the London Underground system, and bus routes. One major pedestrian/bicycle route flanks the Thames River and another follows the open-space spine that traverses the length of the peninsula and terminates in the GMV, which has its own green core in the Village Square and in Southern and Ecology Parks. Buses run between the village and the North Greenwich subway station.

Development Process

Oil began flowing from the United Kingdom's North Sea fields in 1975, and by the mid-1990s, Britain was a net exporter of oil and gas. The trend quickly reversed, however, and toward the end of the decade, domestic oil and gas production was declining and prices were increasing. Moreover, the media was awash with reports detailing global warming and forecasting shortages of energy, potable water, and developable land.

Hence, when voters returned the Labor Party to power in 1997, after 18 years in opposition, the nation as a whole was ready to move in a sustainable direction. Sir John Egan of the Department of Trade and Industry launched an effort called "Rethinking Construction," and Lord Richard Rogers headed a task force charged with determining how to reuse brownfields while abetting regeneration. Deputy Prime Minister John Prescott decided that the 63.8-acre (25.8-hectare) site on Greenwich Peninsula was an ideal place to showcase his team's ideas.

EP announced an international competition to design and develop GMV as "a tangible living model" that would evince advanced theories of urban design and best construction practices. A preliminary master plan approved by the borough of Greenwich formed the basis of the competition brief. The word *sustainable* was prominent in all related documents, and it packed a uniquely European meaning. Europeans believe that for a project to be sustainable, not only must it be environmentally sensitive and financially viable, but it also must engender a sense of community—in part by including a diverse range of residents.

Before the first round of competition proposals arrived at EP headquarters, remediation efforts were well underway. Other components of the peninsula master plan were also taking shape. At the tip of the peninsula, the Millennium Dome, funded by National Lottery pro-

ceeds, was emerging on the London skyline, as was the North Greenwich underground station. EP had purchased an additional 24.7 acres (ten hectares) on the peninsula, raising its holdings to 325 acres (131.5 hectares). And the agency offered 99-year leases on the big-box lots adjacent to GMV.

Countryside Properties, a private developer based in Brentwood, England, had been a traditional United Kingdom homebuilder until the 1992 Earth Summit in Rio de Janeiro. Afterward, the company revised its production process, reducing waste and improving energy efficiency and water conservation. Chairman Alan Cherry formed a team to submit a proposal. Since the competition was attracting big players in the design and development world, he selected a partner with an international profile and strong financials (Taylor Woodrow, a public corporation operating in Europe and North America), a Swedish architecture firm with unique experience in sustainable housing projects (Erskine Tovatt), and a London nonprofit organization (Moat Housing Association) to manage the affordable housing component.

Upon winning the competition, Countryside and Taylor Woodrow formed a joint venture company, Global Millennium Village Limited (hereafter referred to as "the developer"), to proceed in partnership with EP, the land-owner. Erskine Tovatt Arkitekter (now Tovatt Architects

and Planners) continues as master planner, designer of Phase I, and supporting designer in Phase II. Moat still manages the affordable component.

Master Plan

Envisioned as a contemporary—and sustainable—version of a traditional English village, the primary design challenge was to transform a barren site, relate it to existing social structures and infrastructure, and endow it with the capacity to grow organically into a self-managing community that the designer hoped would embody "respect for human dignity, equality, and freedom."

These challenges suggested that, for starters, GMV should be dense and diverse. New housing developments in England average ten units per acre (24.7 units per hectare). In London, the figure can exceed 50 units per acre (123.5 units per hectare). Upon completion, GMV is expected to average 75 units per acre (185.25 units per hectare). This density will reduce sprawl and create a residential base to support later phases of retail and office space. The designer devised several ways of enhancing diversity. As is typical of traditional European towns, building depths and heights vary and uses are mixed. Equally, if not more, important is the affordable housing component, projected to constitute 30 percent of units.

The master plan features a landscaped village square in the first phase. Cafés, shops, and restaurants will surround the square, which will host outdoor markets and musical performances. The square is located at the terminus of the peninsula's green-space spine. Completed in September 2003, the rest of the initial phase comprised Ecology Park, Southern Park, and a cluster of 299 flats in three buildings designed by Erskine Tovatt.

GMV shares characteristics with other Erskine Tovatt–designed communities. High perimeter walls on the north, in combination with deep roof overhangs ("weeping roofs"), deflect winter winds and create warmer microclimates in sheltered courtyards. Interior walls open to the courtyard via balconies, terraces, large windows, and covered galleries. Artful use of color, materials, articulation, and variable building heights and depths are intended to endow the village with an ambience that is sophisticated, cozy, and whimsical.

Located in the northwest corner of the site, between Ecology Park and Village Square, phase one consists of seven buildings ranging in height from four to eight stories arranged around a courtyard. The units in this phase are a mix of one- to four-bedroom townhouses and one- and two-story condominiums.

Designed by Erskine Tovatt and United Kingdom–based Proctor and Matthews Architects, phase two consists of six clusters of low- and medium-rise structures. The clusters rise to eight stories. Each court has three or more buildings juxtaposed to form interior courtyards. The unit and bedroom mix is the same as that of the first phase, but also includes 14 live/work units. These units feature sliding partitions that allow residents to adapt their interior space. The live/work units form a mews adjacent to the parking garage so that, if businesses grow, they are able to expand into the garage.

Scheduled for construction between 2007 and 2013, the next three phases will comprise a series of buildings arranged around interior courtyards—much like the site design in phase two.

Green Design and Construction

The project's green components fall into four categories: parking and transport; landscape; building construction; and combined heat and power (CHP). While mixed-use developments have the potential to significantly reduce the need for automobile travel, some GMV residents do own cars. The developer plans to build an average of 0.7 parking space per residence, plus 275 spaces for nonresidential purposes, for a total of 2,345. Parking is located underground and at the periphery of the village to reduce emissions impact.

After removing contaminated soils and capping the ground, EP terraced the river and planted more than 12,000 trees, including a reintroduced Leisham black poplar. All in all, GMV has 14 acres (5.6 hectares) of dedicated open space. Ecology Park—two lakes surrounded by marsh and woodlands—is a major component of that network. Visitors traverse the park via boardwalks punctuated with observation huts. A gatehouse on the Thames serves as a visitor center. The four-acre (1.6-hectare) area provides habitat for many species, including warblers, swifts, and skylarks. Ecology Park fulfills two other functions: flood protection and environmental education.

The developer is concerned with both primary energy consumption and the energy embodied in manufacturing/transporting building materials. The former is reduced with passive solar design, high levels of thermal insulation, efficient appliances and windows, daylighting of interiors, and controlled lighting of common areas. The latter has been lessened by careful use of alternative and recycled materials, such as furnace slag to replace cement.

A CHP system deploys gas-fired turbines to generate electricity. Typically, 100 kilowatt-hours of electricity produce 145 kilowatt-hours of waste heat. At GMV, the developer uses that power to heat water. It is distributed to homes via super-insulated pipes for supplemental space heating and as potable hot water. Use of CHP in combination with passive design and high-grade insulation means that GMV is self-sufficient in terms of hot water and heating needs. The community is, however, connected to an electrical grid, buying and selling as needed.

The developer has minimized water use by careful specification of fixtures and fittings, such as low-flush toilets, low-flow taps, and highly efficient appliances. The amount of construction waste has been reduced via an on-site separation and recycling program.

As a public/private partnership and as a model development, GMV has been subjected to an unusual amount of probing. Stringent audits from a construction think tank, the Building Research Establishment (BRE), have led to "excellent" ratings for each subphase completed as of March 2006. Per contractual arrangements with EP, the developer must periodically report on a set of sustainability milestones.

Financial Viability

Just how profitable or unprofitable GMV will prove to be may take years to ascertain. EP's initial £47.8 million

investment in remediation, infrastructure, landscaping, and civic components has certainly defrayed some of the development costs. The British government also subsidizes the development of the affordable units through its Housing Corporation subsidiary. Nonetheless, in 2006 the developer's costs are running about £290.25 per square meter (£27 per square foot) higher than other projects in London. Typically, units in a low- to mid-rise building with minor site contamination and a minimal sustainability agenda cost of about £1,505 per square meter (£140 per square foot) to construct. At GMV, the figure is closer to £1,795.25 per square meter (£167 per square foot).

Jonathan Gimblett, one of the project development managers, says that most of the premium is due to higher design costs, more expensive materials, and the innovative nature of the project. He estimates the sustainable premium is 6 percent. Notably, it costs roughly £10,000 extra per home to earn BRE's Ecohomes Excellent rating.

Flats in the village typically sell for £3,762 to £4,730 per square meter (£350 to £440 per square foot). Market absorption has been strong (flats are selling faster than those of competitors in the area) because prospective buyers say they appreciate the project's design, sense of community, focus on sustainability, amenities, and lower projected utility bills. The developer regards GMV as research-and-development investment that will lead to innovation elsewhere. Still, with lower costs, profit margins would increase and, likewise, would motivate other developers to follow suit with greener projects—a national priority.

Hence, the developer is experimenting with three strategies for minimizing costs: build faster, more efficiently, and in a denser fashion. Sophisticated construction management techniques have reduced the duration of each

Designed in a contemporary style, residences are outfitted with the most advanced sustainable technologies available, reducing environmental impacts. The units make use of passive solar design and high levels of thermal insulation.

subphase by 10 percent, with additional gains anticipated through better sequencing, improved procurement practices, and greater use of modular and prefabricated construction (i.e., off-site construction of bathrooms and cladding sys-

tems). And the developer is working with suppliers and contractors to decrease product-associated waste. That, in turn, will lower landfill costs. Cutting in half the number of dumpsters, for example, has generated a direct savings of £150,000.

Phases three, four, and five will be denser than the first two phases, but not solely to bolster profits. The 2004 London Plan calls for higher density in order to efficiently accommodate population growth. And some residential towers at the adjacent Delta Meridian project will rise to 30 stories. Hence, the developer is seeking higher density for better integration with GMV's evolving urban context. Expenses will increase due to a higher percentage of affordable housing and the need for more community facilities.

The developer paid approximately £741,000 per hectare (£300,000 per acre) for the site. Due to the innovative nature of the project and associated risks, the developer and EP will share profits above and beyond a fixed threshold. "This is a high-level, government-driven project," says Gimblett. "For every £1 invested, EP recovers its original investment partly through the financial value created as a result of the success of the development, which is principally by way of a profit-sharing arrangement, and the remainder through the resulting improvements in local social and economic conditions, which benefit the wider community."

Experience Gained

Johannes Tovatt, business partner of master planner Ralph Erskine, who died in 2004, believes that developers who want to engage in a project of this nature need to set reasonable goals at the beginning of the process with regard to payback time and flexibility. He adds, "Whatever one talks about today won't mean a lot in a year's time because these projects are so vast. Sometimes, only a fraction of the original design is implemented. Begin with less defined outcomes so the project is more flexible. Build adaptability into the process."

The developer stressed the importance of getting everyone—the GMV team, local councils, bankers, contractors, tradespeople, and buyers—on the same page, so that they would share a common understanding of a sustainable community.

The first two phases of the village make use of about 250 distinct light fixtures, sockets, and bulbs. Architectural variation is important, but elements that fail to add tangible value should be standardized. A reduction to five light fixtures, for example, would be less expensive and easier to maintain in the long term.

As noted earlier, GMV has been subject to many audits, in part so that lessons learned could be disseminated to the construction industry and into a set of six additional "Millennium Communities" that EP is pursuing in various locations. One BRE report focused on the waste reduction program, which includes several principles: brief subcontractors on goals; establish benchmarks; allocate a clear and accessible space for waste bins; engage workers with briefings and poster campaigns; publish results; reuse as much of the waste as possible on site; and identify new outlets for—and ways to use—waste products.

Upon completion, Greenwich Millennium Village is expected to average 75 housing units per acre (185.25 units per hectare) and approximately 30 percent of the units will be affordable.

Greenwich Millennium Village

LAND USE INFORMATION

Total site area (acres/hectares)	63.8/25.8
Number of dwelling units (phases one and two)	701 built, 166 under construction; 228 planned
Number of dwelling units expected at buildout	2,956
Gross residential density (units per gross acre/hectare)	Phase one: 101/250 Phase two: 51/126 Expected at buildout: 75/186

RESIDENTIAL UNIT INFORMATION

Unit Type	Size (sq f/sq m) Typical Sale	Built Construction (2006)	Range of or Under Prices/Rents
Market-Rate Units			
One-bedroom	570/53	280	£112,000–£220,000
Two-bedroom	871/81	332	£210,000–£260,000
Three-bedroom	1,258/117	95	£230,000–£650,000
Four-bedroom	1,226/114	8	£300,000–£3,500,000
Two-bedroom live/work unit	1,279/119	12	£260,000–£300,000
Three-bedroom live/work unit	1,430133	2	£260,000–£300,000
Affordable Units			
One-bedroom	538/50	22	£94 per week
Two-bedroom	78573	65	£100 per week
Three-bedroom	1,000/93	48	£105 per week
Four-bedroom	1,516/141	3	£111 per week

DEVELOPMENT COST INFORMATION

Public Contribution
Estimated EP investment in GMV (remediation, landscape, and traffic improvements): £48.7 million

Private Contribution

Estimated Developer's Costs (all phases)

	Amount	Percentage
Land purchase and construction costs	£487,972,442	76
Soft costs and general development costs (i.e., architects and consultants)	£92,714,764	14
Marketing and selling	£35,264,126	5
Contributions to local improvements	£25,214,612	4
Total developer's costs	£641,165,944	N/A
Total Project Costs	**£689 million**	

DEVELOPMENT SCHEDULE

Site acquired	1998
Planning started	1998
Construction started	1999
Residential sales/leasing started	2000
Commercial leasing started	2006

Estimated Phase I completion	September 2008
Estimated Phase II completion	2006
Estimated project completion	2013

BUILDING RESEARCH ESTABLISHMENT

	GMV Achievements for First 286 Units (%)	Target Goals for First 286 Units (%)	Final Target Goals at Buildout (%)
Reduction of primary energy source consumption	65	none	80%
Amount of energy used to manufacture construction materials	25	15	50%
Reduction in water consumption	20	15	30%
Reduction in construction costs	12	5	30%
Reduction in construction duration	none	10	25%
Reduction in defects upon handover	70	50	zero defects
Reduction in construction waste	59	none	50
% of affordable units	16	none	30
Area devoted to mix of uses	4,300 sq f/ 400 sq m	none	43,000 sq f/ 4,000, sq m

DEVELOPMENT TEAM

Developer
Greenwich Millennium
Village Ltd.
Countryside Properties PLC
London, United Kingdom
www.countryside-properties.com

Taylor Woodrow PLC
Watford, Hertfordshire
United Kingdom
www.taylorwoodrow.com

English Partnerships
Thames Gateway Team
London, United Kingdom
www.englishpartnerships.co.uk

Moat Housing Group
Sevenoaks, Kent
United Kingdom
www.moat.co.uk

Architects
Tovatt Architects & Planners
Drottningholm, Sweden
www.tovatt.com

Proctor and Matthews Architects
London, United Kingdom
www.proctorandmatthews.com

John Robertson Associates
London, United Kingdom
www.jra.co.uk

EPR
London, United Kingdom
www.epr.co.uk

Planning
EDAW PLC
London, United Kingdom
www.edaw.co.uk

Landscaping
LDA Design
London, United Kingdom
www.lda-design.co.uk

Harvest Lakes

PERTH, AUSTRALIA

HARVEST LAKES IS ONE OF AUSTRALIA'S largest residential communities to be developed with a sustainable approach to urban design, construction, water conservation, and energy efficiency. The development is well underway and approximately 80 percent of the 1,000 lots planned have been sold. As of early 2007, individual homeowners have built 500 houses. On completion, the development is expected to house some 3,500 people.

Developed by LandCorp, the property development agency of the Western Australian government, the 284-acre (115-hectare) project is in the city of Cockburn, a rapidly growing municipality of 80,000 people located approximately 12 miles (20 kilometers) south of Perth, the capital of Western Australia. Situated just east of the Kwinana Freeway, it is within easy commuting distance of the city. It is also within a short drive of the Cockburn central station, a future stop on the Southern Suburbs Railway, a rapid transit system now under construction. There are regularly scheduled buses to Perth, and a major bus interchange located two miles (three

SPECIAL FEATURES

- Affordability
- Diversity
- Innovative stormwater management system
- Passive solar orientation of all houses
- Wetland restoration
- Green building features
- Community and environmental center

Detailed area plans mandate that 12 sustainable features, such as solar orientation and natural ventilation, must be included in the design of every home at Harvest Lakes. The plans are flexible enough to allow considerable diversity in the design of individual houses.

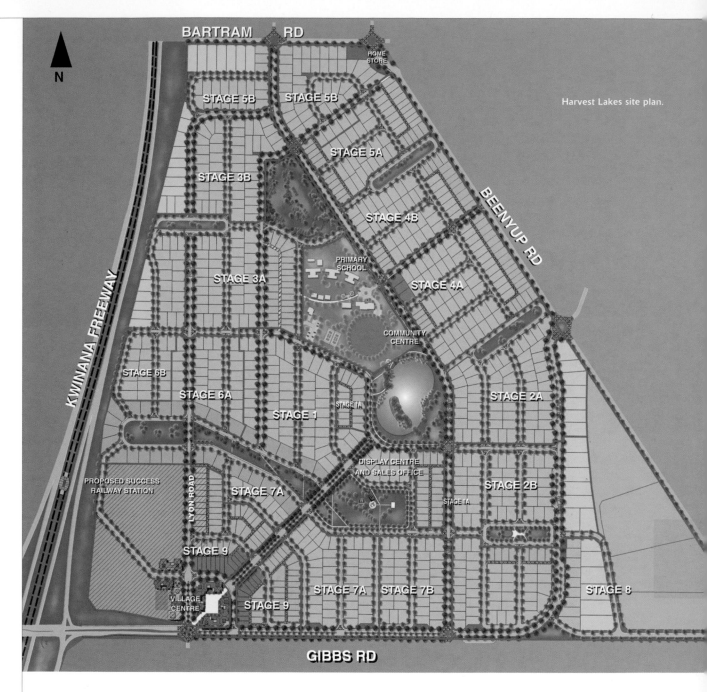

kilometers) from Harvest Lakes provides park-and-ride facilities. A trail connection between Harvest Lakes and the nearby Kwinana Freeway bicycle system also encourages the use of alternative transportation.

The development corporation, which reports to the Western Australian State Minister for Planning and Infrastructure, is tasked with providing a financial return to the government while focusing on a triple bottom line approach to broader social, environmental, and economic

goals. As the state's specialist property development agency, LandCorp strives to be a leader in trendsetting sustainable development practices. Through sensitive planning, building design, and management, it ensures that protection of the environment and energy conservation are central to all its projects, from industrial parks to marinas, schools, mixed-use centers, and residential developments.

At Harvest Lakes, LandCorp followed sustainability standards in the site planning and land development process. These include mandatory sustainable components for all homes, mandatory 5 Star Home Energy Rating (a government program for residential construction), on-site educational programs, an on-site community and environmental center, a model home showcasing sustainable design features, and incentives for compliance with energy efficiency measures. Although not involved in the construction of individual homes, the company utilizes a variety of innovative techniques to ensure that property buyers and their builders follow sustainability guidelines in the design, construction, and maintenance of homes.

Harvest Lake is one of the largest developments in Australia to be designated as "GreenSmart" by the Australia Housing Industry Association.

Development Process

Conceptual planning for the project began in 1996, detailed planning began four years later, and the Community Development Plan was completed in 2002. The first residential lots were sold the same year.

The developer has worked closely with the City of Cockburn and state agencies throughout the planning process and has encountered few issues. Regulations called for the project to be submitted to the local authority, the City of Cockburn Council, so that the site could be rezoned from agricultural to residential use. Next, a detailed subdivision plan was submitted to the Western Australia Planning Commission, which circulated it with various servicing authorities for sign-off and provided "conditions of development."

A step-by-step homebuyer approval process is used to ensure that all houses built at Harvest Lakes meet sustainability goals and conform to the Detailed Area Plan (DAP), which is a set of design guidelines adopted by the City of Cockburn specifically for the development. In this process, each lot owner must first obtain a minimum 5 Star Home Energy Rating from an accredited assessor and submit detailed plans for approval. A consultant engaged by LandCorp assists homeowners at this stage by reviewing plans prior to submission to the local government to ensure DAP compliance. After plans are approved, lot owners can apply for a building permit from the local government.

The objectives of the DAP guidelines are to achieve compliance with the Building Code of Australia Energy

This formerly degraded wetland on the Harvest Lakes site was rehabilitated and now serves as a visual centerpiece for the development as well as an important element of the project's stormwater management system. No stormwater runoff leaves the site.

Provisions, incorporate passive energy conservation, and promote attractive and consistent development. The mandatory features required by the DAP include:

- minimum 5 Star Home Energy Rating;
- house orientation that maximizes winter solar access;
- cross ventilation;
- minimization of east- and west-facing windows, adequate summer shading, or energy efficient glazing;
- a solar hot water system or integrated gas and solar hot water system;
- energy efficient fixtures;
- water-wise plumbing fixtures, irrigation systems, and landscaping;
- environmentally sustainable building materials; and
- minimization of construction waste.

Research conducted by LandCorp with prospective homeowners prior to the development of Harvest Lakes showed that, although environmental sensitivity was deemed important, community values rated even higher. Based on this finding, the development corporation determined that creating a "sense of place" would be key

to the success of the project and the most effective means through which to promote its sustainability objectives.

Early delivery of the community and environmental center, the first to be built to sustainable design guidelines in Western Australia, was pivotal to the development's image. Today, the purpose-built community hub, which includes the environmental center, a primary school, educational wetlands, and public open space, provides a popular focal point for a wide range of activities. LandCorp developed these facilities in association with local authorities.

Eight pieces of public art by Western Australian artists located throughout the development help to promote the developer's message of sustainability and environmental concern. This effort was conceived as part of the original community plan and was designed in conjunction with an education component.

Master Plan

The master plan for Harvest Lakes designates approximately 20 phases of residential lots arranged around a central area that includes a primary school, the community and environmental center, and open space. The main entrance into the development from the southwest is a landscaped boulevard that helps create a sense of arrival for the estate. Several finger parks and an undeveloped tree-lined ridge punctuate the site with green areas. The configuration of the roads, trails, open areas, and parks is intended to encourage community interaction.

Bird viewing stands in the community's Eco Park provide a chance for residents to enjoy nature.

Although the northern portion of the site, which is situated next to previously developed areas with existing

utilities and services, would have been the most logical place to initiate development, the first phases of Harvest Lakes took place in the center of the site because it was judged to be the most attractive portion. This plan required the installation of infrastructure throughout the entire area. In spite of creating a large initial expense, it was believed to be pivotal to the image and success of the development, especially in its early phases. The development of parks in the first phases also added to initial costs.

There are eight major lot types available at Harvest Lakes, ranging from medium-density parcels that average 24.29-units per acres (60 units per hectare) to smaller "cottage" lots with narrow street frontage and rear alleys for access to parking. Relatively large "special character lots" are generally located on desirable park-facing streets.

Climate-responsive design features—outdoor pergolas, louvered windows, and energy efficient window glazing—help minimize sun exposure and encourage passive energy conservation at "The Elements" model home built by LandCorp and National Homes, a Perth-based homebuilder.

In the future, plans call for more compact development at the western edge of the site, near a railway line and proposed transit station. Now in the planning stages, this area, known as Harvest Edge, will include a neighborhood shopping center, single-family homes on small lots sold as house/lot packages, and apartments. Under a different approach than that used in the rest of the estate, LandCorp has created designs for each of the houses to ensure that they make up a unified and attractive streetscape. With Harvest Edge, the developer aims to meet the needs of smaller households and combat urban sprawl and wasteful land utilization practices through denser development. But this initiative has met with some opposition. Residents of the area have objected to the proposed density levels and it has taken a careful public consultation process to educate the community on the benefits of compact development. In addition to sending information about the development to residents in the area, LandCorp conducted focus groups and sponsored workshops and a series of facilitated meetings between stakeholders.

The Harvest Lakes Village Center is planned for the southwest corner of the development, near the main entrance. With a combination of retail, commercial and residential uses, it is envisioned as the heart of the community.

Green Building Design and Construction

Harvest Lakes' holistic approach to sustainable development includes land and energy conservation techniques, water management, and green design and construction practices.

LAND CONSERVATION

With environmental sustainability the underlying objective through all phases of the land development process, LandCorp undertook comprehensive site investigations to establish opportunities and constraints for development prior to the initiation of site planning. As a result, two degraded wetlands were upgraded and retained for public open space, three significant areas of remnant vegetation were rejuvenated and retained for public open space, and a tree-lined ridge traversing the site was retained as a prominent landscape feature near the entrance to the Harvest Lakes. To promote the most efficient use of land, road widths and building setbacks were reduced from the typical sizes found in the area. As is standard in most jurisdictions in Australia, the local regulations call for 10 percent of the site to be open space, but due to its sustainable practices, the company received permission to provide a slightly smaller amount—8 percent.

ENERGY CONSERVATION

The Harvest Lakes site plan addresses energy conservation through the solar orientation and configuration of all land parcels: east-west lot exposures are minimized and north-south exposures are maximized. Approximately 75 percent of all lots are oriented to maximize the benefits of solar design. In addition, solar-powered lighting is used in public open spaces.

Mandatory energy conservation requirements for individually built homes include minimum solar hot water systems and energy efficient fixtures. House designs in which living areas are north facing and sleeping areas are south facing are encouraged, as are shading features such as awnings, deep eaves, and porches.

Components such as rainwater collection tanks and photovoltaic solar panels are used at "The Elements" to demonstrate simple ways of conserving resources and reducing impacts on the environment.

WATER MANAGEMENT

Water-sensitive urban design principles guided the creation of a water management system at Harvest Lakes that increases aquifer filtration and reduces stormwater

runoff, so that no water leaves the site except in major storm events. The two existing degraded wetlands on the property were rehabilitated and integrated into the water management system—one as a permanent water body, the other as a seasonal wetland. The permanent wetland, a lined basin, provides a collection point for stormwater and is used to irrigate public open spaces. It also provides a year-round open water habitat for waterfowl. The unlined, seasonal wetland captures stormwater flows and helps in the recharge of the underground water table.

Eight large-scale pieces of public art throughout the development help promote the message of environmental sustainability. This interactive sculpture is reminiscent of the reeds and grasses that help filter and clean the water in nearby wetlands.

It is estimated that the water management system used at Harvest Lakes will produce an additional recharge to the aquifer each year equivalent to the annual water consumption of 415 homes in Perth.

The role of individual homeowners is also addressed. All homes are required to include water-conservation features including low-flow fixtures. Homeowners are also required to install low-water landscaping. All front yards have irrigation controllers with separate settings for turf and garden areas to enable reduced capacity for specific areas. DAPs and on-site education programs also encourage homeowners to conserve water. A program to educate the community on the importance of protecting waterways from stormwater pollutants is also in effect. It uses signs and pictures on stormwater drains to discourage the disposal of pollutants such as car wash liquid, oils, paints, and unwanted household substances into the stormwater drain system.

BUILDING DESIGN AND MATERIALS

Lot buyers at Harvest Lakes design their own homes and select their own builders. To ensure that homes meet sustainability standards there are mandatory standards referred to in the land sale contract. These DAPs promote passive energy conservation, solar orientation, adequate shading, ventilation, and other practices. Harvest Lakes' DAPs were developed in consultation with leading homebuilders and specialists in the areas of planning, environment, and urban design. They are incorporated into the local government's Town Planning Scheme rather than attached to the sale of individual lots through covenants.

The obligation for meeting the standards has become stricter at each phase of development. In the early phases, residents were obliged to comply with two out of 12 standards; in later phases the requirement rose to 6 of 12. Today, new residents are required to comply with all 12 standards in the construction of their homes. LandCorp estimates that sustainable features add approximately A$3,000 to the total cost of each home.

LandCorp does not monitor DAP conformity during construction, but the company does conduct an inspection at construction completion and provides incentives for those who comply with development standards. Owners who build their home within 18 months of settlement are given a cash contribution of A$1,200 for items such as landscaping and fencing. According to the company, the ongoing monitoring of compliance with design guidelines is largely done through the local community and residents association.

GREEN CONSTRUCTION PRACTICES

The site development process employed a number of green practices. Significant trees and natural habitats were retained and incorporated into public open spaces when possible. Surplus trees were recycled and used in the construction of boardwalks and park benches and cleared vegetation has been reused as mulch. Builders are required to prepare and implement waste-management plans before they can begin construction on individual homes.

The construction of the Community and Environmental Center, established in conjunction with the local government, was undertaken with sustainability principles in mind. The center is Australia's only multi-purpose community facility to feature an environmental workshop and interpretive center that is specifically designed to provide information and education on environmentally sustainable lifestyle practices. Significant features of the center include trombe walls (sun-facing masonry structures that passively store heat), sustainable building management systems, solar hot water systems, energy-efficient lamps and appliances, graywater recycling, and cross ventilation. It is expected that these features will result in an approximately 25 percent reduction in energy consumption

LandCorp also worked with the Western Australia Department of Education and Training in building the state's first ecologically designed primary school. The school is located adjacent to the community center and the two facilities share parking.

Community Education and Involvement

Community education and involvement are important components of LandCorp's efforts to create a sustainable development that is embraced by its residents. An innovative Community Development Plan guides growth and recommends methods to facilitate residents' involvement in environmental protection and sustainability initiatives. The company also provides new homeowners with litera-

ture showing how careful selection of household appliances and plumbing fixtures can, in the long term, reduce water consumption by up to 35 percent.

A tangible example of how to go green is provided by "The Elements," a model home built by LandCorp and National Homes, one of the state's most prominent homebuilders, to showcase cost-effective sustainability measures that can easily be incorporated into new and existing homes. As noted by Carl Curtis, the company's development manager, the house illustrates that, "It's really not so complicated to build sustainably."

The Community and Environmental Center, built by LandCorp in association with local authorities, is an important hub of activities and educational programs such as "Building Green" workshops.

Marketing

Since its opening, Harvest Lakes has enjoyed outstanding land sales success. At the first sale in late 2002, over 700 individual lots were sold. Since that time, there has been such strong interest in purchasing lots that potential buyers often can be found camping out at the sales office prior to the day of a sale. As a result, the company does not announce or advertise sales releases until just before they take place. LandCorp discourages speculators; at each release, purchasers may buy only one lot at a time.

Clusters of lots are released in stages and buyers select their properties from plans that indicate parcel dimensions and configurations as well as allowable house size. Prospective buyers who register their interest and pay a small deposit are placed on a priority list and are then notified when the sales process can proceed.

An outside marketing and sales agent appointed by LandCorp maintains a sales center. To date, buyers have been primarily professionals with young families. Most are second- or third-time homebuyers from throughout the Perth area.

A variety of lot sizes, from 3,767-square-foot (350-square-meter) "cottage lots" to 19,375-square-foot (1,800-square-meter) "character lots," helps ensure a diverse and sustainable community at Harvest Lakes. This selection of lot sizes accommodates a range of family types—young families, single parents, empty nesters, and retirees. In future phases, even more focus will be placed on affordability.

The Harvest Edge portion of the development is planned to demonstrate that high-quality, moderately priced homes on relatively small lots can be designed for one- or two-person households without compromising property values.

Experience Gained

Harvest Lakes offers a practical model for sustainable development. It has educated builders and land buyers in tangible ways to reduce impacts on the environment at a major residential project.

In the early stages of the project there was concern about market acceptance of design guidelines with mandatory requirements. But the image of Harvest Lakes and positive word of mouth has meant there has been little need for expensive marketing or advertising.

The higher-density Harvest Edge portion of the development was met with more controversy than expected by LandCorp. In retrospect, the company would have introduced this concept earlier in the project development process so that residents of the area would be aware of it when they purchase their lots. Today, however, the Harvest Edge concept is being embraced by the residents of Harvest Lakes. The changing nature of demographics in Australia—the aging of the baby boomer generation, the increase in single-parent families, and the rise of telecommuters—has helped to increase public acceptance of a more diverse mix of housing types within developments.

This picnic area is defined by a simple structure made of recycled wood beams. All landscaping comprises drought-tolerant materials.

LandCorp has been pleasantly surprised by the success of Harvest Lakes. Gross estimated sales in early 2007 total A$160 million. The initial land cost was A$4 million and estimated development expenditure in early 2007 is A$80 million.

As a result of its success and its high level of national recognition, Harvest Lakes has provided an impetus to other developers to adopt sustainable practices.

Harvest Lakes

LAND USE AND BUILDING INFORMATION

Site area (acres/ hectares)	84/34
Total number of dwelling units at completion	1,000
Retail gross leasable area (sq f/sq m)	53,820/5,000 (village center)

LAND USE PLAN

Use	Total Acres/Hectares	Percentage of Site
Rural residential	21.10/8.54	13.0
Special character lots	9.34/3.78	5.8
Traditional lots	98.72/39.95	61.0
Laneway lots	4.048/1.638	2.5
Cottage lots	23.134/9.362	14.3
Mixed use lots	2.1696/0.8780	13.4
Medium density	2.1009/0.8502	1.3
Medium density	1.0465/0.4235	0.65
Total residential	**161.61/65.4**	**57**
Public open space	23.2/9.4	8
Primary school/community center	9.9/4.0	3.5
Retail (mixed-use village center) (comprises office, retail, medium density and open space)	19.5/7.9	6.9
Roads/parking (excluding village center)	69.2/28	24.4

RESIDENTIAL INFORMATION

Lot and Unit Types	Average Lot size (units per acre/ units per hectare)	Units Planned
Single-family lots	12.5–60/30.89–148.26	1,000
Harvest Edge apartments	60–80/148.26–197.68	40
Harvest Edge house and lot packages	40–50/98.84–123.55	60

DEVELOPMENT COST INFORMATION

In million Australian dollars

Site Acquisition Cost	**6.6**
Site Improvement Costs	
Excavation/grading	14.9
Sewer/water/drainage	9.4
Paving/curbs/sidewalks	6.0
Landscaping/irrigation	7.3
Fees/general conditions	7.6
Other	6.5
	51.7

Construction Costs

Construction Tax	13.5
(Contribution to Water Authority for sewage hookup)	

Soft Costs

Marketing and PR	2.4

Other

Portion of Community Cnter construction	1.5
Community Association budget	2.0
Elements House	0.3
	3.8
Total Development Cost	**$78 million**

DEVELOPMENT SCHEDULE

Site acquired	October 1992
Planning started	February 1996
Site development started	March 2002
Residential sales/leasing started	November 2002
Commercial leasing projected	2010 (Village Center)
Projected residential completion	2008

DEVELOPMENT TEAM

Developer
LandCorp
Perth, Western Australia
www.landcorp.com.au

Architect
Sharni Howe Architects
Northbridge, Western Australia

Planner
Roberts Day Group
East Perth, Western Australia
www.robertsday.com.au

Landscape Architect
McNally Newton
Northbridge, Western Australia
www.mnla.com.au

Consulting Engineers
Sinclair Knight Merz Pty Ltd.
Perth, Western Australia
www.skmconsulting.com

Hidden Springs
ADA COUNTY, IDAHO

HIDDEN SPRINGS IS A 1,756-ACRE (711-hectare) planned community located in the Boise Front foothills of Ada County, Idaho. When completed in 2008, the community will have 840 residential units and a small town center. Developed by Martin Community Development, Hidden Springs was envisioned and implemented as an environmentally sensitive community. Nearly 60 percent of the site is open space dedicated to a variety of uses, including preserved lands, hiking, agriculture, wetlands, and wildlife preserves. The project features an innovative wastewater reclamation system, community-supported agriculture, and comprehensive design guidelines. The community has received recognition as a model for smart growth from organizations such as the Lincoln Institute of Land Policy, the Sonoran Institute, and the National Association of Home Builders.

SPECIAL FEATURES

- Extensive open space
- Innovative wastewater reclamation system
- Community programs that connect residents to the natural environment

Site and Context

Located ten miles (16 kilometers) northwest of Boise, Hidden Springs sits in a rural setting in the Dry Creek Valley. An agricultural area, the Dry Creek Valley was once home to Basque farmers. Hidden Springs contains a 130-year-old working farm, which a group of community members is

Development within Hidden Springs is guided by strong architectural and landscape guidelines overseen by a design review board. Massing, building height, exterior colors, and roof pitch vary by lot type and neighborhood.

WELSH STUDIOS

HIDDEN SPRINGS

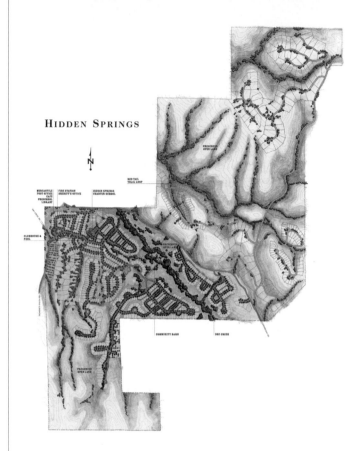

HIDDEN SPRINGS

Hidden Springs site plan.

- **Rural character and farming traditions.** Hidden Springs will maintain the rural traditions of the property by incorporating older outbuildings into the landscape designs where practical, and will dedicate some of its open space to appropriate agricultural uses.

- **Create small town atmosphere.** Traditional neighborhood design will be the foundation for Hidden Springs' small-town lifestyle.

- **Respect for the natural environment.** The developer and the residents will respect the natural environment.

- **Traditional home design.** The developer will encourage the design and construction of homes that are comfortable and durable, using energy and resources efficiently and responsibly.

- **Prioritize quality of life and healthy living.** The developer has set aside, and will care for, large and diverse areas for outdoor living and recreation.

- **Maintain high educational standards.** The community will support neighborhood schools and lifelong learning opportunities.

- **Pursue demographic diversity.** Builders will offer a variety of houses, so that people of many ages, incomes, and backgrounds can live at Hidden Springs.

- **Establish value and values.** The community of Hidden Springs will provide enrichment, enjoyment, and value for many generations to come.

These principles have helped to ensure continuity of the vision despite changes in ownership, development staff, vendors, and consultants.

Master Plan

Hidden Springs' land plan identifies over 1,000 acres (405 hectares) as permanent open space used for trails, agriculture, wetlands, and wildlife refuge areas. The plan is divided into distinct neighborhoods, each with their own housing types and design themes. Hidden Springs also has a town center, a public charter school, a private preschool, and a community-supported produce farm.

The residential design guidelines for Hidden Springs were drafted to promote sustainable treatment of the semi-arid, high-desert terrain. In contrast to conventional subdivisions in the area, the plan establishes the preservation of the more visually sensitive foothill slopes as open space and clusters homes in a village on the val-

trying to preserve as a museum. For a semi-arid, high desert climate, the site is relatively well irrigated, as the development gets its name from several subsurface springs found on the land. The site is bisected by Dry Creek, which is fed by melting snow in the foothills. Homes are nestled into the surrounding lower foothills, with site elevations varying by 900 feet (274 meters).

Because Ada County did not have a master planned community ordinance in place, entitlement took two years. In 1997, Hidden Springs became the first community approved under the Ada County Planned Community Ordinance, the first of its kind to be adopted by an Idaho jurisdiction. The ordinance allows for the development of new communities under the guidance of a specific plan based on smart growth principles.

Sustainability as a Core Value

Hidden Springs was envisioned as a sustainable community in the design tradition of Idaho's small towns. The developer's vision is based on eight principles, which serve to guide the long-term planning and construction of the project:

ley floor or tucked within hidden side valleys, where they will not dominate the landscape.

Hidden Springs' housing types are diverse, ranging from condominiums in the town center to custom homes on 1.5-acre (0.61 hectare) sites. Houses are designed in a variety of traditional styles on fully landscaped parcels to enhance neighborhood streetscapes. Development within Hidden Springs is guided by strong architectural and landscape design guidelines overseen by the Town Design Review Board. There is no arbitrary minimum square footage or price requirement for new homes at Hidden Springs. However, massing, maximum building height, exterior colors, and roof pitch vary by lot type and neighborhood within the community. The guidelines include detailed illustrations showing encouraged and discouraged design solutions. The town center is located near the community's primary entrance and features

a fire station, preschool, and a mixed-use building that houses The Dry Creek Mercantile, a café, business offices, a community mail center, and a library. Set around a traditional village green, the town center serves as a gathering place for community activities. To facilitate community interaction through residents' daily trips to the town center, Hidden Springs does not have postal delivery. Planning for the viability of future commercial and higher-density housing, the developer set aside land next to the fire station for a mixed-use development of retail space and condominiums. The first phase is currently under construction as the Marketplace at Hidden Springs.

Hidden Springs abuts the foothills of the Boise Range. The plan preserves the environmentally sensitive slopes as open space and clusters homes in a village on the valley floor or tucked within hidden side valleys, where they will not dominate the landscape.

In addition, zoning allows home-based businesses, which include a hair salon, chiropractor, massage therapist, event planner, mortgage brokerage, financial planner, and real estate brokerage.

A network of 24 trails winds through the development, connecting amenities, neighborhoods, and foothills. Amenities include parks, playing fields, two pools, a club-

house, common open space, a community barn, a village green, and pocket parks interspersed throughout the community. The Dry Creek Mercantile, the clubhouse, and the new barn host programs and events throughout the year.

Homes are designed in a variety of styles, but take their design cues from vernacular architecture. Builders participate in a green construction program and must meet minimum standards set by the developer.

The Hidden Springs Charter School, at the center of the community, is a public institution governed by a board of trustees and founded by community members. The school opened in fall 2001 and currently serves 470 students in kindergarten through ninth grade.

The Smart Start Preschool, which opened in 1999, serves students aged three to five. The quality of both the pre-school and charter school, whose students have among the highest test scores in the state, have given Hidden Springs' an advantage in the market.

Green Building Design and Construction

Hidden Springs has received national recognition for its combination of integrated development planning, environmental sensitivity, and resource-efficient infrastructure. In 2005, the National Wildlife Federation (NWF) deemed Hidden Springs a Wildlife Habitat Community, only the seventh in the nation to receive the recognition. In addition, more than 35 homeowners have had their yards certified as a NWF Backyard Wildlife Habitat sites.

As houses and lots are sold and resold, a transfer fee of .25 percent of the price funds trail improvements, landscape restoration, wetland and open space enhancements, and educational programming. A resident Open Space Program Manager, employed by the Hidden Springs Town Association, is responsible for overseeing such initiatives as well as working with the developer to create habitat plans for existing and future development phases. The Hidden Springs Open Space Council, a group of resident volunteers, organizes a variety of stewardship and education programs and publishes a monthly newsletter called Habitat Happenings, which features articles on wildlife sightings in the community (pronghorn antelope, mule deer, coyote, badgers, and raptors) and educational programs on wildlife, conservation, and environmental stewardship.

One of Hidden Springs' sustainable strategies, its wastewater reclamation system, was key to the viability of the development, since the site is far from existing municipal sewer services. Annual rainfall of 12 inches posed an additional challenge for the development team. To help address these problems, Hidden Springs' wastewater is recycled through a two-step reclamation process: The wastewater travels from each neighborhood to a series of ponds, where it undergoes intensive aeration and natural filtration before the treated water is pumped out to irrigate farm fields and common areas and returned to the aquifer.

Another such resource-saving effort is the development's traffic management plan, which was designed to reduce the number of vehicle trips per day from a typical 12 per household to eight. Pedestrian access to all of the community's amenities, including the charter school and the town center, decreases the number of automobile trips residents may require on a daily basis.

Hidden Springs' land conservation, wastewater reclamation, and traffic reduction plans are complemented by the development's green building guidelines. In order to construct energy-efficient residences, builders are encouraged to participate in the U.S. Department of Energy's Building America Initiative or the Environmental Protection Agency's Energy Star® program. The goal is to use resources efficiently during the construction process and employ guidelines that result in energy savings for residents. As demand in the Boise housing market has increased, the developer has implemented more aggressive standards for higher quality design and green building. The developer and builder team have committed to constructing the remaining phases of homes to Energy Star standards.

Marketing

An early effort to position the community as a latter-day Mayberry failed because consumers perceived the marketing effort to be contrived. A more authentic and sophisticated marketing strategy was subsequently put into place. The current creative pitch is "The Antidote to Anywhere, USA," which contrasts Hidden Springs' unconventional design and features against the relatively undifferentiated Boise market. Since its early stages, Hidden Springs has leveraged its extensive local and national media coverage with great success.

To ensure a higher degree of professionalism and control of on-site sales and marketing, the developer initially established an in-house brokerage entity dedicated to Hidden Springs properties. This action was counter to the local trend of developers and builders enlisting established real estate offices to sell new homes. The result was confusion, skepticism, and resistance from the brokerage community, which affected sales rates in a market that has a high degree of broker co-op sales. Since then, the developer has listed Hidden Springs with a well-established local brokerage and broker co-op sales are now in line with the market.

Boise is primarily a market of small homebuilders. The Hidden Springs builder program struggled initially, as most local contractors were reluctant to abandon their existing plans in favor of investing in redesigns to fit the vision of Hidden Springs. The developer had to work extensively to educate builders in the merits of green construction practices and siting homes in an alley-loaded configuration. Over time, as lot supplies and increasing demand has shifted, the community has proven to be a desirable and profitable location for several local builders who have remained with the community since the beginning. In fact, many of the people involved in the development are residents; the developer, seven builders, and seven Realtors reside in Hidden Springs.

Initially, Hidden Springs had a limited product offering, primarily targeted to families with school-age children. The pricing was also narrow, competing at the top of the

Nearly 60 percent of the Hidden Springs site is preserved open space and used for trails, agriculture, wetlands, and wildlife refuges.

WELSH STUDIOS

Boise market. The marketing program was expanded to target one- and two-person households, which turned out to be about two-thirds of the development's market. Over half of the buyers have been transferees from outside Idaho, compared to about one-quarter in other new-home developments. Buyers are drawn by employment in the nearby technology campuses. There are also a few retirees, whose numbers have increased in recent years. Although the majority of residents are middle to high income, the more affordable units on smaller lots near the pool and clubhouse have helped diversify the product types and buyers. Zoning allowed accessory units, which were offered on many homes with the idea that they would provide an affordable rental option to lower-income residents. Few such units were built and most of them are being used by visiting relatives or as home offices.

Architectural guidelines include detailed illustrations showing encouraged and discouraged design solutions.

Financing

Hidden Springs was initially developed as a partnership between an entity of The Carlyle Group of Washington, D.C., and an entity of Grossman Company Properties of Phoenix, Arizona. Carlyle Realty contributed the initial equity, while Grossman contributed the land, which it had owned for many years. However, below-plan financial performance of Hidden Springs' early phases led both entities to exit the partnership in 2001. The current owner, Developers of Hidden Springs LLC, is an entity of Minneapolis-based GMAC ResCap. Since 1997, Frank Martin has led the Hidden Springs development team.

The lack of similar master-planned developments in the area set the stage for Hidden Springs to be a cutting-edge community. However, the innovative land planning, architecture, and premium pricing may have proved too far ahead of the market. Early phases performed basically in-line with the market, given the relatively narrow product offering and price point. However, the *pro forma* necessitated a greater sales velocity to ensure solvency for the project, due to the significant upfront development costs. The rural location presented several development challenges, such as a lack of infrastructure and paved access roads, increasing development costs. In addition, Hidden Springs struggled in the first phases against the perception that the community was too far from Boise.

WELSH STUDIOS

However, in recent years, new development has sprawled to the bedroom communities west of Boise. Hidden Springs now enjoys the advantage of being "close in."

Despite the nationwide cooling of the real estate market in 2006, Hidden Springs posted its second highest single-year home sales in its eight-year history. One hundred sixty-three homes were sold, compared to 192 in 2005 and 112 the year before. Current lot pricing ranges from $80,000 to $315,000 and unit prices now range from $335,500 to over $1 million, selling at a premium in the market. There are 13 approved builders, and each home must be started within six months of the lot closing and completed within 12 months. If construction does not commence, Hidden Springs' speculation-discouraging buyback provision kicks in. With the Boise market seeing an influx of investors in recent years, Hidden Springs has prohibited builders from knowingly selling to investors, in favor of selling to permanent residents who are critical to community building.

Because the town center building was viewed as such an integral part of the community fabric and a critical marketing tool, it was constructed before the first home-owner moved in. The developer was not required to complete it until the fiftieth residential occupancy permit

Hidden Springs' charter school helped distinguish it from competing communities. It opened in fall 2001 and currently serves 470 students in kindergarten through ninth grade.

was issued, in part as a vehicle trip reduction strategy. The developer has also subsidized its rents and operations during the development phase, though it is expected to become self-sustaining at buildout.

Experience Gained

The development team cites several reasons for the success of Hidden Springs. Foremost is the project's appeal as a destination community. Its rural setting, architecture, community events, open space, charter school, and overall sensitivity to the land distinguish Hidden Springs from its competitors, most of which are traditional single-product subdivisions. However, the developer admits that the project involved a steep learning curve. The lessons learned relate more to implementation than to the nature of innovative sustainable design in community development:

■ Establish a set of guiding principles that will help align all stakeholders with the vision of the community throughout its lifecycle.

■ Avoid too many cooks in the kitchen by establishing clarity in ownership structure, management control, and decision-making to ensure empowerment and accountability.

Hidden Springs' fire station is located in the town center at the entrance to the community.

- Partner with a local builder or builders in the first phase to set the bar for design and energy-efficient construction practices.

- Develop in small phases in an area that is as fragmented as the Boise market.

- Plan to front-load, and subsidize if necessary, distinctive amenities to help build momentum in early phases and establish credibility in the market.

- Make environmental preservation and conservation central to the planning process. Open space can be part of the palette of community-building programs that engage residents and connect them with each other and the natural environment.

- Differentiate a development through community-building events and programs.

- Build community loyalty. It generates strong referrals. (Many Hidden Springs residents are on their second or third move-up home.)

- Be prepared for strong resident participation that may challenge the developer at times. At Hidden Springs, for example, some residents strongly opposed the reduction of the farmstead from 100 acres (40 hectares) to 35 acres (14 hectares) to accommodate a shift to higher density development in the valley floor in response to market demands.

- Choose battles carefully. Hidden Springs' attempt to establish its own on-site sales operations alienated builders and brokers.

- To hedge risk, improve overall absorption rates, and create diversity in the community, define a broad-based product and price segmentation plan to meet the needs of a variety of income levels.

Hidden Springs

LAND USE INFORMATION

Site area (acres/hectares)	1,756/711
Number of residential units	40
Percentage of residential development complete	80
Gross residential density (units per acre/hectare)	.48/0.19
Average net density (per acre/per hectare)	1.41/0.57

LAND USE PLAN

	Area (acres/hectares)	Percentage of Site
Residential	594/240	34
Roads	91/37	5
Developed open space (parks, common areas)	42/17	2
Undeveloped open space (natural open space)	1,005/407	57
Town center/mixed-use/school	17/7	1
Sewer and power facilities	7/3	1

RESIDENTIAL INFORMATION

Unit Type	Unit Size (sq f/sq m)	Range of initial sales prices
Cottage	1,600/49	$170,000s
School Ridge	1,800–2,200/167–204	$170,000–$220,000
Village	2,200–2,600/204–241	$240,000–$270,000
Foothills	2,400–3,000/223–279	$265,000–$300,000
Cottonwood	1,650–2,700/153–251	$335,000–$525,000
Maple	2,200–3,700/204–344	$435,000–$620,000
Aspen	2,600–4,000/242–372	$580,000–$689,000
Marketplace	1,835–2,420/170–225	$300,000s+
Custom	3,000–6,000/279–557	$800,000–$1,000,000+

DEVELOPMENT COST INFORMATION

Site Acquisition Cost	$8,750,000

Site Improvement Costs

Excavation/grading	$9,425,000
Sewer/water/drainage	$10,300,000
Paving/curbs/sidewalks	$4,920,000
Landscaping/irrigation	$2,810,000
Telecom/power	$1,700,000
	$29,155,000

Construction Costs

Office and retail	$1,400,000
Amenities	$3,200,000
Fire station	$600,000
	$5,200,000

Soft Costs

Architecture/engineering	$3,180,000
Project management	$4,800,000
Marketing and sales	$5,900,000
Legal/accounting	$1,015,000
Taxes/insurance	$1,500,000
Town association	$500,000
Construction interest and fees	$3,800,000
Licenses, bonds, permits	$460,000
	$21,155,000
Total Development Cost	**$64,260,000**

DEVELOPMENT SCHEDULE

Planning started	January 1995
Site purchased	February 1997
Construction started	November 1997
Sales started	September 1998
Phase I completed	December 1999
Project completed	December 2008 (estimated)

DEVELOPMENT TEAM

Owner
Developers of Hidden Springs LLC
Minneapolis, Minnesota

Developer
Martin Community Development LLC
Boise, Idaho
www.hiddensprings.com

Site Planner
Hart Howerton
San Francisco, California
www.harthowerton.com

Architects
Mithun Partners, Inc.
Seattle, Washington
www.mithun.com

Nagle Hartray Danker Kagan McKay Architects Planners Ltd.
Chicago, Illinois
www.nhdkm.com

Glancey-Rockwell and Associates
Boise, Idaho
www.grboise.com

Other Key Team Members
Givens Pursley LLP
Boise, Idaho
www.givenspursley.com

RiveRidge Engineering
Boise, Idaho
www.rvrdg.com

Stoltz Marketing Group
Boise, Idaho
www.stoltzgroup.com

Group One, Inc.
Eagle, Idaho
www.group-one.com

Holiday Neighborhood

BOULDER, COLORADO

LOCATED AT THE NORTHERN EDGE of Boulder, Colorado, the 27-acre (11-hectare) former Holiday Drive-In Theater site is being redeveloped as a new urban community in an area dominated by suburban growth patterns. Holiday Neighborhood contains 334 homes designed in a wide range of styles, building types, and prices, including 138 affordable properties, and 5,000 square feet (465 square meters) of commercial space—a gourmet pizza restaurant, a bakery/coffee shop, a fitness center, an eco-friendly dry cleaner, and office condominiums. The project also has a community garden, pedestrian walkways, bike paths, a two-acre city park, and several pocket parks. From the beginning, the aim of the developer, a public/private partnership, has been to combine the best of locally based sustainable design and development practices with, the affordability, the arts, and a healthy lifestyle.

Holiday Neighborhood emphasizes sustainability's "three E's"—economy, equity, and environment—through high-density, clustered,

SPECIAL FEATURES

- Affordability
- Infill redevelopment site
- Transit accessible
- Green building features
- Innovative stormwater management system
- Construction waste recycling program

Holiday Neighborhood emphasizes sustainability's "three E's"—economy, equity, and environment—through high-density, clustered mixed-use development that encourages walking, biking, and transit use.

ELIZABETH MORGAN WOLFERT

183

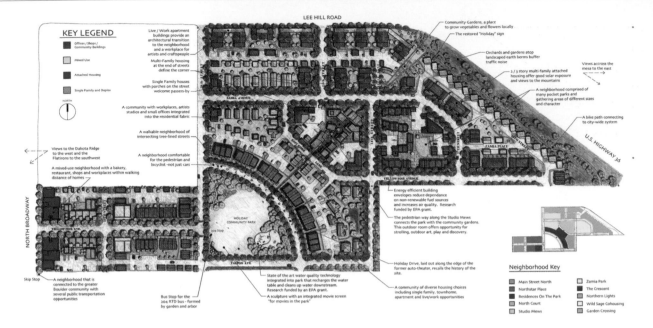

KEY LEGEND

- Offices / Shops / Community Buildings
- Mixed Use
- Attached Housing
- Single Family and Duplex

NORTH

LEE HILL ROAD

Community Gardens, a place to grow vegetables and flowers locally

The restored "Holiday" sign

Orchards and gardens atop landscaped earth berms buffer traffic noise

Views accross the mesa to the east

2 / 3 story multi-family attached housing offer good solar exposure and views to the mountains

A neighborhood comprised of many pocket parks and gathering areas of different sizes and character

A bike path connecting to city-wide system

U.S. HIGHWAY 36

Live / Work apartment buildings provide an architectural transition to the neighborhood and a workplace for artists and craftspeople

Multi-Family housing at the end of streets define the corner

Single Family houses with porches on the street welcome passers-by

A community with workplaces, artists studios and small offices integrated into the residential fabric

A walkable neighborhood of intersecting tree-lined streets

A neighborhood comfortable for the pedestrian and bicyclist -not just cars

Views to the Dakota Ridge to the west and the Flatirons to the southwest

A mixed-use neighborhood with a bakery, restaurant, shops and workplaces within walking distance of homes

NORTH BROADWAY

ZAMIA AVENUE

ZAMIA PLACE

YELLOW PINE AVENUE

HOLIDAY COMMUNITY PARK

YARROW AVE.

Skip Stop

A neighborhood that is connected to the greater Boulder community with several public transportation opportunities

Bus Stop for the 304 RTD bus - formed by garden and arbor

State of the art water quality technology integrated into park that recharges the water table and cleans up water downstream. Research funded by an EPA grant.

A sculpture with an integrated movie screen "for movies in the park"

Energy efficient building envelopes reduce dependance on non-renewable fuel sources and increases air quality. Research funded by EPA grant.

The pedestrian way along the Studio Mews connects the park with the community gardens. This outdoor room offers opportunity for strolling, outdoor art, play and discovery.

Holiday Drive, laid out along the edge of the former auto-theater, recalls the history of the site.

A community of diverse housing choices including single family, townhome, apartment and live/work opportunities

Neighborhood Key

- Main Street North
- Northstar Place
- Residences On The Park
- North Court
- Studio Mews
- Zamia Park
- The Crescent
- Northern Lights
- Wild Sage Cohousing
- Garden Crossing

mixed-use development that reduces energy and encourages walking, biking, and transit use. Its sustainable features include passive and active solar heating; solar orientation, roof overhangs, and awnings to minimize heat gain in summer; recycled and other low-impact building materials; energy-efficient building systems; state-of-the-art lighting guidelines; and innovative stormwater management strategies.

Above: Holiday Neighborhood site plan.
Below: The site was formerly occupied by the Holiday Drive-In Movie Theater, which closed in 1989. The developers decided to retain the iconic sign to reinforce the project's name and identity.

The project is the result of a partnership between local housing authority Boulder Housing Partners (BHP)—a quasi-governmental agency—and six private developers. BHP acted as the land developer and sold finished lots to its development partners. As Cindy Brown, BHP's co-executive director for development, notes, "Projects undertaken by BHP must meet a triple bottom line by accomplishing social, financial, and environmental goals." In the case of Holiday Neighborhood, these goals often complement each other. The financial goal of generating a surplus in the land development phase, for example, has enabled BHP to invest in 49 rental housing units, which it is buying back from its development partners and earmarking for low-income households.

Site and Context

Although immediately bounded by local roads as well as U.S. Highway 36, the site is largely surrounded by open space to the north and east. To the northwest sits a National Guard Armory, on which a local developer recently proposed building a grocery store and residential condominiums. Limited residential and commercial/industrial development has taken place near the site's southern and western edges.

ABOVE BARRETT STUDIO ARCHITECTS; RIGHT ELIZABETH MORGAN WOLFERT

After the Holiday Twin Screen Drive-In Theater closed in 1989, the land remained vacant for several years. Although the landowner had signed a letter of intent with a big-box retailer to build a warehouse store on the site, a community planning process determined that this was not what Boulder wanted on one of its last undeveloped parcels.

In March 1997, the city purchased the land for $4.8 million, or about $4 per square foot ($43 per square meter). The following year, the city sold the site to BHP, a public entity separate from the city. The agency took over the responsibility for the land loan; its goal for the site was to create a desirable, diverse, sustainable, and affordable community. The entire North Boulder area is being developed within the context of a community plan that emphasizes new urbanism.

Sustainability as a Core Value

One of the BHP's primary goals for the Holiday Neighborhood was to limit its environmental impact. BHP envisioned the neighborhood as a diverse community in which walking would be a pleasure and public transportation, trails, and bike paths would be easily accessible. These features would reduce automobile dependence. To receive a building permit, the builders must comply with the Boulder Green Points Building Program, which requires residential builders to meet rigorous criteria designed to conserve land, water, energy, and other resources.

In 2001, the Sustainable Futures Society (SFS), a Denver based organization dedicated to sustainable development practices, secured an EPA Sustainable Development Challenge Grant to help green Holiday Neighborhood. The EPA challenged SFS to select several key aspects of sustainable design, incorporate them into the neighborhood, and evaluate the air and water quality benefits by comparing them with traditional development. SFS convened a meeting, facilitated by the Rocky Mountain Institute and attended by SFS, Holiday Neighborhood's architects and developers, and city officials to discuss the project's sustainability focus. At this first meeting the developers chose water quality, energy efficiency, energy systems analysis, and materials recycling/acquisition as key areas on which to focus. As Jim Logan, architect of Wild Sage pointed out at this early meeting, energy-efficient design is a great match with the Holiday Neighborhood's affordability goals, because it will result in lower-than-average utility bills.

SFS explored a wide range of cutting-edge technologies that could be used to reduce Holiday Neighborhood's impacts on water quality, stormwater runoff, and energy

use. While many of these proved to be too expensive or otherwise impractical to implement, others were incorporated into the project.

The Holiday Neighborhood project took green features a step beyond those required by Boulder's Green Points

Program, establishing sustainability guidelines for the neighborhood that challenged development teams to produce innovative designs and efficient technologies that were sufficiently cost-effective to turn a profit with an affordable project. All of the builders selected to develop projects within the Holiday Neighborhood were already familiar with affordable and sustainable development, and all specified insulation, building materials, appliances, and other features that surpassed the green guidelines.

Holiday Neighborhood includes community gardens, bike paths, and pocket parks.

The neighborhood's public open space is also green amenity. The open space is organized as a series of pedestrian spaces, paths, and outdoor environments that serve as public living rooms and passages. Transit options make the neighborhood's residents and workers less reliant on cars, and all Holiday Neighborhood residents receive free city bus passes to encourage transit use.

ELIZABETH MORGAN WOLFERT

Master Plan

Acting as the master site developer, BHP hired a master planner, Boulder-based Barrett Studio Architects, to create a concept plan for Holiday Neighborhood. From the beginning, BHP aimed to create a variety of housing types in the neighborhood, including a cohousing community. Public input into the project also began early on, with a kick-off barbeque on the site and a series of public meetings designed to determine what various stakeholders wanted to see happen there. Affordable housing was near the top of everyone's list. Consequently—and to meet city requirements described in the Approvals section below—BHP required 40 percent of the neighborhood's homes to be affordable to low- and moderate-income households (those earning less than 80 percent of area median income). To help developers meet this goal, BHP discounted land sales. It also held two acres (0.8 hectares) for a city park and dedicated another 70-foot-long (21-meter-long) corridor to the city for a noise buffer and bike path along the edge of the site.

Holiday Neighborhood contains a variety of housing types at various levels of affordability. The affordable Northern Lights project was built with community volunteers.

BHP structured its planning process to be inclusive, inviting public involvement throughout. In a city famous for public debate and opposition to development, Holiday Neighborhood faced no significant opposition. The site

plan is designed around Holiday Park, the living room of the neighborhood, which will be located on the site of the former drive-in theater screen. To the west of the park, mixed-use development acts as a gateway to the neighborhood off North Broadway. North and east of the park,

residential and live/work properties will include single-family detached dwellings and attached housing, artists' studios, small offices integrated into the fabric of the neighborhood, a community garden, and pocket parks. Easy Rider Lane, near the center of the neighborhood, is named after the first film screened at the drive-in, and the theater's original sign, now restored, sits along the edge of Holiday Neighborhood off U.S. Highway 36.

Development Process

It took more than seven years just to get the Holiday Neighborhood project underway. When negotiations for the site began in 1996, several members of the local real estate community opposed the deal, arguing that the public sector should not be involved in development. Boulder's focus on providing affordable housing—with a stated goal of making 10 percent of the city's housing stock permanently accessible to households earning less than 60 percent of area median income—was a critical component in the city's commitment to purchase the site. Despite opposition, the city council authorized the sale, provided a $1 million grant, and allowed city reserves to be used to back an interim loan for the purchase.

After securing the land, BHP entered the city's planning approval process. Although the city's planning board supported the Holiday Neighborhood concept site in 1999, the plan itself created a barrier to development because it called for an overall density of 20 units per acre (about 50 units per hectare), twice the density specified in the city's subcommunity plan for the area. It took the city a year to draft and adopt an ordinance that created a density bonus to allow the level of development required by the site plan. An inclusionary zoning ordinance passed in 2000 requires 20 percent of housing in all new residential developments (except condominium conversions) to be permanently affordable to households earning less than 80 percent of area median income. The ordinance that created the bonus required double that amount—a total of 40 percent—affordable units in denser projects. Further site review and approval of the technical document for Holiday Neighborhood took until the end of 2002.

After the initial Holiday Neighborhood site plan was completed, BHP issued a letter of interest, to which it received about 45 responses. After two rounds of interviews, BHP—on the basis of the applicants' strengths and past histories, as well as their commitment to the project's clearly stated affordability and sustainability goals—selected six development partners to design and develop residential and commercial buildings in specific sections of the neighborhood. BHP developed the necessary infrastructure and sold fully entitled and finished lots to its development partners.

A groundbreaking ceremony was held on the site in December 2002. The infrastructure for the entire neighborhood was developed in a single phase, since doing so was more cost effective. BHP obtained a construction loan for the entire cost of infrastructure development and selected a contractor in early 2003. Infrastructure construction—including streets, utilities, sidewalks, curbs, gutters, and rough grading—began in March 2003 and was completed that September.

The Main Street North neighborhood contains 14 residential units and about 27,000 square feet (2,508 square meters) of retail and office space.

As BHP completed infrastructure improvements and obtained the required approvals, it resold the land to its development partners at prices ranging from $11 per square foot for the Northern Lights (fully affordable) project site to $23 per square foot for some of the mixed-use Broadway North project ($118 to $248 per square meter).

Each project within Holiday Neighborhood has its own name and identity. Coburn Development was selected to develop the largest portion of the site as five separate projects: Studio Mews has 32 residential units and 12 commercial (artist studio/office) units, as well as a pedestrian path and outdoor gallery/meeting space; NorthStar Place combines 33 townhouses and loft-style condominiums with eight commercial units; Crescent, a development facing Holiday Park, includes 40 condominium units in four elevator buildings; Holiday Squares contains eight townhouse-style units in four duplex buildings; and Z Park, with 25 detached single-family homes and carriage houses. Naropa University, with Wolff/Lyon Architects, was chosen to develop North Court, which has 68 residential units (flats and townhouses) and nine studios for artists and craftspeople. Wolff/Lyon also was named developer of Main Street North, a section containing 14 residential units (one- and two-bedroom flats) and about 27,000 square feet (2,508 square meters) of commercial space. The Affordable Housing Alliance, a nonprofit group dedicated to providing homeownership opportunities, was chosen to develop Northern Lights—14 duplex and carriage-house units built with sweat equity and volunteer labor. Peak Properties and Development Corporation built the 55-unit Garden Crossing project and Block 6's eight townhouse/duplex units with roof gardens. Wonderland Hill Development Company was tapped for the 34-unit Wild Sage Cohousing project.

Green Design and Construction

While all of the individual projects at Holiday Neighborhood are sustainably designed and constructed, the design and construction of the 1.5-acre (.6-hectare) Wild Sage Cohousing project represents an unusual model for sustainable communities: environmentally sound practices driven by a participatory process.

Wonderland President Jim Leach likens his company's tiered decision-making process, which involves future residents in the planning, design, and development through a series of workshops, to "building custom homes—only we are building custom neighborhoods." While the process involves challenges and frustrations, the importance of cohousing, he believes, lies in the fact that it "demonstrates the value of community."

TOP: CONOR MERRIGAN, BOTTOM: STUART GROGAN

The fees potential residents paid to attend Wild Sage workshops were later applied to the purchase price of their homes. The design workshops paid particular attention to the development's exterior spaces and circulation patterns. The back doors of most units open onto small patios, which in turn open onto paths that lead to the central courtyard facing the common house. Garages and parking spaces are located at the edge of the community to encourage informal interaction among residents. Likewise, the common house's location at the center of the community encourages residents to gather there and on the green space around it.

Wild Sage contains seven different unit types, ranging from 693-square-foot (64-square-meter), single-level carriage houses above garages to 2,712-square-foot (252-square-meter), three-level end units. All units are attached, sharing one or two common walls. Market-rate, affordable, and Habitat for Humanity–built homes are mixed throughout the project, and the affordable units are indistinguishable from the market-rate homes. Two of the seven unit types were available to all three economic groups, one was developed for both affordable-housing and market-rate purchasers, and the remaining four were developed solely as market-rate units. The construction budget for the residential space was $85 per square foot ($915 per square meter).

From the beginning, architect Jim Logan stated his intention to exceed Boulder Green Points Building Program requirements and to make every practical effort to limit Wild Sage's consumption of fossil fuels. The primary aspect of the green strategy at Wild Sage is energy efficiency and sustainability. Clustering and downsizing housing units create a great deal of energy efficiency. Future residents agreed early on that solar energy was an important goal, and reached consensus that the community would not use forced-air heating or central air conditioning. Although the design team initially explored the use of alternative energy sources such as fuel cells, microturbines, and photovoltaic panels, the team ultimately settled on a more traditional system that will be converted to an active solar system in the future.

The Studio Mews neighborhood is made up of 32 residential units and 12 mixed-use commercial (artist studios and office) units, as well as a pedestrian path and outdoor meeting space.

Each of the project's eight buildings is preplumbed for radiant solar heating and has a single hydronic baseboard mechanical heating system run by a central, high-efficiency boiler that is zoned by unit. Each mechanical

CONOR MERRIGAN

room sits atop an open space that can be used to store hot water from the active solar system. The community began installing donated, used solar panels on two seven-unit buildings in mid-2006; savings from this system will be invested in an account that will eventually pay for the installation of solar panels on the remaining buildings.

All exterior walls are insulated with 100 percent recycled wet-blown cellulose and covered with durable fiber cement siding. Roofs are insulated with R50 insulation, and all flat roofs—designed to hold solar panels—are covered with a white single-ply membrane, which reduces the urban heat-island effect. Wild Sage uses approximately 40 to 60 percent as much energy as a comparable housing project.

Innovative stormwater management techniques also contribute to Wild Sage's sustainability. Low-impact development techniques are geared toward infiltration rather than removal. Rooftop runoff is directed to shallow, vegetated trenches or swales, where it irrigates ornamental and edible plantings and gradually infiltrates an underlying sand bed, reducing both the need for supplemental watering and the amount of pollution in runoff.

Marketing and Management

The marketing process began with an exercise to come up with a name and an identity for the site. BHP gathered all of its development partners to discuss this issue, and found—at first—a wide range of opinions. Eventually, the group agreed on Holiday Neighborhood. The landmark Holiday Drive-In Theater sign offered one way to reinforce this name and identity, but BHP was careful to avoid using any type styles or graphics in its marketing materials that might be confused with the Holiday Inn motel chain. All of the development partners then selected names for their own individual projects.

BHP managed a coordinated marketing process for Holiday Neighborhood, and each of the development partners contributed to the marketing budget. BHP created a marketing brochure/folder into which it placed informational cut sheets; each development partner then added its own materials for its specific marketing purposes.

The Holiday Neighborhood Master Association governs the community. BHP formed and wrote the CC&Rs for the association, which first convened in December 2004, and the association's board of directors originally consisted of three BHP staff members. As occupancy benchmarks were met, their seats on the board were turned over to elected residents. The first two resident members were elected at the association's first meeting and a resident replaced the last BHP employee in February 2006. Each project at Holiday Neighborhood also has its own homeowners association.

Experience Gained

BHP and its development partners learned a variety of lessons in the development, design, construction, and marketing of Holiday Neighborhood:

■ In order to accomplish community goals, a project leader must be dedicated to the public good. BHP was willing to sell the land at a discount, accept a lower financial return, and charge a lower development fee than most private sector developers could have done. Even so, difficult decisions and tradeoffs were required. At Holiday Neighborhood, innovative water treatment strategies affected the size and usability of the park. Likewise, the size of the community garden shrank, as developers needed more land on either side of it to squeeze in additional affordable units. And BHP

ELIZABETH MORGAN WOLFERT

had to hold onto money that could have been spent on additional amenities in order to cover its costs and purchase units it could rent to low-income families.

- Development partners should be chosen for their expertise. BHP selected developers that already had demonstrated success in building comparable projects elsewhere. A developer with a strong record in mixed-use projects, for example, built the neighborhood's commercial section. Similarly, Habitat for Humanity and the Affordable Housing Alliance led the project's "sweat equity" efforts in which low-income families put in a substantial amount of time building their own homes.

- New Urbanist and scattered-site mixed-income development attract homebuyers. Holiday Neighborhood's market-rate homes have sold more quickly and at higher prices than similar products elsewhere in Boulder. People like being able to walk to a neighborhood restaurant, coffee shop, health club, or salon. They enjoy sitting on their front porches, interacting with neighbors and keeping an eye on the street.

- Cohousing developments can play a community-building role that spreads beyond the project itself. Wild Sage Cohousing residents became skilled at communication and conflict resolution, and have been able to use these skills for the benefit of the broader neighborhood. Several Wild Sage residents are leaders in the Holiday Neighborhood homeowners association, which frequently meets at the Wild Sage common house.

- Crucial to the success of the project, comments BHP's Cindy Brown, were people willing to think big: a city manager who said "Do it" and a board of commissioners willing to take risks to reach public goals. "My small organization fronted thousands of dollars, as did the city of Boulder, which helped BHP make the land payments during the difficult early years and provided other essential support. BHP took on the entire entitlement risk to keep the project running, which helped the developers a lot." Looking back on this process, Brown continues, "If I were doing the project again, I might try to share the entitlement risk with the development partners."

In the Wild Sage cohousing neighborhood, all units are attached with garages located on the perimeter of the community. Front doors open to sidewalks that lead to a large common house, where community meetings, dinners, and activities are held.

- While it may be politically controversial for a public entity to act as a land developer, BHP has found this an effective way to accomplish its social goals.

- Everything takes longer and costs more than originally projected. Members of the BHP team laugh when they look back on their original timeline, which called for the project to be completed between 1997 and 2001.

- Ultimately, one major reason for Holiday Neighborhood's success is that BHP set its terms for affordability and green design guidelines early in the process, and kept them in the forefront throughout the course of development.

Holiday Neighborhood

LAND USE INFORMATION

Total site area (acres/hectares)	27.29/11.04
Total number of dwelling units	334
Gross residential density (units per gross residential acre/hectare)	30/121
Average net residential density (acres/hectares)	49/20
Total commercial space (sq f/sq m) (includes restaurants, personal services, and professional and technical office space)	58,264/5,413

LAND USE PLAN

	Acres/Hectares	Percentage of Site
Residential	13.72/5.55	50
Mixed use*	2.70/1.09	10
Commercial**	0.80/0.32	3
Roads/parking	8.33/3.37	31
Open space	1.74/0.71	6***
	27.29/11.04	100

*Ground-floor commercial uses with residences above.

**Commercial space along North Broadway only.

***City park only; small green spaces are incorporated into other land uses throughout the site.

RESIDENTIAL UNIT INFORMATION

Project (Unit Types)	Unit Size (sq f/sq m)	Number Units	Range of Initial Sales Prices
Block 6 (townhouses and duplexes)	1,200–2,100/ 112–195	8	$140,000– $450,000
The Crescent (condominium apartments)	803–1,591/ 75–148	40	$129,000– $625,000
Emergency Family Assistance Association (two-bedroom townhouses)	1,100/102	3	NA
Garden Crossing (one-bedroom carriage house units and two- and three-bedroom townhouses)	660–1,628/ 61–151	55	$110,000– $301,180
Holiday Squares (townhouse-style condominiums in duplex buildings)	960–1,040/ 89–97	8	$145,000– $409,000
Main Street North (one- and two-bedroom flats)	620–940/ 58–87	14	$106,000– $270,000
North Court (one- to three-bedroom flats and three-bedroom townhouses	770–1,340/ 72–125	68	$104,000– $305,000
Northern Lights (one-bedroom carriage house units and two- and three-bedroom duplexes)	720–1,247/ 67–116	14	$102,000– $169,000
Northstar Place (townhouses and loft-style condominiums	847–1,450/ 79–135	33	$126,000– $409,000
Studio Mews (townhouses and loft-style condominiums)	580–1,124/ 54–104	32	$102,000– $381,000
Wild Sage Cohousing (one-bedroom carriage house units and two-and three-bedroom townhouses)	693–2,712/ 64–252	34	$94,000– $493,000
Z Park (carriage houses and single-family homes)	605–2,440/ 56–227	25	$145,000– $799,000

DEVELOPMENT COST INFORMATION

Site Acquisition Cost	$4,756,000

Site Improvement and Infrastructure Construction Costs

Dry utilities	$255,399
Superstructure	$3,766,673
Fees/general conditions	$141,891
Off-site improvements	$172,763
	$4,336,726

Soft Costs

Architecture/engineering	$233,470
Construction interest and fees	$53,543
	$287,013
Total development cost	$9,379,739

DEVELOPMENT SCHEDULE:

Site acquired	March 1997
Planning started	Fall 1998
Infrastructure construction started	2003
Residential sales started	February 2004
Residential leasing started	May 2004
Commercial leasing started	Early 2003
Estimated project completion	Early 2008

DEVELOPMENT TEAM

Master Site Developer
Boulder Housing Partners
Boulder, Colorado
www.boulderhousing.org

Development Partners
Peak Properties & Development
(Garden Crossing and Block 6)
Boulder, Colorado
www.peak-properties.com

Affordable Housing Alliance
(Northern Lights)
Boulder, Colorado
www.wlarch.com/projects/
northern.html

Coburn Development
(The Crescent, Northstar Place,
Studio Mews, and Z Park)
Boulder, Colorado
www.coburndevelopment.com

Wonderland Hill Development
Company
(Wild Sage Cohousing)
Boulder, Colorado

Wolff/Lyon Architects
(Main St. North and North Court)
Boulder, Colorado

Master Site Planner
Barrett Studio Architects
Boulder, Colorado
www.barrettstudio.com

Oleson Woods Apartments

TIGARD, OREGON

IN CONTRAST TO THE PREVAILING PATTERN of small apartments surrounding it, Oleson Woods Apartments in Tigard, Oregon—a suburb just south of Portland—consists primarily of three- and four-bedroom townhouse-style rental units that are suitable for large families. Located between an existing 30-year-old, two-story garden apartment development and single-family homes, the townhouses are clustered around a wooded natural area, a courtyard, a play area, and a preserved wetland. The architectural focal point of the site is the community center, where tenants have access to services as well as meeting space.

With Oleson Woods, owner and developer Community Partners for Affordable Housing, Inc. (CPAH) has taken advantage of an environmentally sensitive site to pursue multiple goals. The project was conceived as a healthy, energy-efficient community, where wildlife and native vegetation could thrive alongside tenants. This was achieved through programs that educate community members about the many plants

SPECIAL FEATURES

- Affordable
- Multifamily rental housing
- Green building features
- Wetland preservation
- Extensive open space
- Environmental education program

The large on-site wetland, which might have been treated in a strictly technical manner, is instead embraced by the site design, becoming an educational resource and a visual amenity. Private courtyards overlook a pond, where seasonal blossoms and several bird species are visible.

Oleson Woods site plan.

and animals surrounding them and the ways they can protect their own health along with the environment.

Apartments are available to those earning 46 percent of the area median income. Oleson Woods has helped address an imbalance between available jobs and housing by providing workforce housing that is convenient to employment centers.

Site and Context

Oleson Woods is in Washington County near the geographic center of Tigard, an outer-ring suburb of Portland that grew around a number of shopping centers in the 1970s and 1980s. Local leaders have struggled, with some success, to create a civic identity for Tigard and to forge a sense of community among residents.

The community has the highest job-to-residence ratio in the Portland metropolitan area, with 18,000 jobs to only 2,300 housing units. And an estimated 9,800 new jobs are forecasted in the coming years. But very few of those jobs pay family wages, and most are in the shopping centers, including nearby Washington Square, a large complex that claims to be one of the country's top-grossing malls per square foot.

Accessed via 91st Avenue, the site is angled in between the intersection of two arterial routes, Oleson Road and Hall Boulevard. Originally, one large parcel contained the existing apartment complex, but the property was subdivided and the apartment complex is now adjacent to the Oleson Woods site. Due to the presence of a substantial natural wetland that provides scarce habitat for a number of native animal species—some of which are threatened—this land was designated as a sensitive area.

Most of the surrounding blocks are occupied by single-family homes, but the project is also across the street from the public 18-hole Red Tail Golf Course and a short distance from Washington Square. Also within walking distance are schools and a library. A few steps from the site, a bus stop provides service to the Washington Square Transit Center, where commuters can make transit connections to downtown Portland and the Max Light Rail line. A hard-rail commuter line is scheduled to be added to the network in the next five years.

Development Process

CPAH was founded by Loren Kerkof, a Catholic priest at St. Anthony Church. In the early 1980s, he began to form partnerships with local leaders to establish the nonprofit organization, and the group hired executive director Sheila Greenlaw-Fink in 1995.

In a two-county area where the median income is $40,740 for a family of four, residents of CPAH properties tend to be families with a yearly household income under $20,000. The organization partners with schools, libraries, police, and youth programs to bring on-site services to its housing projects, which now include 175 units that house more than 500 individuals. Three-fourths of family heads are employed, and about half of those work in food services or retail.

CPAH's history as a developer commenced in 1997 when it acquired two existing apartment buildings— an 84-unit low-income housing complex and a 32-unit HUD-assisted apartment building—for rehabilitation. In 2002, CPAH completed its first new construction project, the 26-unit Village at Washington Square, where sustainable materials and construction methods were specified. CPAH's first project following Oleson Woods, the Watershed at Hillsdale, broke ground in September 2006 on a brownfield site in nearby southwest Portland.

With the exception of the Watershed at Hillsdale, the Oleson Woods development and design team is the same for all of these projects. In addition to CPAH, the team includes the Housing Development Center (HDC), a non-profit housing development consultant; Carleton Hart Architecture of Portland; and Macdonald Environmental Planning, also of Portland.

Before beginning plans for Oleson Woods, CPAH had documented the need for affordable housing for larger families and was determined to offer large (three- and four-bedroom) units in its new project. CPAH commissioned independent market studies to make sure the mix of residential unit types and rent goals would fit a well-defined need; studies showed that there were only three three-bedroom rental units available for every five families with three or more members. The county's U.S. Census data for 2000 showed that the amount of overcrowded renter households had increased by 170 percent over the preceding

Oleson Woods was conceived as a healthy, energy-efficient community where wildlife and native vegetation could thrive alongside tenants. It contains minimal impervious surfaces and paths are made with stone pavers instead of concrete.

decade. During the same decade, the number of rent-burdened households (those paying more than 30 percent of their total income for rent) rose by nearly 60 percent.

In 2002, the Olsen Woods site was purchased from the owners of the neighboring 30-year-old apartment complex. CPAH learned about the availability of the site through the HDC, and along with the architect, the team began to evaluate the possibilities there. They had already started to analyze the possibilities for purchasing and renovating the existing apartment complex, which has a typical mix of studio and one-bedroom apartments. However, they chose to take advantage of the unbuilt parcel in order to provide new family-sized apartments.

When it was purchased, the parcel was landlocked and had no public access. The county planned to extend an existing road that would link it to Oleson Road sometime in the future, but in order to move ahead with the development, CPAH negotiated with the owner of the neighboring apartment complex (and the former owner of the

Oleson Woods site) for a through-street right-of-way and gateway. In addition, CPAH was able to secure a parking easement from the same owner to accommodate 12 cars. By making use of existing paved areas, these easements significantly reduced the need for new paving in connection with the project.

As plans took shape, the developer faced negative reactions from nearby residents. Reticence about accepting low-income housing in the area was coupled with outcries from those for whom the wooded site had served as a de facto park. In facilitated meetings with residents of nearby developments, CPAH members won neighborhood acceptance by keeping them informed about environmental goals while repeating the message that development of the site was inevitable, and that CPAH would protect open space and habitat more thoughtfully than other developers would.

Because the site was environmentally sensitive, the development team had to deal with a number of reviewing agencies beyond the local jurisdiction of Washington County, ranging from the National Marine Fisheries to U.S. Fish and Wildlife and the U.S. Army Corps of Engineers. Federal funding for affordable housing meant that the Oleson Woods environmental package had to be submitted to HUD for review, too, a process that extended the development timeline considerably.

Financing

Washington County was first to commit funds for the project, with an equity share loan (the county's HOME program) of $700,000. The county's support was critical in obtaining the single largest source of funding for Oleson Woods: annual tax credits providing $3,224,000 in equity from the federal Low Income Housing Tax Credit (LIHTC) program. Since it was created by the Tax Reform Act of 1986, the LIHTC program has given states the equivalent of nearly $5 billion in annual budget authority to issue tax credits for the acquisition, rehabilitation, or new construction of rental housing for low-income households.

Oleson Wood's focal point is its community center, which provides space for meetings, child care, and community service referral. The 1,490-square-foot (138.6-square-meter) building faces the access right-of-way.

A total of $273,000 for the construction of the community center at Oleson Woods came from a community development block grant. The Oregon Housing Trust Fund contributed another $100,000. For the project's sustainable features, the Enterprise Foundation provided a grant of $32,000 through its Green Communities program. The Oregon Housing Weatherization program granted $16,000.

The Network for Oregon Affordable Housing (NOAH), a statewide nonprofit group, provided a first-position mortgage of $1,441,898. A small development loan of $33,795 came from CPAH, and a net cash flow of $20,068 during lease-up helped finance the project.

Master Plan

The choice to build new construction reflected the decision to develop on the site at a much lower density than a typical multifamily project. The zoning code contained a habitat overlay for the site that precluded construction for much of its total area. But the decision to erect three-bedroom units on much of the site, with generous amounts of private and public open space, meant the whole site would be considerably less dense than the level allowed by the zoning code or encouraged by standard smart growth principles.

CPAH and the design team, led by Carleton Hart, developed a vision for Oleson Woods that differs not only from prevailing notions about density (in units per acre), but also from neotraditional street grids with alleys. Instead, the building plans relate to the natural landscape, with sawtooth footprints around the open spaces.

The large on-site wetland, which might have been treated in a strictly technical manner, is instead embraced by the site design, becoming an educational resource and a visual amenity. Private courtyards overlook a pond, where seasonal blossoms and several bird species are visible. The wetland area is protected by a split-rail fence between the water and a walkway that serves the surrounding townhouses.

From the beginning, much of the open space was intended to preserve and create wildlife habitat and to protect and reintroduce native forest. In an early inventory, 55 species of plants and animals were identified on site. Much of the mature canopy of native trees, including white oak, Douglas fir, big leaf maple, and ponderosa pine, was retained. In addition, 200 young trees were planted.

There are six residential buildings at Oleson Woods. Facing two sides of the wetland and one side of the common courtyard are four two-story townhouse structures, each with five three-bedroom units. In one of the two other buildings, both of which face the common courtyard, there are four one-bedroom apartments, and in the sixth there are nine units, including three four-bedroom flats and six three-bedroom townhouses.

The townhouse rows and three additional residential buildings are wrapped around two main open areas on site. One is the protected wetland habitat, which has become a scenic amenity, and the other is the community courtyard and play area. A third open space—a natural wooded habitat—lies in a corner on the north end of the site and serves as another scenic amenity for the neighborhood. In addition to these areas, a large buffer of unused open space contains a new stormwater retention

pond. It lies at the other end of the L-shaped site, directly next to the access easement, and can be expanded to serve the stormwater needs of contiguous developments.

Although it is bounded by one of the townhouse buildings and crossed by a trail, the forested habitat in the northern corner of the site has no doors facing it. This allows for visual surveillance through apartment windows while deliberately making it inaccessible from the units themselves. It is closed off from surrounding streets, yet it is maintained as an educational amenity for visiting groups.

The townhouses are arranged in three linear buildings. The sawtooth layout helps to visually separate each unit and establishes a rhythm for the whole composition. Small, private front courtyards face a walkway and open space beyond, a pattern that demarcates private outdoor space for family use but connects it to the open space. The plan creates an environment where children can play in front of the units and can also be seen as they move around the development.

Small, private front courtyards face a walkway and open space beyond, a pattern that demarcates private outdoor space for family use but connects it to the communal open space. The plan creates an environment where children can play in front of the units and can also be seen as they move around the development.

Next to the wetland is the community center, which contains spaces for meetings, child care, and community service referral. The 1,490-square-foot (138.6-square-meter) building faces the access right-of-way with a gable profile of interlaced timbers supporting a high peaked roof.

Green Building Design and Construction

Many of the sustainable features of Oleson Woods added no cost to the project, but some—such as rated appliances, low-VOC finishes, and extra insulation—called for upfront investments estimated at about $158,000, or 2.7 percent of the total development cost. This estimate does not include the costs of wetland restoration, which was required by current codes and would have been undertaken and monitored independent of the developer's goals.

The sustainable aspects of Oleson Woods include the following:

- **Sustainable building materials.** Drywall, insulation, carpeting, and interior paint all have recycled content. Engineered wood products, fill, and steel all have some recycled content.

- **Energy conservation.** Reduction of energy consumption for Oleson Woods exceeds the specifications of the Earth Advantage program and Energy Star® standards. All qualifying appliances are Energy Star rated, and many light fixtures are compact fluorescent. Resting on concrete with thermal breaks, high-efficiency water heaters with pressure-relief valves drain to the buildings' exteriors.

- **Water conservation.** In the landscape, timed drip or spray irrigation is limited to about 10 percent of the site and will be decommissioned after two years, when plants are established. Fixtures in all units include low-flow toilets, faucets with flow restrictors, and water-saving dishwashers.

- **Indoor air quality.** Composite wood products, including countertop substrate, are free of formaldehyde, and low-VOC sealers, paints, primers, and carpets were used. Bathroom fans and range hoods are vented to the outdoors. Tamper-proof vented windows provide makeup air. No mold-propagating materials were used in wet locations. Bathroom and kitchen flooring is ceramic tile in the community center, and commercial-grade vinyl with welded seams in the residential units.

- **Location.** The Oleson Woods site is located near transit and within an urbanized area.

- **Site plan.** The building footprint is compact in order to preserve a reconstructed wetland, maintain the existing tree canopy, and maximize natural open space.

- **Wetland preservation.** The site's existing wetland was enlarged, protected, and enhanced with native plants, and integrated with the landscape.

- **Stormwater.** Site stormwater is caught in biofiltration swales before being passed on to the wetland and the secondary retention pond. It returns to the underlying aquifers through on-site drywells.

- **Landscape.** Specimens native to Oregon including white oak, ponderosa pine, fir, and big leaf maple have been preserved and are cared for by a professional arborist. In addition, over 200 new trees were planted on site. Specified new plantings are hardy and drought tolerant. The plan contains a minimal amount of hard surface. Certain paths to buildings are made with stone pavers instead of concrete, and pavers are used in individual courtyards. Walking paths in the natural area are made with wood chips provided by the arborist.

Marketing and Management

Within five months of the project's completion, in November 2005, all 32 units were occupied and a waiting list was started. The units would have been filled in much less time, but the application process required tenants to be screened and income-qualified. As of September 2006, turnover has been very low—just one unit. News about the opening of Oleson Woods was disseminated through the chamber of commerce and other local civic organizations and public agencies. Also, information about the development and the units available was posted on local Web sites such as the Housing Connection, which serves all sectors, but especially the affordable and low-income housing market.

A full-time, on-site manager responds to day-to-day tenant issues and also serves as a point of referral for outside services. To support and further environmental goals, CPAH has embarked upon a plan for education and stewardship. It began with the distribution of a resident manual that includes information about the health benefits of the construction methods and finishes used, as well as an overview of the complexity of the wetland environment. It also contains some basic rules for maintaining and protecting all of these benefits, including the need to keep children and pets out of the wetland itself. There is information about the schools, libraries, and shopping opportunities within walking distance. The manual is distributed with other welcoming items, including a sampler of environmentally friendly cleaning products.

Educational compact discs that provide information about the animals and plants found on the site are used in special group sessions and may be viewed at the community center. Stormwater drains and inlets are labeled for the benefit of the many children living at Oleson Woods as well as in nearby apartments.

Experience Gained

Oleson Woods demonstrates that high density does not always go hand in glove with affordable housing or even with sustainability. Attractive, livable, and affordable housing can be developed as a dispersed plan while simultaneously preserving and stewarding scarce natural habitat.

A combination of smart site design and building plans can preserve natural areas as an amenity for the development and the entire neighborhood without becoming a social and law-enforcement liability. As mentioned previously, many windows in the two-story townhouses that look onto this fragile environment allow for visual surveillance, but the lack of doors on that same side restricts physical access and maintains a clear boundary between the residential units and the natural areas.

With vision, aggressive outreach, and excellent design, a housing developer can be a steward for natural habitat. Neighbors of the project engaged a local watershed watch coordinating group, the Tualatin Riverkeepers. While the Riverkeepers initially opposed the project, they ultimately determined it was "the best development" that could have happened at the site, and have assisted with education and outreach, including building chickadee houses with the residents.

Oleson Woods shows not only that a well-preserved habitat benefits surrounding private properties, but also that these benefits can be used as a strategic answer to the resistance faced by developers of affordable and low-income housing. Even when the natural areas cannot be publicly accessed, they present a slate of environmental benefits when properly protected. The presence of bird sounds, natural cooling, and air cleaning—in addition to scenic views—will likely impress many local property owners and help to win critical support for the project.

The following policies make success more likely:

- **Sell green upfront.** Building innovative, green workforce housing is an attractive idea to many potential funders and lenders. However, many of them are not aware of the upfront costs of some green measures, so it is important to clearly explain those costs and the ways they add value to the project and the community.

- **Get buy-in from the entire design and construction team.** Meeting with everyone involved—including subcontractors—as early as possible in the design and construction process will help keep sustainability goals on track. For instance, a subcontractor or general contractor may substitute conventional materials for sustainable materials because they are not committed to the goals of the project or lack experience in sourcing and using green materials.

By embracing a holistic approach upfront and emphasizing the broad values of the project from the beginning, a development team can find a like-minded constituency to support its vision.

Oleson Woods Apartments

LAND USE INFORMATION

Site area (acres/hectares)	3.15/1.74
Percentage complete	100
Gross density (units per acre/hectare)	10.16/25.1
Number of off-street parking spaces	47
(36 on site and 11 on adjacent property easement)	

LAND USE PLAN

Use	Area (sq f/sq m)	Percentage of Site
Buildings	20,805/1,933	15.2
Streets/surface parking	13,118/1,219	10.0
Landscaping/open space	103,317/9,598	74.8
	137,240/12,750	**100.0**

RESIDENTIAL INFORMATION

Unit Type	Number of Units	Area (sq f/sq m)	Range of Initial Rents
One-bedroom flat	4	615/57	$328–$435
Three-bedroom townhouse	21	1,120–1,150/ 104–107	$456–$700
Four-bedroom flat	3	1,340/124.5	$507–$775
Four-bedroom townhouse	4	1,330/124	$507–$775

DEVELOPMENT COST INFORMATION

Site Acquisition Cost	**$518,475**

Site Improvements and Construction Costs

Excavation/grading/sewer/water/drainage/ paving/curbs/sidewalks (on site)	$432,128
Excavation/grading/sewer/water/drainage/ paving/curbs/sidewalks (off site)	$75,355
Landscaping/irrigation	$122,223
Fees/general conditions and profit/overhead	$377,898
All other residential construction costs	$2,697,003
	$3,704,607

Soft Costs

Architecture/engineering	$263,518
Project management	$160,000
Marketing	$4,365
Legal/accounting	$73,812
Taxes/insurance	$65,996
Title fees	$21,180
All financing fees	$371,739
Reserves (lease-up, operating)	$62,468
	$1,023,078

Total Development Cost	**$5,246,160**

DEVELOPMENT SCHEDULE

Planning started	February 2002
Site purchased	July 2003
Construction started	December 2004
Sales/leasing started	August 2005
Project completed	November 2005

DEVELOPMENT TEAM

Developer
Community Partners for Affordable Housing, Inc.
P.O.Box 23206
Tigard, Oregon
www.cpahinc.org

Architect
Carleton Hart Architecture
Portland, Oregon
www.chapc.com

Planner/Project Manager
Housing Development Center
2627 NE Martin Luther King Jr. Boulevard
Portland, Oregon
www.hdc1.org

Landscape Architect
Macdonald Environmental Planning
Portland, Oregon
www.mep-pc.com

Habitat Consultant and Wetlands Scientist
SWCA Environmental Consultants
Portland, Oregon
www.swca.com

Civil Engineer
DL Design Group, Inc.
Portland, Oregon
www.dleng.net

Prairie Crossing

GRAYSLAKE, ILLINOIS

PRAIRIE CROSSING—ONE OF THE NATION'S first conservation developments—demonstrates how ecologically sensitive development can be used as a tool for the conservation of land that is threatened by inappropriate uses. The 678-acre (274-hectare) site, which is located some 40 miles (64 kilometers) north of downtown Chicago, was purchased by Gaylord Donnelley, a Chicago printing executive who lived nearby, and seven neighboring families. The group formed Prairie Holdings (PHC) in 1987, following a 15-year battle over the development of the former farmland. The new owner set out to create a community that would leave a substantial portion of the property in a natural or agricultural condition by clustering houses on small lots. In essence, homebuyers would be trading off private acreage for shared ownership of open space.

SPECIAL FEATURES

- Conservation development
- Restored wetlands
- Transit-oriented development
- Green building features
- Natural stormwater treatment system
- Organic farm

Development Process

George A. Ranney Jr., and his wife Victoria Ranney, who were members of the original investment group and officers of PHC, led the planning for the project. When Donnelley died in 1992, the Ranneys took charge of the development. They

VAUGHN WASCOVICH

were convinced that a substantial market of homebuyers would pay a significant premium —some 30 percent more—to live in a conservation community with smaller lot sizes, but greater amounts of protected open areas and higher-quality design and amenities. They planned Prairie

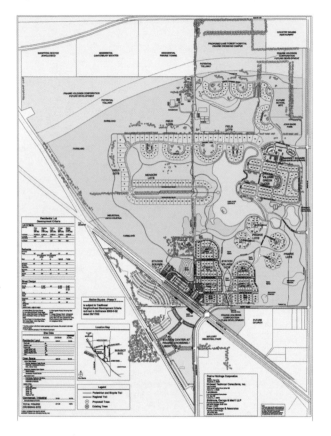

Praiarie Crossing site plan.

Crossing accordingly. The residential development consists of 359 single-family homes and 36 condominiums. Nearly 70 percent of the community is devoted to open space, including a 70-acre (28-hectare) working farm and more than ten miles of trails through a landscape of restored prairies, lakes pastures, and farm fields.

There was no commuter rail service when Prairie Crossing was first planned. The developers worked for nearly a decade with Metra—the region's commuter rail agency—to bring service to the area, giving residents convenient access to downtown Chicago and O'Hare Airport. Once Metra committed to building two rail stops nearby, the developers reconfigured the southwest portion of the site into a denser, pedestrian-oriented neighborhood within walking distance of the stations. The second phase of development, known as Station Village, includes 42

houses that are designed in a New Urbanist–style configuration around a village common; they sit on smaller lots and are clustered more tightly together than phase-one homes. Station Square (phase three), located across the street from one of the rail stations, contains 36 condominiums in three buildings with ground floor retail and underground parking organized around a landscaped square. The 13-acre (5-hectare) mixed-use neighborhood also includes space for several full-service restaurants, a three-story office building, and an outdoor organic farmer's market.

The developer acquired several out parcels located near the train stops—beyond the Prairie Crossing boundary—in a strategic move to ensure that future development on these parcels would be transit-supported and further the overall goals of Prairie Crossing. It is anticipated that these parcels, designated for mixed-use, retail/commercial buildings will be built by third-party developers.

The development team faced many hurdles along the way, including a proposed extension to a nearby landfill and the proposed construction of a power plant and a six-lane toll road. While the former was resolved through negotiations with the landfill owner and the latter two were defeated and postponed indefinitely, respectively, these formidable challenges caused many people to believe that Prairie Crossing would never succeed. To overcome these doubts, the developer decided to build much of the infrastructure and many of the common amenities upfront, including the roads, trails, working organic farm, beach and lakes, restored barn/community center, and horse stables. The developers also knew that the working landscape and natural areas, known as the Liberty Prairie Reserve, on the east edge of Prairie Crossing were a tremendous asset to the project and spent nearly half a million dollars to construct a trail underpass beneath Route 45, so that hikers, bikers, and horseback riders can reach these natural areas without having to contend with highway traffic.

Nearly 70 percent of the community is dedicated to open space uses, including a 70-acre (28-hectare) organic farm.

Master Plan

A critical piece of the planning process was the decision to adopt a set of ten guiding principles for Prairie Crossing: environmental protection and enhancement, a healthy lifestyle, a sense of place, a sense of community, economic and racial diversity, convenient and efficient transportation, energy conservation, lifelong learning and education, aesthetic design and high-quality construction, and economic viability. These principles shaped almost every important decision at Prairie Crossing.

Preservation of open land was the primary organizing framework for this conservation community. Early focus groups confirmed the importance of protecting the existing farmland on the site with conservation easements. When potential residents were asked to select the types of

landscapes they preferred, most of them said they would select the farm views if they were ensured that it would remain farmland in perpetuity. Today, conservation easements permanently protect 193 acres (78 hectares) of the original parcel.

Prairie Crossing worked with multiple architects to develop over 20 house plans, creating visual variety and diversity throughout the community. This strategy was also intended to appeal to a broad demographic, which was especially important in the early development phase when the market was still untested. More than ten architectural firms collaborated on different pieces of Prairie Crossing. They were directed to emphasize midwestern vernacular architecture and energy efficiency in their designs. Many of the single-family homes have large front porches that invite neighborly interaction and enliven the streetscape and are clustered in New Urbanist–style village neighborhoods with sidewalks and alleys.

The Byron Colby Community Center is a refurbished 19th-century timber-frame barn that houses a fitness facility, catering kitchen, and central gathering space.

VICTORIA RANNEY

Sustainability as a Core Value

Although many recent residential developments incorporate environmental features, Prairie Crossing made ecological concerns its starting point, building a community around principles of enhancing and caring for the land.

Rail passengers can reach downtown Chicago in a little over an hour on the North line and O'Hare International Airport is approximately one-half hour on the North Central line.

A prime example is the natural stormwater treatment system that was used instead of conventional storm sewers. The water "treatment train"—the first of its kind in the country—channels rainwater and snowmelt through open swales and wetlands into lakes, ponds, and streams. Each step in the treatment train reduces the volume of runoff, allowing greater water filtration and evaporation as well as the removal of pollutants. The water that reaches the wetlands has been significantly cleansed by the time it flows into Lake Aldo Leopold, an artificial water feature, and three other ponds, which act as detention basins. This treatment train decreases the amount of stormwater conveyed off site by approximately 60 percent compared to the predevelopment agricultural landscape, thus helping to prevent flooding downstream.

The lakes and ponds at Prairie Crossing serve as recreational and ecological amenities. The Illinois Department of Natural Resources uses one of the smaller lakes to restock endangered native fish. More than 120 bird species (the bald eagle included) have been sighted in the area, in contrast to the approximately 15 species that are typically found on conventional chemically farmed lands in the area.

Conservation easements are used to protect open space and natural areas at Prairie Crossing. The Liberty Prairie Conservancy, a land trust that manages a portion of the open space easements, also provides important leadership, educational, and advocacy for environmental preservation and open space protection in the county. The conservancy's largest source of funding is the Liberty Prairie Foundation, which receives most of its funding from the .05 percent assessment on the sale and resale of Prairie Crossing homes.

The community was founded on the belief that conservation and community go hand in hand. Many of the community-building features of the development revolve around the land. The annual program in which residents learn about safe and effective techniques for burning prairie grasses is a good example. After participating in the course, residents form small groups to help each other burn individual yards— a rural tradition, not unlike barn raising.

The working farm, which the Ranneys turned into an organic operation, grows vegetables, fruits, herbs, and flowers, and raises chickens that produce free-range eggs. Community participation is encouraged. This includes opportunities for children at the Prairie Crossing Charter School and a Montessori Adolescent Program to help with the daily farm work. Residents and others can lease farm plots or purchase annual farm shares to receive a weekly basket of fresh organic produce grown by a resident farm couple and staff.

The central gathering place at Prairie Crossing—the Byron Colby community center—is a refurbished 1885 timber-framed barn. In 1992, the barn, which was originally located several miles from Prairie Crossing, was disassembled timber by timber, moved to the development, and reassembled with mortise-and-tenon joints, as it had been more than 100 years ago. With a 24-hour fitness facility on the lower level, a large room on the main level, a loft, and a catering kitchen, the 7,000-square-foot (650-square-meter) barn is an active hub for social and community

events, including wedding receptions, homeowners' meetings, lectures, and concerts. Both residents and nonresidents can lease the facility, which is self-sustaining.

Green Buildings Design and Construction

The single-family houses at Prairie Crossing were built to the standards of the U.S. Department of Energy's (EPA) Building America energy-efficiency and environmental program, which has cut annual heating and cooling bills by up to 50 percent. Prairie Crossing was the first subdivision in the country to use this program throughout the development. The homes include many energy-saving features that have become standard in sustainable developments today, including high-performance glazing, interior airflow retarders, and walls with two-by-six-inch framing, instead of two-by-four-inch members, to allow more room for insulation. The condominiums

Aerial view of Prairie Crossing.

in Station Square have earned a five-star energy rating, the highest rank offered under the EPA's Energy Star® program. A windmill on the organic farm generates electric power for its irrigation pumps, lights, and other needs.

Two LEED certified buildings of the Prairie Crossing Charter School use a geothermal heat-pump system and extensive daylighting, and was built with low-impact

PRECISION AERIAL PHOTO

construction materials. The secondary school's strong environmental curriculum features a variety of hands-on outdoor classes that focus on the prairies, wetlands, and lakes of the community, as well as the organic farm.

Marketing

The developers knew that, if they were to provide high-quality design and construction along with many amenities, the houses would have to be priced higher than most residences in nearby subdivisions. Prairie Crossing homes, which first went on the market in 1994, were priced between $179,000 and $250,000, whereas the average home price in the area was approximately $120,000. The Prairie Crossing homes were marketed to the greater Chicago metropolitan area.

Eve Lee, who headed the initial marketing program, says, "We sold community from the start." A house was built for the sales office. Visitors were offered fresh vegetables from the organic farm. Many of the marketing events revolved around the agricultural seasons. "The goal was to connect people with the land," she explains.

The first ad campaign in the *Chicago Tribune* proved expensive and not especially effective. So the developers changed strategies and sought out venues that were targeted more specifically to potential Prairie Crossing residents. They advertised on classical music and public radio stations, in local and national ecology magazines, and in publications like *Conscious Choice* and *Chicago Parent*. One of the most effective marketing strategies was to involve Prairie Crossing residents in the sales process. A number of homeowners assisted as hosts on the weekends, greeting potential homeowners and responding to questions.

The initial warning given to the developers—that people would not pay more to live in a conservation community—proved to be incorrect. According to a 1999 marketing analysis by Robert Charles Lesser and Company, Prairie Crossing single-family homes sold at prices 33 percent higher than comparable homes in the competitive market area. Lesser estimated a 14 percent value ratio premium over the competition that was attributed, in part, to the project's high level of amenities, conservation ethic, and open space. The higher-quality design and construction and energy-saving features, along with custom options and upgrades, made up the remaining 19 percent.

Although sales lagged at the start and again when the power plant was proposed next to the site in 2000, approximately 35 homes sold each year. Lee notes that potential homebuyers often visited Prairie Crossing up

to eight separate times before deciding to purchase, in comparison to the more typical two to three visits at a more standard development. By the end of the project's single-family home sales, the pace had risen to more than 45 per year.

Experience Gained

Looking back, George Ranney says that the development team was probably overly aggressive in building much of the infrastructure and community amenities upfront, believing now that some of those elements could have been delayed or phased, despite the challenges set forth by the landfill expansion, power plant, and toll road. A feature such as the stormwater treatment system, however, had to be constructed in a single phase. Ranney also notes the importance of building certain signature elements, such as the Byron Colby Barn, to help forge a strong visual identity for the development.

Had it been developed at slightly higher densities, Prairie Crossing would have been more profitable, according to Ranney. Although 78 new houses at Station Village and Station Square were added to the original 317 units, "We could have built more homes and still have maintained the same overall ambience and high quality," he notes. According to Ranney, the investor group of neighboring landowners, some of whom originally envisioned ten-acre farmettes for the parcel, resisted the notion of denser development, as did some political leaders in the Village of Grayslake.

When sales started in 1994, the market for single-family homes built on relatively small lots and priced significantly higher than most homes in the area, was still untested. To appeal to a broad market, the developer offered 12 house plans and added others over the course of the project. In addition, many homeowners requested changes and upgrades and were essentially purchasing semi-custom houses. In hindsight, the developer would have offered fewer house plans, which would have streamlined the design process, saved time, and lowered costs significantly.

Once a year, Prairie Crossing residents are asked to rate their community according to the ten guiding principles.

Lakes and ponds provide both recreational and ecological amenities.

Environmental protection and enhancement generally receive top marks, along with high-quality design. "We're probably weakest on racial and economic diversity," says the developer. But the high demand for Prairie Crossing homes and escalating costs didn't allow for the social and economic diversity originally envisioned for the community. In hindsight, the developers say they might have considered partnering with a nonprofit development corporation to achieve a more balanced housing mix.

The developer didn't want Prairie Crossing to be an insular enclave and looked for ways to physically integrate it into the region. To that end, ten miles of internal trails at Prairie Crossing (that enable residents to walk and bike to the commuter rail stations) will eventually connect to the Des Plaines River trail system linking the state of Wisconsin and Cook County. The developers also created several entities— the Liberty Prairie Conservancy, Prairie Crossing Institute, and Liberty Prairie Foundation—that support conservation and environmental practices both within and beyond the Prairie Crossing community. Like Byron Colby Barn, Station Square will attract people from across the region to Prairie Crossing, further strengthening connections to the larger community.

It was critical to develop a permanent funding mechanism to support the community's environmental agenda. The .05 percent assessment on home sales and resales, which is used primarily for environmental preservation and education, currently generates approximately $80,000 a year. Other conservation communities, including Spring

STEVEN ARAZMUS

Island in South Carolina and Hidden Springs in Boise, Idaho, use similar assessments to fund such programs.

Prairie Crossing broke many rules of conventional development. For example, the Ranneys were advised to build a swimming pool instead of a lake and beach. As it turns out, the beach is a favorite gathering spot for residents, and Lake Aldo Leopold proved to be a strong marketing amenity. When sales started, homes next to the lake commanded a premium of approximately $25,000. By the time all of the units were built, the premium for the top lakefront homes was $100,000.

Conventional wisdom also advised painting the homes in neutral colors such as "transferee beige," as it is sometimes called in the home building industry. The developers were warned that vivid colors would appeal to only a few buyers and could impede resale value. But Vicky Ranney wanted to use colors that would help relieve the long, gray winter months. She hired color expert Todd Schwebel to design a consistent palette of earth tones (based on the colors of the prairie) for the clapboard siding, trim, roofs, and other elements of the homes.

The last development phase, Station Square, features 36 condominiums with underground parking. Two of the three buildings feature shops and services on the ground floor. The 13-acre (5 hectare), mixed-use development also includes space for restaurants, an organic farm market, and a three-story office building.

An important goal for Prairie Crossing was to serve as a model for neighboring communities and offer an alternative to the sprawling subdivision development that prevailed in the area. Prairie Crossing's influence on nearby development is undeniable. The Village of Grayslake currently advises area developers to look to Prairie Crossing as an example of marketable sustainable development. In fact, one recent project was redesigned to follow the Prairie Crossing model; originally planned with five-acre lots, parcels were reduced to one acre and the majority of the site was preserved as permanent open space.

Developments like Prairie Crossing need a community leader to keep them on track. "This is not a role for a construction manager," observes George Ranney. " A founder can take such a leadership position, as did Robert Davis at Seaside, and a long-term project manager can too, as did Frank Martin at Hidden Springs." But Ranney believes that, "It requires an individual who works to sustain the integrity of the vision and who recognizes that the civic aspects of a development can also enhance the bottom line."

HEDRICH-BLESSING

210

Prairie Crossing

LAND USE INFORMATION

Total site area (acres/hectares)	678/274
Total number of dwelling units completed	359
Gross residential density (units per gross acre/hectare)	1.7/0.69
Average net residential density (units per acre/hectare)	3/7.41
Nonresidential development (roads, streets, parks/open space per acre/hectare)	470/190
Total office space (square feet/square meters)	20,000/1,858*
Total retail space (square feet/square meters)	52,500/4,877*

* planned

LAND USE PLAN

	Acres/hectares*	Percentage of Site
Residential	135/55	20
Open space	470/190	69
Other (planned commercial)	73/30	11
	678/274	100

*Total acreage designated for this land use.

RESIDENTIAL UNIT INFORMATION

Unit Type	Unit Size (sq f/sq m)	# Units	# Units Sold	Range of Initial Sales Prices/Rents
Single family	2,300/214*	359	359	$189,000–$650,000
Condominiums	2,000/186	36	18	$329,900–$549,000

* Average lot size of single-family home: one quarter acre

DEVELOPMENT COST INFORMATION

Direct Expenses

Land	$10,561,451[1]
Site improvement	$25,942,977
Construction	$93,862,927
Landscaping	$3,697,599
Community assets	$2,441,412[2]
Total Direct Expenses	**$136,506,366**

Indirect Expenses

Sales/marketing/models	1$2,293,425
Professional fees	$6,695,601[3]
Taxes/insurance	$1,659,169
Independent review/field inspections	$601,083
General and administrative	$9,843,078
Homeowners' Association dues	$1,173,312[4]
Total Indirect Expenses	**$32,266,736**

Other

Open space assessment	$665,000[5]
Total other	**$665,000**

Total Development Costs	**$169,438,102**

1. Includes raw land price plus transaction and predevelopment costs.

2. Includes restored Byron Colby Barn community center, horse stable, organic farm, and other improvements that benefit the community.

3. Includes planning, architectural, engineering, legal, accounting, and third-party general contractor fees. The developer spent more than typical homebuilders developing plans for individual houses. This is due in part to Prairie Crossing's pioneering role working with the U.S Department of Energy's Building America program. The developer also contributed $250,000 in engineering and landscaping for construction of two new commuter rail stations at Prairie Crossing. Design fees amounted to approximately $1.3 million and legal fees amounted to approximately $1.3 million.

4. The developer elected to pay homeowner assessments on unsold residences over a ten-year-long absorption period.

5. Liberty Prairie Foundation Open-Space Assessment. For every unit sold and resold at Prairie Crossing, .05 percent of the sale price is contributed to the Liberty Prairie Foundation, a private nonprofit that promotes local environmental preservation.

DEVELOPMENT SCHEDULE

Site acquired	1987
Planning started	1987
Construction started	1992

Projection completion

Phase I	Single-family houses in clustered neighborhoods	
Phase II	Station Village single-family houses	
Phase III	Station Square condominiums	
Project completion		2007

PROJECT TEAM

Developer
Prairie Holdings Corporation
Grayslake, Illinois
www.prairiecrossing.com

Land Planners
Skidmore, Owings & Merrill
Chicago, Illinois
www.som.com

Calthorpe Associates
Berkeley, California
www.calthorpe.com

Architects
Tigerman McCurry
Chicago, Illinois
www.tigerman-mccurry.com

Worn Jerabek Architects
Chicago, Illinois
www.wwapc.com

Serena Sturm Architects
Northbrook, Illinois
www.serenastrum.com

Landscape Architects
William Johnson, FASLA
Bainbridge Island, Washington

Peter Lindsay Schaudt Landscape Architecture, Inc.
Chicago, Illinois
www.schaudt.com

Terramor at Ladera Ranch

ORANGE COUNTY, CALIFORNIA

LOCATED IN SOUTH ORANGE COUNTY, California, the village of Terramor is situated within the 4,000-acre (1,619-hectare) planned community of Ladera Ranch. Considered the largest "green-oriented" residential village in the state, Terramor contains 1,258 residential units; 37 percent of the homes employ photovoltaic panels.

The premise for Terramor was driven by four key factors: 1) the need to distinguish Terramor from other residential planned communities selling new homes within the same time frame and geographic area; 2) the requirement to incorporate green development practices mandated by the state of California; 3) the developer's desire to remain on the forefront of development trends and practices; and 4) the developer's interest in tapping a newly defined market segment, the "cultural creatives."

SPECIAL FEATURES

- Green development requirements for production builders
- Targeted to environmentally conscious buyers
- Constructed seasonal creek provides community amenity and environmental benefits
- Sustainable landscaping
- Extensive use of photovoltaic panels
- Construction waste recycling program

Terramor's design manual allowed for less complicated styles than in the other villages of Ladera Ranch. The alley-loaded homes open onto courtyards and trails.

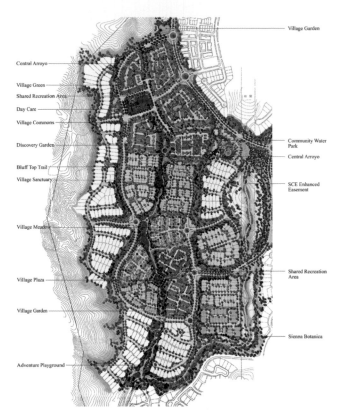

Village Garden

Central Arroyo

Village Green

Shared Recreation Area

Day Care

Village Commons

Discovery Garden

Bluff Top Trail

Village Sanctuary

Village Meadow

Village Plaza

Village Garden

Adventure Playground

Community Water Park

Central Arroyo

SCE Enhanced Easement

Shared Recreation Area

Sienna Botanica

Development Process

Located just a few miles inland from Interstate 5, which stretches from Mexico to Canada, Ladera Ranch is surrounded by the cities of Mission Viejo and San Juan Capistrano as well as other suburban developments in South Orange County.

As master planner and developer of Ladera Ranch, Rancho Mission Viejo, owned by the O'Neill, Avery, and Moiso families and others, contributed the land for Ladera Ranch from the historic 200,000-acre (80,937-hectare) ranch that the family has controlled since 1882. The guiding precept for Ladera Ranch incorporated four cornerstones: 1) the legacy of the land; 2) distinctive village design; 3) intimate neighborhoods ; and 4) neighbor-to-neighbor social interaction. Each of these cornerstones is reflected in the final land plan for Ladera Ranch. For example, stamping each village with a distinctive architectural identity and limiting neighborhoods to 40 to 50 units each are byproducts of the second and third cornerstones. The community's fourth cornerstone is fulfilled by the construction of five village clubs, each with its own distinct architectural theme and amenities, which provide a neighborhood nucleus and entice residents out of their homes to socialize and interact.

The community opened in July 1999 and is approaching buildout of its 8,100 residential units, which range from apartments and townhouses to single-family homes. Today, Ladera Ranch contains over 100 neighborhoods organized within six villages and three mixed-use districts (with higher residential densities, a higher percentage of attached units, and office-retail components). In addition to its schools, daycare centers, shopping centers, office space, restaurants, library, parks, village clubs, water parks, trails, and walking paths, Ladera Ranch has preserved nearly 50 percent of its 4,000 acres (1,619 hectares) as open space.

Ladera Ranch's riverine system, known as the "Sienna Botanica," is a narrow, constructed seasonal creek bed that serves as both a scenic amenity and a natural filter for water runoff. Its landscaped pathway runs the length of Ladera Ranch and is showcased by hardy wildflowers, native shrubbery and ground cover, grassy meadows, and tree canopies. While the Sienna Botanica is part of an innovative environmental benefit and wetlands restoration program, it also creates an attractive addition to community living spaces within Ladera Ranch.

To identify the potential target market for Terramor, the developer commissioned American LIVES, a market research firm based in Carmel Valley, California, to con-

Terramor did not come to fruition without challenges. The developer had to convince ten of the nation's largest homebuilders, some of which had no prior green building experience, to endorse a bold green strategy for Terramor. These homebuilders embraced the developer's requirements with varying degrees of enthusiasm and were ultimately swayed by the strong market and their own past sales success at Ladera Ranch. Following two years of intense planning and collaboration—and the recognition that green is here to stay—many of the homebuilders at Terramor have embraced green building practices.

Terramor at Ladera Ranch site plan.

Home sales at Terramor proved to be highly successful. However, due to the imbalance of housing supply and demand in the late 1990s, when Terramor was introduced to the market, the primary buyer motivation was not the village's green orientation. Instead, buyers were motivated by the availability of homes in a constricted market. It wasn't until residents had the chance to experience the green features at Terramor firsthand that the developer and homebuilders could begin to assess the true value of the village's sustainable development program.

©EDAW/PHOTOGRAPHY BY DIXI CARRILLO

duct surveys among people who had expressed interest in Ladera Ranch. The resulting data indicated a growing interest from a segment of the population dubbed the "cultural creatives" (CCs) by author Richard Florida. In choosing a home, CCs, like the other homebuyer segments at Ladera Ranch, wanted a "nest" that came with a sense of place and community, among other attributes. Ecological best practices and living in harmony with nature were also prominent values.

Rancho Mission Viejo asked American LIVES to take a closer look at CCs. Further research indicated that this demographic, which represented 32 percent of Terramor's target homebuyers, had been purchasing via the secondary market, often in central cities. The fact that they were now showing interest in suburban homes at Ladera Ranch indicated an opportunity to attract a new homebuyer segment. Targeting the cultural creative market segment with a green product would not only add value to the community by addressing the needs and wants of environmentally conscious homebuyers, but could also bolster profits by increasing base values and absorp-

tion. And it gave the developer the validation it needed in order to foster a sustainable community.

The developer and its planning team translated CC values, including green homebuilding and the preservation of nature, into a matrix of planning elements. The project design team added details and dimension to the matrix, which was then incorporated into the village's final design guidelines.

Next, the developer invited a group of national and local builders to compete for particular housing products subject to parameters outlined in Terramor's design guidelines. On presentation night, builders demonstrated that they were "on message." One redrew internal streets for optimum solar access. Others offered contemporary architecture. All styled their presentations for a CC audience.

After selecting builders (on the basis of bids and designs), the developer continued to exercise tight control via a five-stage review process. The first four stages

One of Terramor's development principles was respect for the environment. Therefore, residents have easy access to trails, parks, and 1,800 acres (728 hectares) of permanently preserved habitat.

©EDAW/PHOTOGRAPHY BY DIXI CARRILLO

215

involved design review. The last was home inspection by an independent third party to ensure compliance with Terramor's green building program.

Master Plan

The challenge for the development team was to produce a village plan for Terramor that attracted CCs (without alienating other market segments) and render distinctive architectural designs that would not clash with the rest of Ladera Ranch. The final land plan for Terramor created a tightly knit community that allows most residents to walk from their front doors to any neighborhood or facility in the village without crossing a major street. Instead of opening onto streets, over half of the residences at Terramor are oriented toward the village's Central Paseo, a three-quarter-mile-long (1.21-kilometer-long) pathway that runs down the spine of the community, or along a variety of Terramor's secondary paseos, courtyards, and parks. All of the homes in the community are within close walking distance of the Terramor water park, a 7.5-acre (3.03-hectare) site featuring a resort-style pool and play elements for children.

Nearly 40 percent of homes in Terramor feature photovoltaic panels, making the development one of the nation's largest solar-powered communities.

Secondary streets found within most other residential villages at Ladera Ranch were replaced with a network of arroyos, paseos, courtyards, and greens at Terramor. The paseos, including the Central Paseo, connect to the ten-mile-long Ladera Ranch Trail, which encircles the community and provides access to the 1,800 acres (728 hectares) of preserved open space surrounding Ladera Ranch. The Ladera Ranch Trail is also linked to a regional riding and hiking trail. Two community-wide trail systems also link Terramor to all the villages within Ladera Ranch.

With 1,258 residential units, Terramor has the highest density of homes within Ladera Ranch—8.7 gross units/acre (21.5 gross units/hectare). Housing types range from detached single-family homes and attached condominiums and townhouses to live/work units and clustered court homes.

Vehicular traffic is directed toward the perimeter of the village. Streets have traffic-calming features, such as narrow widths, and many of the homes are alley-loaded.

Green Building Design and Construction

To help reduce overall costs and compensate for green features projected to cost $3.50 to $5.00 per square foot ($38.00 to $54.00 per square meter), Terramor's design

guidelines allowed for less complicated styles than in the other villages of Ladera Ranch. A Spanish Colonial home, for example, could be more rectangular and have less complicated rooflines than a traditional home of the same design.

Terramor's green development program included six categories of design and construction standards: green development program site/landscape design; water conservation; energy; materials and resources; indoor environmental quality; and innovation. Each category was tied to one primary goal. For example, the goal for the water conservation category was to reduce the use of potable water by at least 20 percent. The goal for the energy category was to reduce annual energy costs and associated atmospheric pollution by at least 20 percent.

Today, the average residence at Terramor uses 20 percent less energy and potable water than a comparable house in Orange County.

Terramor builders were required to exceed California's stringent Title 24 energy code requirements by 20 percent. They were able to achieve this benchmark through any number of creative design solutions, including passive solar design, extra insulation, and instantaneous hot water systems. Additionally, the builders were required to provide 110-volt electrical outlets for charging neighborhood electric vehicles (NEVs). Each builder demonstrated a NEV at their model homes and offered the vehicles as an optional purchase for homebuyers.

Among the more popular green features at Terramor are photovoltaics, Energy Star–certified appliances, fluores-

cent lighting indoors and low-voltage lighting outdoors, low-flow water fixtures, formaldehyde-free insulation, low-VOC paints and carpets, and drip irrigation systems.

Builders also employed on-demand hot water pumps, tankless water heaters, moisture sensors, water purification systems, and central vacuums. Among the list of options for the home interiors were renewable resources such as cork or bamboo, materials with a high level of recycled content, and certified wood for trim and finish work.

Each builder had to participate in a mandatory recycling program for construction waste and demolition and land clearing material. Builders initially tried on-site separation of waste materials, but the high cost of training workers failed to produce low contamination rates. A trash hauler was hired to sort the material instead. From

2007 ©TOM LAMB/LAMB STUDIO

2007 ©TOM LAMB/LAMB STUDIO

start to finish, about 65 percent of site construction materials were recycled.

Common area landscaping at Terramor is 90 percent native or drought-tolerant plants. The availability of specified trees and most shrubs at local nurseries reduced the number and length of vehicle trips required for delivery. Green waste produced at Ladera Ranch was used as mulch at Terramor.

Residents can walk to the Village Club, an amenity that features a pool and a skate park.

All village-wide landscape irrigation at Terramor is plumbed for reclaimed water when available from Santa Margarita Water District (the reclaimed water storage facility is located within the community). Supplemental water needs are met by a computerized drip system that can detect a single malfunctioning valve. On-site weather stations ensure that water is delivered when and only to the extent needed.

Marketing

The market research that was conducted for Terramor, which also identified the "cultural creative" homebuyer segment, assisted the developer in forging a brand for the village—"360° Living." The identity permeated all aspects of the village, including Terramor's green development program. Two factors drove the brand selection process: it had to be accurate, without overreaching, due to the CC's emphasis on authenticity; and it couldn't alienate other key market segments. The developer chose 360° Living because it represented the full spectrum of CC values and emphasized Terramor as both a lifestyle and a place.

Automobiles are de-emphasized in Terramor, while walking and neighborhood electric vehicles (NEVs) are encouraged. Each home has an NEV charging station in the garage and homeowners can purchase the vehicles at a reduced cost.

Terramor's grand opening weekend attracted 12,000 people, according to local newspaper reports. Prospective homebuyers visited model home complexes that included displays of the various green features. Many green-related vendors also had displays organized under a large tent where home shoppers could browse before or after touring the various models. At one booth, a nursery offered tips on landscaping with native plants. At another, an automobile dealer offered certificates for $1,000 off of electric vehicles. Displays described waste management efforts, photovoltaic panels, and, of course, 360° Living.

With a strong real estate market (at the time, demand in Orange County was exceeding supply by 10,000 units a year), homes at Terramor sold at a quick clip and the village was completed three years faster than anticipated.

A post-marketing survey of buyers indicated that 88 percent of Terramor residents were willing to pay an additional $124 per month for green features, especially when it came to energy savings. Additionally, 57 percent of respondents think that builders are not paying enough attention to green development.

From concept to finish, the Terramor marketing team worked closely with the developer, builders, and homeowners to create and present a well-articulated vision of the community. This endowed all parties critical to the success of the community with a common vision and language.

©EDAW/PHOTOGRAPHY BY DIXI CARRILLO

Experience Gained

When a developer makes an effort to stay on message, it pays dividends: more coherent communications, better products, and improved sales.

The green development program at Terramor was about 70 percent complete prior to the selection of participating builders. The developer's design team worked closely with builders to flesh out the remaining 30 percent. This set a cooperative tone that persisted throughout the development process. Builders even shared information with one another about green suppliers and materials.

Many involved in Terramor regretted the suboptimal orientation of streets. Rectifying this situation with shading elements on west-facing windows proved to be time-consuming and difficult for some builders. When developers are starting from scratch, they must address orientation issues and apply passive solar design principles appropriate to the local climate. Often, streets can be organized in an east-west pattern. Another option is to double-load streets so that one row

Public plantings are 90 percent native or drought-tolerant species. Supplemental water needs are met by a drip irrigation system.

has the principal living area on the north side and the second row's living quarters are on the south side.

Communicating the value of sustainable features to homebuyers is crucial. However, sales staff and marketing materials must be careful not to commercialize or oversell green design. Instead, marketing programs should communicate the benefits of sustainable development and building features, especially when they involve monetary savings.

ABOVE: DAN GRAY ; LEFT: ©EDAW/PHOTOGRAPHY BY DIXI CARRILLO

Terramor

Site area (acres/hectares)	300/121
Number of dwelling units completed	1258
Gross residential density (units per gross acre/hectare)	8.7/21.5
Average net residential density: (units per net acre/hectare)	11.7/28.8

LAND USE PLAN

	Acres/hectares	Percentage of Site
Residential	150/61	52
Roads/parking	20/8	7
Open space	110/45	38
Recreational/daycare	10/4	3
	290/117	**100**

RESIDENTIAL INFORMATION

Unit Type	Unit Size (sq ft/sq m)	# of Units	Range of Initial Sales Prices
Single-level and 2-Story Attached Condominiums	921–1,279/ 373–518	142	$275,000– $333,000
Single-level and 2-Story Attached Condominiums	1315–1,669/ 532–675	152	$340,000– $378,000
Tuckunder Townhouse Condominiums	1,617–1,754/ 654–710	151	$389,000– $421,000
2- and 3-Story Townhouse Condominiums	1,612–2,055/ 652–832	149	$457,000– $533,000
2- and 3-Story Live/Work Townhouse Alternative	2,059–2,082/ 833–843	24	$560,000– $565,000
Single-family Detached Cluster Court Homes	1,625–2,150/ 658–870	107	$426,000– $472,000
Single-family Detached Courtyard Homes	1,790–2,095/ 724–848	104	$460,000– $500,000
Single-family Attached Alley Court Homes	2,220–2,534/ 898–1,025	109	$515,000– $545,000
Single-family Attached Alley Court Homes	2,556–2,987/ 954–1,209	75	$572,000– $615,000
Single-family Detached	2,358–2,982/ 954–1,207	89	$600,000– $685,000
Single-family Detached	2,770–3,675/ 1,221–1,487	77	$675,000– $772,000
Single-family Detached	3,712–4,168/ 1,502–1,687	79	$825,000– $864,000

Site Acquisition Cost	N/A*
Site Improvement Costs	
Excavation/grading	$18,000,000
Sewer/water/drainage	$5,000,000
Paving/curbs/sidewalks	$2,500,000
Landscaping/irrigation	$6,000,000
Other	
dry utilities	$1,000,000
	$32,500,000
Soft Costs	
Architecture/engineering	$2,200,000
Overhead (includes construction interest and fees)	$12,000,000
Marketing	$300,000
Legal/accounting	$75,000
Taxes/insurance	$3,200,000
Title fees	$100,000
	$18,550,000
Total Development Cost	**$51,000,000**

* Family-owned ranch land

DEVELOPMENT SCHEDULE

Site acquired	1996
Planning started	2001
Construction started	2003
Project completion	2006

DEVELOPMENT TEAM

Developer and Master Planner
Rancho Mission Viejo
San Juan Capistrano, California
www.ranchomissionviejo.com

Architect
William Hezmalhalch
Architects, Inc.
Santa Ana, California
www.wharchitects.com

Land Planning Consultant
EDAW Inc.
Irvine, California
www.edaw.com

Master Landscape Architect
Land Concern, Ltd.
Santa Ana, California
www.landconcern.com

Market Research
American LIVES
Carmel Valley, California
www.americanlives.com